HUMAN CULTURES THROUGH THE SCIENTIFIC LENS

Human Cultures through the Scientific Lens

Essays in Evolutionary Cognitive Anthropology

Pascal Boyer

OpenBook Publishers

https://www.openbookpublishers.com

© 2021 Pascal Boyer

ISBN Paperback: 9781800642065
ISBN Hardback: 9781800642072
ISBN Digital (PDF): 9781800642089
ISBN Digital ebook (epub): 9781800642096
ISBN Digital ebook (mobi): 9781800642102
ISBN XML: 9781800642119
DOI: 10.11647/OBP.0257

Cover photo: Marc-Olivier Jodoin on Unsplash at https://unsplash.com/photos/-TQU ERQGUZ8
Cover design by Anna Gatti

Contents

1. Anthropology, Useful and Scientific

An Introduction

The essays gathered in this volume were all intended as contributions to what I would like to call a *useful* and *scientific* anthropology, two words that may seem a tad presumptuous and require an explanation.

First, the useful part. The essays address specific questions such as the following:

- Why do some social institutions seem 'natural' to many people across different cultures?

- How do people form their views of the economy?

- Why do human beings engage in ritual behaviors, either pathological (in compulsive disorders) or culturally sanctioned (like ceremonies)? What are the common features of these behaviors?

- How do people detect that someone has a mental disorder? Does this differ from one culture to another?

- What motivates conflict between groups?

- Do ethnic conflict and discrimination have an impact on people's health? If so, how does that happen?

- What explains the differences between religions?

- Why are some political institutions stable and not others?

These are all questions of some social importance. It is not difficult to see that it would be a Good Thing, so to speak, to make progress in

 https://doi.org/10.11647/OBP.0257.01

addressing such issues. I do not claim that the essays gathered here are *more* useful than other attempts in the social sciences, but simply that the main motivation here is indeed to be useful, to provide models and findings that help us move closer to a proper explanation of these phenomena. That is the goal, the ambition, if perhaps not the actuality.

What about 'scientific'? In my view, the main way for scholarship to be useful, indeed useable, in these domains, is to proceed in a scientific manner. By using this term, I certainly do not mean to claim or imply that the various statements contained here are true. In fact, making such a claim would be quite the unscientific thing to do. The implication is simpler and more modest, meaning that the models proposed can and should be examined in terms of empirical data, and that they may be found to be false or in serious need of revision on the basis of such data.

In all these essays we adopt the perspective of an 'integrated' social science, that addresses questions about cultures and societies in a deliberately eclectic manner, combining results and models from evolutionary biology, experimental psychology, economics, anthropology and history (Morin, 2016; Sperber, 1996; Tooby & Cosmides, 1992). This approach is sometimes derided as 'positivistic' and 'reductionistic', and that is exactly what it is. It is blithely reductionist (explaining what happens at a high level of complexity in terms of the combinations of simpler, lower-level elements) and mostly positivist (if the term simply denotes the scientific aspiration).

Why Science Isn't and Should Not Be True to Life

To some people, it may seem that this way of describing and explaining social phenomena robs them of much of their substance. The models may be compelling but they miss out the rich texture and detail of actual social interactions. We talk about rituals in general without considering the particular and highly varied social contexts in which they take place; we examine people's views of economic processes, but we ignore the subtle individual differences in their construction; we consider widespread assumptions about madness, but not how they are modulated in each case... to these objections, the proper reply would be: Yes, *YES!* We do that, and that is exactly what we should do. Far from being a problem, the exclusion of so much information is precisely the main virtue of this way of proceeding.

The point will seem quite obvious to some and strikingly wrong-headed to others. For some people, doing science consists in discovering 'what really happens', beyond error, prejudice and received wisdom. Scientists are seen as people who describe things the way they really are. So it seems that one's theories should always be 'true to life.' That is very misleading.

In some sense, of course, scientific theories are 'true to life' because evidence is the only tribunal that judges right and wrong. An embarrassing, unexplained fact carries more weight than a satisfactory, elegant theory, and that is what makes scientific activities so frustrating sometimes.

In another sense, scientific theories are not, cannot be, and should not be 'true to life.' Producing a theory does not mean taking into account all possible aspects of the phenomena you describe. On the contrary, it means that you focus on some aspects that can be described in terms of abstract generalizations, assuming, for the sake of simplicity, that all other aspects are 'equal'. The notion of 'all else being equal' seems entirely natural and compelling to some people; and it seems utterly alien to many others. As the Russian writer Alexander Zinoviev put it, the two styles of thinking are diametrically opposed: 'the scientific principle produces abstractions, the anti-scientific principle destroys them on the grounds that such and such has not been considered. The scientific principle establishes strict concepts, the anti-scientific principle makes them ambiguous on the pretext of thus revealing their true variety' (Zinoviev, 1979, p. 209).

Why Social Science Is Impossible (Or Nearly So)

Where do we stand, in our understanding of social phenomena? How much do we know? It often seems like we are nowhere near where we should be, given the amount of available information about human cultures and history. Analogies with other sciences are certainly difficult, but it may seem that we are at the same stage as chemistry was, say around the beginning of the nineteenth century. At the time, chemists had at their disposal a vast number of facts about different substances and their interactions, but very little by way of a systematic understanding of these facts. Why would an acid and a base combine to form water and a salt? (For that matter, the distinction between acids and alkali would have been difficult to explain).

One obstacle on the way to social science is, as it turns out, human minds themselves. The problem is that, in a sense, we already have all sorts of ideas about societies, what could be called a 'folk-sociology' (Boyer, 2018, pp. 216–237). Folk-sociology consists in a set of partly tacit assumptions, that we all use when trying to describe or explain social facts and processes.

For instance, one major feature of our folk-sociology, found in the most diverse societies, is that we spontaneously construe human groups as agents. We talk about villages or social classes or nations as entities that want this, fear that, make decisions, fail to perceive what is happening, reward people or take revenge against them, are hostile towards other groups, and so on. All these terms suggest that, in some implicit way, we consider that what happens in social groups is very much the same as what happens in a human mind.

Another assumption of folk-sociology is that power is a kind of substance attached to particular individuals, and its operation is analogous to a physical force. This is manifest in such phrases as 'she has power,' 'she lost power,' 'his power increased,' and so on. This is not just a Western or European way of speaking. Such metaphors are familiar from many tribal societies, chiefdoms, and early states. We say that people 'have' and 'exercise' power. We conceive of someone with power as able to 'push' others toward certain behaviors (as a physical force can move objects), we say that people who did not follow the leader are 'resisting,' that they are not 'swayed', they resent being 'pushed around', etc.

These conceptions of social facts and processes are based on loose and misleading conventional metaphors (Lakoff & Johnson, 1980). We vaguely perceive that social groups are not literally agents and that power is not literally a force, but it is very difficult to think outside the metaphors. Try to describe political power without ever using notions like 'pushing' and 'resisting'; or try to describe international relations without ever saying that 'Russia wanted this' and 'England realized that...', and so forth. Indeed, the metaphors are so entrenched that they may seem self-evidently true—which is why some social scientists, in the past, tried to argue that nations really were like agents and political power really was a force.

Now folk-sociology is a real hindrance, when you try to think about cultural phenomena in a scientific manner, because it hides the very problems we should try to solve. Seeing the nation or the ethnic group as agents conceals difficult questions, such as: why do people favor their group against others? Why would people behave as loyal members of an ethnic group, rather than defect to another one? In the same way, seeing power as a force makes it impossible to describe the complicated dynamics, whereby the preferences of some people (the leaders) seem to have effects on the behaviors of others (the followers). The notion of power as force indeed makes it impossible to understand how power relations change: why was the East German communist party so powerful in 1988 and so powerless in 1990?

Can we really discard folk-sociology? It is difficult for two reasons. The first one is that our social understandings are largely implicit. As the old saying goes, it is difficult to reason people out of something they were not reasoned into. The view that power is a force, for instance, is not usually an explicit, conscious representation of what political power consists of. A second, more familiar reason is that our ideas about society are not just a matter of detached consideration. They guide our own social interaction, and what happens in that interaction does matter to us. While abandoning your folk-theories in the domains of physics or biology does not come at much of a price, giving up on some ill-conceived notion of political power or gender roles may be a more delicate affair.

If all this is true, then doing social science in the scientific manner might seem well-nigh impossible. There may be both a natural inclination and some strong incentives *not* to consider social and cultural processes in scientific terms. On the contrary, there may be powerful reasons to adopt and preserve theories that are not entirely coherent, or do not have much supporting evidence, simply because they fit both our intuitive expectations and our particular projects.

That may explain why the results are decidedly mixed, why we are very much in the same position as chemists before Galton. While we can admire the great insights of luminaries like Montesquieu or Ibn

Khaldun, the prospect of a cumulative social science seems to recede almost as fast as we proceed.

Why Cultural Stability Is a Mystery

A standard answer to many questions in social science, such as those listed at the beginning of this introduction, is that people have particular mental representations, e.g., about what rituals to perform, or what the economy is like, or what is morally repugnant behavior, because those notions 'are in their culture'. So, the fact that you consider, e.g., the economy as a large pie that can be divided in different ways, or a shaman's rituals as required in order to combat witchcraft, these are notions that 'are in the culture' which would explain why people entertain them.

That cannot be a very good explanation, because it is not an explanation at all. To adopt a phrase from physicists, it is not even wrong. It makes little sense to say that most Zulu people like spicy foods, or that Mongols consult shamans because those preferences are in their culture—because what we mean when we say that some notion is 'in the culture' is simply that it is common among people in a particular place. So we are in effect saying that many Zulu people like spicy foods because many Zulu people like spicy foods. That is not a good start.

The only way that kind of strange statement could make sense would be if we assumed that ideas and values, representations and preferences, are always transmitted identically from generation to generation. That is, we might be implying that Mongols resort to shamanism because *previous* Mongols did that too. In this sense, 'it is in their culture' would mean 'they adopted whatever their forebears did'.

That would be almost reasonable. Of course, it would also be largely false. Cultures change as much as they persist. But at least we are now talking about something that is not entirely tautological, and in fact introduces the most important theme in the study of cultures: What is 'in the culture' depends on what is transmitted from one individual to another.

That is of course an old idea, but it is only very recently that social scientists took it seriously enough to build formal models of what is now called 'cultural evolution'. A convenient date of birth for that movement might be the publication of *Culture and the Evolutionary Process* by Boyd and Richerson (1985). The starting point of the model was that cultural material comes in different packets of information, called memes, transmitted from individual to individual. The notion of memes had originally been proposed by Richard Dawkins (1976), and it then formed the starting point of many attempts to describe cultural material. In this selectionist perspective, trends in cultural evolution, for instance, the persistence of a particular tradition or its downfall, the fact that some ideas can diffuse to large communities or on the contrary remain confined to a few individuals all stems from the relative selective success of different memes. This way of thinking transposed to cultural material the successful models of genetic evolution by random mutation and selective retention.

There was a limitation in these selectionist models, however. Memes were construed as abstract realities that replicate by passing from one mind to another, but there was no explanation of how that happened. Or, people assumed that 'imitation' would be the explanation. This was consistent with another one of our folk-sociological assumptions, namely, that human cultures are by default stable. Social scientists for a long time assumed that there was nothing special to explain in the fact that many Venetian and Xhosa customs or ideas were very similar to what the Venetians and the Xhosa of the previous generation had been doing or thinking. In that view, stability is not mysterious, in fact it is invisible! And only change requires a special explanation.

But it is stability that is mysterious. The Xhosa views about marriage or agriculture are conveyed through a vast number of communicative interactions between individuals. But human communication is a place of high entropy—it resembles a game of Chinese Whispers more than serial photocopying. What you get at the end is very different from the beginning, not just because of distortion, but mostly because of reconstruction (Morin, 2016). Distortion does happen when you make copies of copies of copies... but in Chinese Whispers, each individual in the chain is trying to construct something that would make sense, given what they heard. Human communication, even about 'cultural' matters like marriage or agriculture, is even more entropic, as people are in many cases not even trying to reproduce what they heard.

The 'epidemiology of culture' promoted by Dan Sperber and others (and illustrated in several of the essays in this volume) assumed that these facts about human communication were crucial for understanding the apparent stability of some aspects of human cultures, or the fact that different individuals across space and time seem to have roughly similar mental representations (Sperber, 1985). Human communication has to be reconstructive, because much of what is conveyed is not said and need not be said. That is true of the simplest everyday conversations, as studies in linguistic pragmatics demonstrate (Grice, 1991). Sperber and others argued that this fact was essential to understanding human cultures. What makes them stable or changing is not the 'memes', the explicit statements and gestures, but the way these are completed, in the minds of the receivers, with all sorts of additional content (Sperber, 1985).

So, where does stability come from? The main factor here is not imitation or repetition, but similarities in the 'additional content' I just mentioned. That is where the view of communication inherited from pragmatics was combined with a view of the human mind promoted by cognitive psychology (Tooby & Cosmides, 2005). Human mental capacities were no longer described as a unified, multi-purpose computer that would absorb what the environment threw at it, but as a series of learning systems shaped by natural selection, and specialized in handling recurrent challenges of ancestral environments—how to find nutrition and avoid predators, for sure, but how to find the best possible mate, how to recruit social support, how to defend one's group against enemies, and many more, as described by what is now called evolutionary psychology (Buss, 2016).

Why Social Science Is Possible after All: A Field Without a Name

I of course assume that, against the odds, we can build scientific accounts and that we are in fact gaining ground in our models of human cultures.

In this volume, my co-authors and I consider what could be described as questions of political science (What makes institutions stable, and compelling?), cultural anthropology (Why perform rituals? How do people detect mental illness?), sociology (How does ethnicity impact health?) and economics (Do people's view of the economy match their economic behavior?).

The list may seem a tad disparate, but it is not haphazard. These questions all spring from a common way of seeing human cultures, as the product of the interaction of evolved human capacities and preferences with variable environments. We take seriously the fact that natural selection provides not just an explanation for what we know of human nature, but also a source of rich hypotheses for what is still to be discovered. We also take as self-evident that economic models and game theory provide rich models for interactions between agents, that experimental psychology or neuroscience are the best sources for understanding human minds, and that the variation in human norms and concepts provides a wonderful opportunity to describe the envelope of human nature.

Is there a discipline that studies all that? Not if the term 'discipline' denotes traditional academic divisions. But those matter less and less to actual scholarly projects. Our field-without-a-name is making great progress, and it will prove both scientific and useful.

References

Boyd, R., & Richerson, P. J. (1985). *Culture and the Evolutionary Process*. Chicago, IL: University of Chicago Press.

Boyer, P. (2018). *Minds Make Societies. How Cognition Explains the World Humans Create*. New Haven, CT: Yale University Press.

Buss, D. M. (Ed.) (2016). *The Handbook of Evolutionary Psychology (Second Edition)* (Vol. I and II). Hoboken, NJ: John Wiley & Sons.

Dawkins, R. (1976). *The Selfish Gene*. Oxford: Oxford University Press.

Grice, H. P. (1991). Logic and conversation. In H. P. Grice (Ed.), *Studies in the Way of Words* (pp. 1–143). Cambridge, MA: Harvard University Press.

Lakoff, G., & Johnson, M. (1980). *Metaphors We Live By*. Chicago, IL: University of Chicago Press.

Morin, O. (2016). *How Traditions Live and Die*. Oxford: Oxford University Press.

Sperber, D. (1985). Anthropology and Psychology: Towards an Epidemiology of Representations. *Man, 20*, 73–89.

——. (1996). *Explaining Culture: A Naturalistic Approach*. Oxford: Blackwell.

Tooby, J., & Cosmides, L. (1992). The psychological foundations of culture. In J. H. Barkow, L. Cosmides, & et al. (Eds.), *The Adapted Mind: Evolutionary Psychology and the Generation of Culture.* (pp. 19–136). New York: Oxford University Press.

——. (Eds.). (2005). *Conceptual Foundations of Evolutionary Psychology.* Hoboken, NJ: John Wiley & Sons Inc.

Zinoviev, A. (1979). *The Yawning Heights* [translated by Clough, G.]. London: Random House.

2. Institutions and Human Nature

Introductory Note

One of the most enduring and most damaging assumptions in the social sciences is the belief that it makes sense to talk about nature and culture, or to part the 'innate' from the 'acquired' in describing human behavior. Almost as misguided is the recommendation that we should describe behavior as some combination or mixture of these elements—an insipid counsel for moderation that only results in a stubborn incuriosity about what is being 'mixed' and how (Pinker, 2002).

Against all this, many biologists, anthropologists and psychologists have, for decades, tried to illustrate how these oppositions dissolve, when we consider human capacities and preferences from an evolutionary standpoint (Ridley, 2003; Tooby & Cosmides, 2010). It is part of mankind's evolved nature that we can acquire from our conspecifics vast amounts of information that constitute our ecological niche (Tooby & DeVore, 1987). This is possible because genetic selection fashioned a whole suite of learning mechanisms that orient the growing mind's attention to specific cues in the environment, and govern that mind's inferences. That is how we can acquire detailed and valuable information about, e.g., the physical relations between solid objects, the invisible beliefs and intentions that explain agents' behaviors, the nature of the social bonds between people around us, the syntax of the local language, the best ways to extract resources from the natural world or to establish cooperation and garner social support. All this requires extensive learning, which requires extensively prepared systems—for a survey, see Boyer (2018, pp. 1–30) and Tooby & Cosmides (1992).

How does this relate to the study of institutions? To be more specific, Michael Petersen and I were trying to address the very general

    https://doi.org/10.11647/OBP.0257.02

question, why do people adopt some institutions as quite 'natural', in the familiar sense, while others are much less compelling? Why is marriage apparently so self-evident, that in most cultures throughout history, no-one needed an explanation for it? Why would the rules of a deliberative democracy be a much more fragile construction?

We can describe institutions as the 'rules of the game' in complex social interaction (North, 1990). These rules can be very different, from time to time and place to place. From that diversity, many people would conclude that genetic evolution by natural selection is irrelevant. But historical or cultural differences are, just like commonalities, an outcome of our evolved dispositions (Sperber & Hirschfeld, 2004). That is what Michael Petersen and I tried to illustrate in this article, using the contrasted cases of marriage institutions, criminal justice, and commons management as our examples. These display vast cultural and historical differences, and in fact some institutions are only found in some human societies. But in these different cases and, we would argue, many more besides these, we can see highly intuitive specific expectations at play, which make some parts of the local, historically specific institutional arrangements very easy to acquire, which in turn makes it relatively easy for people to coordinate their behaviors around common rules. The intuitive expectations are shaped by evolved learning systems, and in turn they shape the various institutions.

An important consequence of this model is that explanations of institutions are, by necessity, domain-specific. For instance, cultural rules about marriage are strongly constrained by human intuitions about mating, about the ways humans combine sexual access, care for their offspring and economic cooperation. By contrast, judicial rules are influenced by our moral intuitions and expectations concerning cooperation. So, to explain two different domains of institutions, we need to investigate two separate mental systems, each of which has its own domain of application, its computational rules, and its associated emotions.

That is why general models or theories of institutions are, in our view, incomplete. True, political scientists and economists have put forward important models of, e.g., the conditions under which there is demand for and supply of institutional rules, especially in complex modern societies—in the article we discuss some of these, especially from the neo-institutional economics literature. But institutions are not just systems of rules, they are also systems of rules mentally represented by individuals—in fact, in many cases they consist in individual mental representations about the mental representations of other individuals (Heintz, 2007). That is why, at some point in our explanations, we must consider the role of evolved domain-specific intuitions, which means that we leave aside a general theory of institutions and produce theories of particular kinds of institutions.

References

Boyer, P. (2018). Missing links: The psychology and epidemiology of shamanistic beliefs. *Behavioral and Brain Sciences*, 41, e71. https://doi.org/10.1017/S0140525X17002023

Heintz, C. (2007). Institutions as Mechanisms of Cultural Evolution: Prospects of the Epidemiological Approach. *Biological Theory, 2*, 244–249. https://doi.org/10.1162/biot.2007.2.3.244

North, D. C. (1990). *Institutions, institutional change, and economic performance.* Cambridge; New York: Cambridge University Press.

Pinker, S. (2002). *The Blank Slate: The Modern Denial of Human Nature.* New York: Viking.

Ridley, M. (2003). *Nature via Nurture. Genes, Experience and What Makes Us Human.* New York: Harper Collins.

Sperber, D., & Hirschfeld, L. A. (2004). The cognitive foundations of cultural stability and diversity. *Trends in Cognitive Sciences, 8*, 40–46. https://doi.org/10.1016/j.tics.2003.11.002

Tooby, J., & Cosmides, L. (1992). The Psychological Foundations of Culture. In J. H. Barkow, L. Cosmides, et al. (Eds.), *The Adapted Mind: Evolutionary Psychology and the Generation of Culture.* (pp. 19–136). New York: Oxford University Press.

——. (2010). Groups in Mind: The Coalitional Roots of War and Morality. In H. Høgh-Olesen (Ed.), *Human Morality & Sociality: Evolutionary & Comparative Perspectives* (pp. 191–234). New York: Palgrave MacMillan.

Tooby, J., & DeVore, I. (1987). The Reconstruction of Hominid Behavioral Evolution through Strategic Modeling. In W. Kinzey (Ed.), *Primate Models of Hominid Behavior* (pp. 183–237). New York: SUNY Press.

The Naturalness of (Many) Social Institutions

Evolved Cognition as their Foundation[1]

with Michael Bang Petersen

Abstract: Most standard social science accounts only offer limited explanations of institutional design, i.e., why institutions have common features observed in many different human groups. Here, we suggest that these features are best explained as the outcome of evolved human cognition, in such domains as mating, moral judgment and social exchange. As empirical illustrations, we show how this evolved psychology makes marriage systems, legal norms and commons management systems intuitively obvious and compelling, thereby ensuring their occurrence and cultural stability. We extend this to propose under what conditions institutions can become 'natural', compelling and legitimate, and outline probable paths for institutional change given human cognitive dispositions. Explaining institutions in terms of these exogenous factors also suggests that a general theory of institutions as such is neither necessary nor in fact possible. What are required are domain-specific accounts of institutional design in different domains of evolved cognition.

---

1   An earlier version of this chapter was originally published as Boyer, P., & Petersen, MB. (2011). The naturalness of (many) social institutions: Evolutionary and Cognitive Background, *Journal of Institutional Economics* 8(1): 1–25, https://doi.org/10.1017/S1744137411000300. Reprinted with permission of Cambridge University Press.

https://doi.org/10.11647/OBP.0257.03

1. Introduction

General accounts of social institutions should provide plausible and testable answers to questions of institutional design, such as, why do social institutions have the specific features that we observe in human societies? Why do we observe common institutional features in otherwise very different cultural environments? Or, why do some institutions seem natural and compelling to participants, while others are considered alien or coercive? Here, we develop the view that present institutional theories do not properly address such design questions, and that this can be remedied only by taking into account what we call the 'naturalness' of institutions, their connection to human expectations and preferences that result from evolution by natural selection. This perspective may help us understand commonalities across cultures, but also why some institutions are more successful and compelling than others and why they change in particular directions.

To some extent, this suggestion echoes a defining feature of the neo-institutional approach. From the beginning, neo-institutionalism has been oriented towards developing realistic models of the actors, countering the *Homo economicus* model inherent in older institutional accounts and emphasizing the cognitive limits of human decision makers (Brousseau & Glachant, 2008). From this perspective, important lines of inquiry have been developed with regards to, first, how institutions carry a range of unintended consequences given the cognitive limits of their designers, and, second, how a function of institutions is to counter such limits (North, 1990). At the same time, however, this perspective of bounded rationality provides only a partial description of human cognition. While one line of research within the cognitive sciences has been preoccupied with the biased and fallible nature of human cognition, a complementary line of research has developed the view that human cognition is in fact 'better than rational' (Cosmides & Tooby, 1994).

Evolutionary psychologists have argued that human cognition includes a multitude of domain-specific cognitive programs, each optimally geared (within evolutionary constraints) to solve particular problems in the course of human evolutionary history (Barkow, Cosmides, & Tooby, 1992). The inferential power of these specialized programs comes from their content-rich nature. That is, they are loaded with inbuilt assumptions about their domain. Environments that fit these inbuilt assumptions appear intuitive and readily understandable.

Our aim is to outline the argument that institutions are effective not *despite* human cognition but, in part, *because* of human cognition. Essentially, we argue that the content-rich nature of evolved intuitions provides a foundation which can be and is often used in the design of many social institutions. Institutions that fit these intuitions, we propose, develop more easily, require less effort to conform to, and are more culturally stable.

While evolutionary psychology is increasingly incorporated into social theory (Alford & Hibbing, 2004; Hodgson, 1999; McDermott, 2006; Petersen, 2010), and some economists have been keen to integrate an evolutionary logic into their models (Dopfer, 2005; Enright, 1984), many social scientists may be unfamiliar with the approach. By way of developing our account, we therefore present a series of illustrations of how our knowledge of human evolution and cognition provides the tools for a causal, naturalistic understanding of social institutions such as marriage rules and norms, legal systems and social exchange mechanisms. In each instance, our point of departure will be the existence of specific cross-cultural features in the design of these institutions and how these can be seen as the institutionalization of evolved intuitions. From this, we show how these insights can inform the study of institutions, the naturalness of (many) social institutions and develop a range of novel predictions on how institutions develop and change.

2. Explaining Common Features

We focus here on named social institutions, that is, sets of norms and rules in which all culturally competent members of a group have explicit, accessible mental representations. For instance, *football* in England, *marriage* in the USA, *potlatch* among the Tlingit or *meeting* for Quakers are social institutions of the kind we consider here. The important point here is that people have some notion that, for example, there is such a thing as *potlatch* in their social environment and they have some notion of how observed behaviors can be seen as exemplars of these abstract notions, or violations of their rules (Searle, 1995). These named bundles of concepts, norms and behaviors are what we call 'institutions' in the rest of this article (Ostrom, 2005). This is only a subset of 'institutions' in the neo-institutional sense, some of which remain implicit, such as, for example, a sense of fairness or simple habits.

Institutional models generally emphasize the contribution of both *formal* and *informal* aspects of such institutions, the former including laws, contracts, administrative rules and procedures, while the latter include implicit norms and routines. Here, we want to explore the cognitive processes that underpin both aspects of institutions. An institution such as 'marriage' in the USA combines legal norms and emotional preferences, contracts and moral intuitions; in short, both formal and informal aspects. The question for us is, what makes certain 'packages' of informal and formal norms natural and compelling to participants?

In many domains, fairly similar institutions can be found in diverse cultural environments. For instance, despite obvious differences, many human groups know of interaction norms that (seemingly) correspond to what an English speaker would call 'marriage' (we will discuss, presently, whether that similarity is an illusion). An interesting fact is that such diverse institutions share not just very general properties, for example, conditions and limits of sexual relationships and parenting, but also many other features, for example, the association between long-term sexual intimacy and economic solidarity, the fact that the union is in principle exclusive, the fact that its inception requires public ceremonies, etc. These are common features, most of which may not be universal, but all of which are so widespread that this recurrence requires an explanation.

In the social sciences, different frameworks suggest very different ways of considering institutions and their common features. For instance, a culturalist account is the default position of much anthropological reflection on institutions. In this view, the latter are the way they are because they are congruent with the particular concepts, values, norms, etc. widespread in a particular place (Gudeman, 1986). A recurrent problem of anthropological culturalism is, of course, the presence of recurrent features of social institutions, which in a purely localist framework would have to constitute massively improbable coincidences. This is true for marriage but also for the emergence of similar patterns in, for example, commons management, sports or political structures. To a large extent, classical functionalist accounts are fraught with similar problems. They require that most institutions emerge as solutions to particular classes of problems or situations, and survive to the extent that they fulfill that role in congruence with other institutions. However, again, this has proved insufficient to account for the recurrence of particular institutions (e.g., raising children in families) compared with other, possibly efficient alternatives (e.g., raising children in kibbutz-like communities) (Merton, 1996).

A more promising account of institutions appeared in economics with the development of neo-institutional models. These extended the notion of institution to encompass both formal and informal, tacit or explicit 'rules of the game' that constrain interaction between economic agents (North, 1990). These rules decrease transaction costs and information costs in particular. Within the neo-institutional tradition, there are different accounts of how institutions are created. Since there is not the space to review such models in detail, for such surveys, see Knight and Sened (1995), North (2005) and Brousseau and Glachant (2008). Briefly, *conventional* accounts assume that institutions emerge out of the recurrent features of repeated economic interactions—they are simply regularities turned into rules (Sugden, 1986). *Competitive* accounts suggest that institutions develop out of original, small-scale norms by conferring competitive advantages to newcomers who participate in the new arrangement (Greif, 2006). Finally, *bargaining* models emphasize power asymmetries between parties in the creation or modifications of institutions (Knight, 1995). However, none of these accounts point to easy, natural answers to questions of design. Whether specific institutions are shaped by bargaining or convention is not sufficient to account for highly specific features, such as, for example, the link between intention and responsibility in the law, or the connection between economic sharing and sex in marriage norms.

Here, we present a complement to neo-institutional accounts. Institutions comprise rules or norms that most agents obey, expect most others to obey and expect most others to expect them to obey (Bicchieri, 2006). But, for a rule or a norm to become an institution, it must be widely distributed in the minds of the members in a group (Sperber, 1996). In order to explain how institutions are developed and changed, we therefore need to understand how people adopt, modify and transmit rules and norms (Heintz, 2007). Most importantly, we need to understand which types of rules and norms are particularly likely to be transmitted and adopted without much modification, while others require significant effort, skill and special knowledge.

This leads to our main contention, that institutions are best understood against the background of a set of human psychological dispositions that influence the effort needed to adopt and accept certain social arrangements. To introduce this cognitive account of institutions, we illustrate how our evolved psychology makes an impact on the developments of common features in three different domains of institutional design.

3. Illustration (I). Marriage Norms and Mating Strategies

Institutional Framework

In most societies, there is a distinction between occasional or informal sexual encounters and arrangements (which may be approved, tolerated, frowned upon, prohibited, etc.) and more stable and formalized unions. The initiation of the latter kind of union is generally, at least in principle, marked by some public event. There are shared norms about what each party should expect from the other, given such ceremonies, and about how they should behave towards third parties. Finally, sanctions are associated with the violation of these norms. Why is all this so common?

A standard, and plausible initial answer would be that such norms reduce uncertainty in social interaction, a general feature of social institutions. Marriage norms and wedding ceremonies certainly have that effect, in several ways. First, marriage between two individuals conveys to third parties that the individuals concerned have rights in each other that (*mutatis mutandis* the local norms) are not available to other members of the group. There is, for example, a certain amount of resources or help that a husband may expect from a wife or vice versa, or a woman from her in-laws, but not from others. Second, marriage conveys to third parties that the individuals concerned have (again, with local variations) withdrawn from the pool of potential mates. The fact that there is a long-term stable union between the partners modifies third parties' mating strategies and preferences towards either one of the partners. Ceremonies do not just signal this to a large number of people, but also inform them all at the same time in the same way. Third, marriage conveys to each party that the other is (at least overtly) committed to fulfilling their obligations as per the local norms. Regardless of intentions, the public commitment signal creates expectations against which either party can measure behaviors.

In other words, the most important effects of weddings seem to consist in signaling. In all human societies, weddings are of interest and great concern to outsiders, which is why for instance the ceremonies are often quite literally very noisy affairs (van Gennep, 1909). Internal signals between the married parties are equally important. The potential benefits of an efficient marriage are in part public goods, and in many cases cannot be achieved without sacrifices, given the spouses' divergent preferences (E. Posner, 2000). So marriage requires honest, hard-to-fake signals of commitment. These are provided in many societies by costly conditions for marriage, for example, the obligation for brides to leave their kin groups, for grooms to provide bride wealth, or to show adequate means to support a family, etc. Such conditions serve (in part) as signals, which may explain why, when they are relaxed as happened in many Western societies, they are replaced with informal signals such as occasional gifts (E. Posner, 2000). The occurrence of informal, 'spontaneous' signals varies inversely with the precision of the group-wide representation of marriage roles.

All this is fine, but falls short of a satisfactory answer to questions of design. Coordination and uncertainty-reduction effects do not explain why marriage is universally about two parties, so that polygamy is a series of two-party contracts, not a group arrangement; why polygyny is common and polyandry exceedingly rare; why a single institution binds sexual, economic and offspring-related norms in most societies; why divorce is often available but fixed-term marriage is generally not; and other such common features.

Evolutionary Background

The institutions may make more sense in the context of specific preferences and competences that arise from human evolution. Obviously, natural selection results in particular mating preferences and processes in each species, and ours can be no exception (Symons, 1979). It would be surprising if human competences and preferences in this domain had no influence on the design of marriage. Indeed, human reproduction and parenting display expected features given the specific history of our primate lineage (Van Schaik & Van Hooff, 1983).

As in most other mammals, there is in humans a large asymmetry of reproductive costs between human males and females. The latter's costs include a long gestation, an even longer nurturing period, with their associated energy and opportunity costs, as compared with the lesser cost incurred by males. This, as in comparable species, means that sexual selection has been important in favoring distinct behaviors and preferences in males and females. Females need to be much choosier than males in mate selection. Also, females should prefer males with demonstrable capacity and willingness to nurture their offspring. Differences between male and female preferences result in an equilibrium that includes relatively long-term paternal investment in children's nurturing, conditional on fathers' certainty that the children are their own biological offspring, as well as a certain but limited amount of philandering and 'mate poaching' in both sexes.

These evolutionary factors predict a whole variety of human behaviors which are actually observed in most human societies, such as: the general disposition towards long-term paternal investment; sexual differences in attractiveness criteria (Buss, 1989); differences between criteria for long- and short-term mates (Kaplan & Gangestad, 2005); the ways in which attractiveness is turned off by childhood cohabitation and other cues, leading to incest avoidance (Lieberman, Tooby, & Cosmides, 2003); the specific triggers of and gender differences in sexual and romantic jealousy (Buss, 2000); mechanisms of sexual coercion and attempts by men to control women's sexuality and increase paternal certainty (Wilson & Daly, 1998); the general pattern of serial exclusive monogamy (and polygyny) observed in human societies (Van Schaik & Van Hooff, 1983); the male tendency to reject step-children (Anderson, Kaplan, Lam, & Lancaster, 1999; Anderson, Kaplan, & Lancaster, 1999; Daly & Wilson, 1988); the influence of male presence/absence on young women's choices of reproductive strategies (Ellis, 1993); and many other behaviors.

Naturally, most computations required by such behaviors are largely unconscious — only their results are available to conscious inspection. To cite but one example, it seems that women's choice of early sexual activity and early pregnancy are directly affected by paternal presence during a critical period in early childhood (Ellis et al., 2003). This can be explained as learning from the environment which reproductive strategy is most appropriate, given low paternal investment in offspring (Quinlan, 2003). Obviously, young women never represent reproductive choices as a search for optimal fitness. They are responding to such proxies as the attractiveness of particular mates or a desire for children, and other here-and-now preferences for particular kinds of behaviors, all of which are the outcome of non-conscious cognitive processes.

An Integrated Perspective

An important point here is that human preferences and behaviors in the mating domain include the expectation of stable long-term unions between men and women that associate privileged or exclusive sexual access with economic solidarity. Note that this is largely intuitive, that is, most humans hold this expectation without necessarily having the explicit model or principles that would explain it. Also, this expectation is of course more abstract than the norms for such long-term unions in particular societies, which can vary in many respects such as number of people involved (polygyny versus monogamy), exclusiveness (e.g., societies with sanctioned 'visiting' lovers), required paternal investment in offspring (from full responsibility to occasional visits) and, most important, filiation and inheritance rules.

All this suggests that human beings are equipped with an evolved, domain-specific learning system that is prepared for and attentive to information about the particular ways in which marriage unions are locally defined and organized. In this perspective, the transmission of culturally specific information about marriage norms 'free-rides' on information supplied by our intuitive expectations. That is, people easily acquire their local marriage norms because the assumptions (e.g., that the union is heterosexual, that it is about long-term mating, that it associates sexual access with resource sharing, etc.) are among the evolved cognitive equipment of the species.

This would explain why many aspects of marriage norms are not the object of explicit, deliberate transmission, and seem to 'go without saying' while others are the object of explicit norms. For instance, the assumption that marriage binds a man and a woman is intuitive enough that it is not actually specified in most cultures. By contrast, the permissible number of simultaneous unions, or the precise manner in which they can be broken up, are matters of explicitly transmitted information. The expectations that married people will contribute to each other's welfare, or that an officially declared union must be officially dissolved, do not have to be made explicit. In this perspective, the social institution seems to consist in particular parameter settings of a marriage template that is spontaneously created by normally developing minds.

4. Illustration (II). Criminal Law and Moral Intuitions

Institutions

The emergence of 'the law' as a separate domain of norms and behaviors, distinct from other social norms, is confined to large polities with literacy (Goody, 1986; Maine, 1963). However, most human groups do have explicit norms for conflict resolution and the punishment of wrongs, even if these are not defined as different from ordinary, non-legal decision making (Hoebel, 1964). From these norms and procedures to the literate, codified legal systems of large states, there is a continuum of social complexification, along which some central aspects of legal norms are preserved. Legal systems all modify personal, face-to-face conflict resolution on the basis of norms that are: (a) explicit; (b) (at least partly) de-contextualized (e.g., construed as the right way to sanction theft, rather than this particular act of theft); (c) (at least partly) impersonal, as they in principle apply to whole classes of agents or even to all possible agents; and (d) therefore more predictable than informal ones.

Why these common features? One possible explanation is that legal institutions are just economically efficient sets of conventions. Richard Posner, for instance, considers that standard economic models of utility maximization explain most features of legal systems (R. A. Posner, 1981). Economic rationality would account for differences between the custom-bound legal systems of small-scale traditional societies, and the legal codes of large-scale industrial polities. For instance, the former generally maintain strict (no-fault) liability, so that one (or one's kin group) is responsible for whatever damage one has caused, whether or not one is guilty of a wrong or of negligence. This, as Richard Posner argues, makes sense in economic systems where the cost of information is particularly high, so that long inquiries into circumstances and intentions would be problematic. In the same way, the fact that litigants are generally asked to pay for arbitrage, in other words to hire a judge, makes sense as there is no institution for the public provision of magistrates (R. A. Posner, 1981).

Economic efficiency can certainly account for specific differences between the legal norms of various places, but it seems insufficient to explain the common features of these systems and the ways in which people generally find them compelling (Cosmides & Tooby, 2006). This is particularly clear in the domain of criminal justice, where apparently obvious features of the institutions, e.g., tacit assumptions about the relative severity of different crimes, only make sense against the background of cooperation in ancestral conditions. The naturalness of (many) social institutions arrangements are based on complex intuitive assumptions about behavior, intentions and fairness.

Relevant Cognitive Systems

In the last 20 years, convergent findings in developmental psychology, behavioral economics and cross-cultural psychology have suggested that human beings in very different groups evaluate the moral valence of actions on the basis of largely tacit, emotion-laden common intuitions (Haidt, 2007). Intuitive morality is independent from (and only partly affected by) explicit, culturally specific understandings of and teachings about right and wrong (Greene, 2005). Intuitive morality also underpins a sense of fairness that is quite distinct from economic rationality (McCabe & Smith, 2001). Rather than survey these models and findings, we will only mention those points directly relevant to the issue of criminal behavior and appropriate punishment.

Human minds in a variety of cultural environments develop the following specific intuitive processes. First, there is a domain of moral principles and norms, distinct from other evaluative dimensions of action. Indeed, even preschool children have definite intuitions about the difference between moral rules and mere social conventions (Elliot Turiel, 1994). Second, the judgment that a behavior is permissible, commendable or wrong occurs as a fast, automatic consequence of representing the specific action and context. These intuitions may then be explicated, nuanced or (more rarely) reversed by explicit reasoning, but the latter is quite literally an afterthought — deliberate, slow and often produced in order to justify a pre-existing intuition. Third, intuitive moral appraisals are generally accompanied by congruent emotions. Emotional appraisal is part of the processes leading to moral evaluation, which is why experimental manipulations of the emotion can trigger significant changes in moral judgment (Haidt, 2001). All this is particularly visible in young children's moral development. In contrast to the classical, Kantian picture of children gradually building moral understandings by acquiring more complex modes of reasoning (Kohlberg, 1981), experimental evidence suggests that moral development consists in the calibration of prior intuitions (E. Turiel, 2002).

Experimental evidence also shows that people are intuitively convinced that wrong behaviors vary in seriousness — that much is assumed by young children even for completely novel behaviors (E. Turiel, 2002). Another common intuition is that the punishment should fit the crime, as it were — such that a schedule of graded punishments is required (Nichols & Knobe, 2008). Again, these thoughts are not entertained as the result of deliberate reasoning on moral matters, but as the intuitions that start the process of moral reasoning.

Another important aspect of moral intuitions is a motivation to punish norm violators, even in third parties who are not harmed by the transgression. This preference is not based on learning from trial and error, since the potential consequences of either punitive or non-punitive strategies are manifest only in the long run. Such punitive attitudes are universal in human groups and virtually non-existent in other animals. There are various interpretations for this evolutionary novelty. Punitive sentiments may have helped recruitment to collective action (Yamagishi, 1992). They may also signal cooperative attitudes, as those who punish transgressors are signaling their attachment to local norms and their willingness to incur costs in their defense (Fessler,

2001), which would explain why people tend to be more punitive when observed by others (Robinson, Kurzban, & Jones, 2007). Finally, punitive attitudes may be an attempt to eliminate the fitness advantage enjoyed by free-riders (Price, Cosmides, & Tooby, 2002) or recalibrate their motivations (Petersen, Sell, Tooby, & Cosmides, 2010). What is certain is that the motivation for third-party punishment is general in human groups, and strong enough to override the cost involved.

An Integrated Perspective

In the same way as for marriage, evolved psychological capacities and processes constrain legal norms. They provide a set of understandings that need not be explicitly transmitted as a condition for participation, and therefore make institutions 'learnable' to the extent that they are congruent to intuitive understandings (Cosmides & Tooby, 2006). Legal institutions do not require that one learn concepts of right and wrong, the need for appropriate sanctions, or that one acquire the motivation for third-party punishment. Also, the ways in which legal institutions publicize decision making seems to derive from moral intuitions. As we noted, people have definite intuitions about the role of reputation in cooperation. It may be no surprise that legal institutions turn reasoning and decision making, ordinarily private mental events, into publicly scrutable processes. Courts work in the open, laws are inscribed in stone or in books, and penalties are made visible, for instance, by using stigma as a salient form of punishment (Kurzban & Leary, 2001; E. A. Posner, 2007). All these aspects of the law seem self-evident to most practitioners, as indeed they should be if they are based on common pre-existing intuitions.

In return, institutions do modify social interactions in the legal domain. Obviously, the existence of public representations of norms and processes make punishment more predictable and the domain of lawful behavior more easily delineated, which translates as an advantage in transaction costs (R. A. Posner, 1981). But the effects may be even deeper, as most people tend to reify or essentialize the law as independent from actual people's decisions and the workings of their minds. To the extent that the motivations for particular judgments seem both stable and impersonal, they reinforce this tacit form of legal idealism, a notion that laws are not made but discovered, which itself may make them more compelling.

5. Illustration (III). Commons and Exchange Intuitions

The cognitive framework may also make sense of some common features of particular economic institutions. Consider, for instance, Elinor Ostrom's description of the principles that allow efficient management of common-pool resources such as fisheries, water distribution, etc., in which a resource must be pooled and might be depleted by opportunistic unregulated use (Ostrom, 1990). According to Ostrom, the following principles are necessary, though not sufficient, to preserve the semi-formal institutions that manage commons: (1) some rules must clearly define the set of agents authorized to use the commons and the conditions for entry; (2) the rules must be adapted to the specific nature of the resource; (3) the rules must be designed by the users; (4) rule observance must be monitored by the users or agents accountable to the users; and (5) rule violation must be sanctioned by graded punishment (Ostrom, 1990).

Why are commons institutions the way they are, and why these recurrent features? An institutional account does not directly address them, as it is focused on different issues, both theoretical (showing how efficient commons-management systems emerge despite collective action problems) and pragmatic (deriving recommendations for efficient commons management). All the rules mentioned above require a complex background of psychological processes and preferences. For one thing, commons management implies definite judgments about distributive justice, about which divisions of resources count as acceptable, given different agents' contributions or needs (Fehr, Schmidt, Kolm, & Ythier, 2006). Psychologists have shown that such judgments are mostly based on early developed intuitions (Enright, 1984). Young children in very diverse cultures use similar principles of distributive justice, combining a principle of equality (equal shares as the best distribution) with context-based intuitions about merit and need (Sigelman & Waitzman, 1991). Obviously, these early judgments are then calibrated during development as a function of local forms of exchange. But the underlying principles subsist. They result in specific fairness intuitions that cannot be explained in terms of standard rational choice models (Fehr et al., 2006).

The cognitive mechanisms required for commons management also include the capacity and motivation to identify violators of agreed norms. Experimental findings suggest that people are specifically sensitive to cheating (taking benefits without paying costs in a social contract) and quickly identify which behaviors constitute cheating. The underlying cognitive system is domain specific, in the sense that social contract violations are not processed in the same way as violations of social norms in general, or exceptions to other kinds of rules (Cosmides & Tooby, 2005).

As Ostrom and others have demonstrated, efficient use of commons requires a whole lot of specific 'tools' (institutions in the neo-institutional framework) such as rules, norms and models to overcome collective action problems. However, these tools need not be provided by the institutions themselves. To a large extent, norms and rules 'free-ride' on competencies and motivations for fair exchange that are part of our evolved cognitive equipment.

6. What Are Evolved Domain-Specific Systems?

Evolved Systems as Specialized Learning and Decision Mechanisms

The perspective developed in relation to these three examples highlights how institutional designs are directly facilitated by the structure of human cognition. In this way, they complement the focus of previous accounts of the interplay between cognition and institutions. In the extant literature, the focus has been on the general cognitive limitations of human cognition and how the latter affect the workings of institutions. One strand of argument has been preoccupied with how the fallibility of institutional designs can be traced back to the fallibility of the cognitive capabilities of their designers (Pierson, 2004). Another strand of research has focused on how institutions can buffer the limits of human cognition (Knight & North, 1997). Hence, institutions — refined through trial and error — provide external constraints on behavior which simplify individual choice and guide it toward rational outcomes. A third strand of research has focused less on the limits of fixed cognitive processes but rather argued for the plasticity of cognitive processes and how they are molded by the institutional environment of the individual (Dequech, 2006). While these avenues toward integrating insights on human cognition and institutions are highly important, they are based on an incomplete description of the current state of knowledge in cognitive science.

In our view, the content (and not just the limits) of a variety of special and species-typical cognitive systems, as observed by evolutionary anthropologists and psychologists, is relevant to issues of institutional design and maintenance. As we noted above, human beings have an intuitive mating psychology that includes attractiveness judgments, relationship maintenance and reproductive strategies (Buss, 1989; Symons, 1979). They have specialized social exchange mechanisms for cheater- and cooperator-detection (Cosmides & Tooby, 2005) and a highly specific moral psychology (Haidt, 2007). They also have a coalitional psychology which monitors the establishment and maintenance of groups with common interests, vigilance towards defection, rivalry towards other groups, etc. (Kurzban & Neuberg, 2005), as well as systems that monitor ethnic cohesion and attitudes towards others (Schaller, 2006) or gender relations (Sidanius & Veniegas, 2000; Wilson & Daly, 1992). In fact, sketching the range of evolved cognitive mechanisms underlying common human behaviors would be far beyond the scope of this article (for general surveys, see (Buss, 2005); (Dunbar, Barrett, & Lycett, 2005)).

Several features of these cognitive systems are of particular relevance here:

Cognitive systems are domain specific. Cognitive predispositions are not just general constraints, for example, on the amount of material that can be acquired, on the capacity of attention and memory. Cognitive predispositions also consist in domain-specific expectations about the kinds of objects and agents to be found in the world. Only some items of information trigger operation of a specific system, in much the same way as only molecules of a particular shape and composition trigger the activity of specific enzymes (Barrett, 2005). Many such narrow input–output relationships are species-typical fixations rather than plastic features that can be molded by environmental processes (Tooby & Cosmides, 1992).

Each domain-specific system includes its own decision-making procedures. In most standard models of economists and political scientists, one assumes that people's behavior is guided by a domain-general, utility-maximizing cognitive system. In those cases in which human behavior does not conform to normative models, this is said to result from general limitations of the decision-making system, for instance because of biases (Kahneman, Slovic, & Tversky, 1982) or impulsiveness (Ainslie, 2005; Loewenstein & O'Donoghue, 2005). These putative flaws in decision making are thought to be domain general — they would occur in the same way in, say, keeping friends and keeping lovers, avoiding enemies and avoiding pathogens. However, psychological evidence suggests a different picture, in which each domain-specific system (e.g., concerned with retaining mates, or with recruiting coalitional allies) comes with its own, domain-appropriate decision rules. For instance, if you are dealing with a contractor for house repairs, it may make sense to average the benefits and costs from previous interactions with that specific agent, in order to compute their overall value to you. If dealing with a lover, it would seem intuitively odd to balance cases of infidelity with cases of availability. Even when we use rules of thumb or 'fast and frugal heuristics', these are tailored to the kinds of problems we evolved to encounter (Gigerenzer, 2002; Gigerenzer, Todd, & Group, 1999).

Competencies and preferences are integrated. This is a consequence of the previous point. Each domain-specific cognitive system includes its own decision-making procedures which combine specific preferences and specific competencies. There is no reason to consider that preferences are external to decision-making systems. For instance, consider human coalitional psychology, our capacity to form an alliance with genetically unrelated agents, usually against other groups. It includes as part of a single package both a set of preferences (e.g., a strong aversion for other agents' defection, a desire to make the coalition stronger, a willingness to pay a high price of entry, etc.) and a set of competences (e.g., the monitoring skills to detect other agents' commitment, the signaling skills to express one's solidarity, etc.).

Cognitive systems are learning mechanisms. Each domain-specific system is specialized in picking up particular kinds of information in the organism's environment. Contrary to widespread assumptions outside evolutionary biology, 'acquired information' and 'genetically specified information' are not a zero-sum system. On the contrary, organisms that can acquire vast amounts of information from their environments (e.g., primates) need vastly more specified initial systems than organisms (e.g., invertebrates) that acquire less. Between species, more learning invariably means more 'instinct', so to speak. Humans have a complex coalitional psychology and a complex mating psychology, which means that in both domains they acquire enormous amounts of information from their social and natural environments precisely because sophisticated learning systems in these domains are specified by their genotypes.

Implications for Interaction with Environments

These features have a number of implications for the operations of human cognition which are highly important to institutional researchers. Here, we focus on two implications. We begin by outlining them in relative broad terms, review some of the evidence for these implications in the cognitive science literature and then specifically apply them to institutional analysis.

Cognitive systems operate more reliably in matching environments. Cognitive systems are designed to operate within a specific domain and, therefore, the inbuilt assumptions, categories, competences and learning procedures reflect the evolutionarily recurrent structure of that exact domain. When cognitive systems are applied to problems on the fringes of their proper domain, they will operate less automatically and less reliably.

This has been directly shown in cognitive research. For example, we have evolved to hunt prey and protect ourselves against predators and, therefore, most probably have specialized cognitive systems designed to track the movements of animals, their orientation, and their most likely trajectory (Barrett, 2005a). In modern societies, predatory animals constitute less a threat than, for example, cars but this does not mean that we can effortlessly apply the systems designed for tracking the former to the latter. And, in fact, Joshua New *et al.* showed that subjects are far slower to recognize changes in car orientation than the orientation of animals—even when these animals are visually unfamiliar, unimportant, and barely discernible (New, Cosmides, & Tooby, 2007).

Similarly, we detect violations of rules faster and more reliably when detecting violations corresponds to detecting cheaters on social exchanges (Ermer, Cosmides, & Tooby, 2007). As argued above, rule violation in the context of social exchange is the exact domain of a set of highly specialized cognitive systems while, most likely, generic rule violations are not. This insight is also directly applicable to actual design situations. Human–computer interfaces require much less effort on behalf of the user if these interfaces correspond to the structure of cognitive systems designed for handling real-world objects (Nørager, 2009).

The structure of cognitive systems creates a baseline motivation to shape environments into a format that matches them. Because environments that fit our cognitive systems can be processed effortlessly (given the possibility for reliably applying evolved categories, competences, etc.), people will find matching environments more 'natural' and their exigencies more compelling. Also, creating and upholding non-matching environments require a level of effort that individuals could be unwilling to pay without special incentives.

Again, a number of studies in cognitive science have directly demonstrated this. Most of these studies have focused on an extreme version of the above principle, in the sense that these studies have shown that we simply process and react toward non-matching environments as if they were matching. In the domain of popular culture, one obvious example is pornography that is psychologically represented as if mating opportunities were present, thereby triggering sexual arousal, etc. (Saad & Gill, 2014). Similarly, research shows that people have difficulties in distinguishing between their real friends and people they see on television in the sense that their satisfaction with their friendships is influenced by both (Kanazawa, 2002). These cognitive effects also occur in the direct interaction with others. For example, modern individuals process the anonymous one-shot interactions of mass society (an evolutionary novel phenomenon) as if they were of the iterated kind to which we have most probably adapted (Hagen & Hammerstein, 2006; Price et al., 2002).

Predictions concerning Institutional Design

One may object that this is fine but insufficient. The evolutionary — cognitive model may solve some issues of design, telling us what rules are 'natural', easy to acquire and intuitively compelling for human beings. But, the objection goes, it does not address the major question of institutional development, i.e., why are these cognitive tools and motivations activated in some but not all contexts? Why, as a result, are some commons successful and others less so? Since the cognitive tools are always present, why are they not always used?

Institutions are a part of the external environment of individual actors and, hence, are processed with the same cognitive effects as other parts of the environment. The application of the above insights to institutional analysis is, therefore, straightforward. Doing so should enable researchers to build specific predictions about (a) which institutions or aspects of institutions people are more likely to find 'natural', (b) to what extent people can have an intuitive grasp of the actual workings of their institutions, and (c) how institutional participation can recruit motivations that are there anyway, regardless of the institutional environment.

In essence, we suggest that the structure of evolved cognitive systems and dispositions create a cognitive 'rubber cage' (Gellner, 1985). That is, human understandings are usually constructed and therefore constrained by the structure of long-evolved cognitive systems, and remain inside the cage, as it were. It is not impossible to think beyond our intuitive assumptions or to build institutions that violate them. However, each such extension requires some effort, and the further one moves away from intuitive expectations, preferences and understandings, the more effort is required (Boyer, 1998; Sperber, 1996). The further away one moves from our evolved understandings, (a) the more effort will be required to get them adopted by large numbers of people, (b) the less people will intuitively grasp how the institution works, and (c) the less motivated they may be to participate.

Because divergence from the intuitive set of design features requires effort, such divergence will be less common than convergence (at least, absent other strong environmental pressures for divergence). Of course, this is likely to be a matter of degree. For instance, it is not too difficult for some human groups to extend the scope of marriage-like institutions to, say, encompass homosexual unions. A more radical departure from common intuitions would be to envisage fixed-term marriage contracts or simultaneous polyandric unions. Although such arrangements are not unthinkable or impossible, they are less likely than standard marriage-like systems in human societies, given the intuitive assumptions that normal human minds spontaneously develop about the connections between sex, reproduction and subsistence. Within this approach, it is also possible to specify a number of other specific predictions:

People will prefer intuitive to non-intuitive institutions. Intuitive institutions, quite simply, seem more natural and appropriate to people. For people to prefer a non-intuitive solution to a problem that mimics something which our cognitive architecture was designed to solve, effort is required on their behalf and they need good reasons to put in this extra effort.

Some research has specifically shown this in the domain of punishment institutions. As argued above, punishment has most probably played a key role for evolution of human social life. Recent studies in neuroscience demonstrate that brain regions related to the production of pleasure are activated when subjects engage in the punishment of free-riders (de Quervain et al., 2004). Also, economic experiments have demonstrated that people prefer to tackle collective action problems in institutional contexts that allow for punishment (Gürerk, Irlenbusch, & Rockenbach, 2006). We can observe such effects outside the laboratory as well. Throughout the twentieth century, criminal justice institutions have shifted from punishing to helping the offender (Garland, 1990). Politically, this shift was legitimized by references to criminologists and other experts' observations that punishment did not work to reduce crime in large societies. In this way, criminal justice institutions were pulled away from their intuitive function — to impose costs on anti-social individuals (Petersen et al., 2010)—and instead designed to simply decrease recidivism in a non-moralizing manner. Across countries, however, these attempts have now been significantly reversed and an explicit part of this has been public reactions led by, for example, victim movements. When they reverted to more punitive practices, policy makers often made clear that the reversal aimed at placating public sentiment rather than decreasing crime (Balvig, 2005). In our terms, the return to punitive rhetoric and practices made the institution closer to our evolved intuitions.

This example also illustrates another point: that intuitiveness is especially important for institutions that are directed toward the public. Worries about rehabilitation-oriented systems did not come from within the penal system itself, whose personnel were quite willing to invest the needed effort to think outside their intuitions. Rather, the pressure came from the general public who have much else on their minds than investing cognitive effort in overwriting their punishment intuitions (Roberts, Stalans, Indermaur, & Hough, 2002).

More intuitive institutions are more efficient in influencing behavior. This follows from our argument that intuitive institutions are easier to process. It is important to notice that this is not just because it is easier to learn some kind of institutional rules than others but rather because intuitive institutional rules simply require less learning on behalf of the subjects. For instance, criminal justice practices that rely on evolved concepts of right and wrong influence public behavior, we suggest, not because citizens have uploaded legal knowledge in their minds but precisely because evolved expectations spare them that effort. While laymen, for example, do not know the specific punishments for shoplifting *versus* grievous assault, their behavior can be guided by an intuitive understanding that the latter is more serious than the first (Robinson et al., 2007).

An example from the health sector serves to illustrate this. To avoid poisoning of children, a government-funded health program in the USA encouraged parents to mark poisonous materials with a 'Mr. Yuk' sticker, an emoticon with the facial expression of disgust, to signal that the material should not be ingested. The effectiveness of this program was negligible (Demorest, Posner, Osterhoudt, & Henretig, 2004). One factor is that accidental poisoning does not fall within the evolved domain of disgust but rather within the domain of fear — i.e., hazard management. Adults as well as children react to accidental poisoning with fear rather than disgust (Pooley & Fiddick, 2010). Marking poisonous material with disgust-conveying emoticons does not engage the cognitive machinery for producing the very behavior that the institution aims at activating.

Our claim here, it must be stressed, is not that 'natural' institutions are necessarily more efficient in terms of generating optimal outcomes.

Efficiency is here strictly understood with reference to their power to influence behavior and not whether the resulting behavior is optimal or rational. In fact, given that our evolved cognitive systems evolved in ancestral environments, institutions that seem 'natural' to the human mind might often be ill-suited to solve the problems of modern-day mass society (Carvalho & Koyama, 2010).

More intuitive institutions seem more legitimate. In the domain of social and moral interaction, institutions that promote our welfare in an intuitive way (i.e., by promoting behavior that would have been ancestrally beneficial and sanctioning behavior that would have been ancestrally costly to us) would be, all else being equal, perceived as more legitimate. As classical sociologists have emphasized, legitimacy is at the root of effective governance (Tyler, 2001). If rules are perceived as legitimate, individuals will spontaneously incorporate them into their decisions. Importantly, efficiency in influencing behavior is not necessarily the same as efficiency in solving the problem that the institution is designed for. Our cognitive systems are designed to function within evolutionarily recurrent situations and can be ill suited for solving the problems of large societies. Similarly, there is no guarantee that institutions matching these intuitions are good at solving modern problems.

Evidence concerning the management of common-pool resources can be interpreted along these lines. In relation to common-pool resources, the problem is congestion and, hence, people need to be restrained in their use of the resources. Detailed studies have shown that the institutions that facilitate restraint most effectively are institutions that facilitate face-to-face interaction among the participants (Ostrom, 1990). This allows for a social situation that mimics that kind of situation in which we have evolved to deal with such problems of collective actions. In fact, laboratory experiments show that resources are protected by institutions that emerge as a result of between-participant social interaction, better than by externally enforced institutions, even if the latter yield the optimal use of the resource (Cardenas, Stranlund, & Willis, 2002). The reason is that people do not feel intrinsically committed to the optimal-but-enforced institutions and, therefore, cheat on them whenever possible.

Clearly, then, the efficiency of institutions in regulating behavior is not a matter of their inherent rationality. Rather, it is the extent to which they allow for appropriate cognitive machinery to become activated. In the case of collective action, a number of studies document that the human mind contains sophisticated machinery for committing ourselves to pro-social decisions but that these are extremely sensitive to the extent to which *others* are similarly committed (given selection pressures for making cooperation reciprocal) (Frank, 1988). Coordination of commitment is possible when institutions for common-pool resources are endogenously agreed upon rather than exogenously enforced.

Another illustration of the importance of 'naturalness' for the regulatory potential of institutions is provided by a series of studies of when people accept specific distributions of costs and benefits (Hibbing & Alford, 2004; Smith, Larimer, Littvay, & Hibbing, 2007). People's reactions are modulated, not just by whether or not they benefit from the allocation, but also by the way the institutions orchestrating the allocation matches evolved moral sentiments. Using the Ultimatum Game, Hibbing and Alford, for example, experimentally varied the institutions governing who would be assigned the role of proposer and, hence, be allowed to divide a pot of money between themselves and the other participant — the receiver — who could accept the division or decline (in which case neither participant received any money). Receivers readily accepted (and felt satisfied with) highly unequal divisions (against their interest), if the institutions governing the allocation of roles focused on merit or chance but not if these institutions focused on preferences, that is, granted a participant the power to propose because he/she wanted this role most (Hibbing & Alford, 2004). We have evolved cognitive devices to resist exploitation (Buss & Duntley, 2008), which is why we spontaneously suspect the motives of eager dictators — and, of particular relevance here, feel more dissatisfied with institutions that allow them to move into power.

Non-intuitive institutions will drift towards greater intuitiveness. Non-intuitive institutions require subjects to continuously invest effort to ensure that their rules are correctly recalled. For example, studies in social psychology demonstrate that individuals use effortful cognitive operations to encode and recall expectation-inconsistent information when forming impressions of others (Macrae, Bodenhausen, Milne, & Calvini, 1999). By implication, we expect that popular images and understandings of the rules of non-intuitive institutions will drift towards greater intuitiveness; that is, over time (if countervailing actions are not taken) subjects will be more likely to recall intuition-confirming parts of institutions and mold initially intuition-disconfirming rules into a format that matches intuitions.

One example of this comes from religious institutions and, in particular, Max Weber's classical account of the rise of capitalism (Weber, 2002). Before the reformation, Christians could secure salvation by submitting themselves to the authority of the Catholic Church. After the reformation, this possibility was closed and, instead, the dominant theological paradigm described how certain people were predestined to become saved. With predestination, the normal response to a problem as psychologically significant as the prospect of eternal damnation, i.e., action, was effectively removed. As a result, at the popular level, the theological institution of predestination quickly drifted into the more intuitive informal institution of looking for signs for salvation in the form of success in the current life. Through success and, hence, hard work, one could then 'reveal' oneself as chosen for salvation.

Divergence between non-intuitive official doctrine and public practice and belief is also widespread in the realm of politics (Kuran, 1995). In the literature on political tolerance, for example, it is often noted that people strongly endorse official doctrines about widespread civil rights for everyone, and at the same time display strong intolerance towards specific groups (McClosky & Brill, 2003). In the domain of criminal justice, there is widespread support for the principle of proportionality, i.e., that punishments should 'fit' the crime (Darley & Pittman, 2003), enshrined in modern criminal justice institutions but at the same time people, when considering specific criminals, allow for a number of exceptions to these principles. While such public beliefs do not necessarily reshape official institutions, they nonetheless influence how the institutions in fact work. As these last examples show, a cognitive science account of institutions does not preclude the possibility that institutions are also shaped by environmental factors that can make them divert from natural focal points. Rather, the point is that such divergence will constantly be put under pressure by processes of institutional drift towards greater fit with our evolved cognitive systems.

7. Is a General Theory of Institutions Possible (or Desirable)?

The framework proposed here implies a substantial departure from common assumptions in theories of institutional design. Neo-institutional models, for instance, describe domain-general processes that should in principle apply in similar ways to marriage, exchange or criminal law, or most other domains of institutional norms (Ostrom, 2005). Also, the aim of such models is to provide general economic or political factors that constrain institutional development. By contrast, we have argued that one should explain institutions in terms of domain-specific psychological systems. Human psychology comes with assumptions, capacities and preferences concerning, for example, reproduction and parenting, distinct and separate from those concerning the punishment of wrongdoing or the establishment of reliable exchange relations. These are exogenous factors in the sense that they stem from the evolved cognitive make-up of the species, independently of social institutions.

If this is a valid proposal, then a general theory of institutions as such is not really what social scientists should aim for. That is because a general model, based solely on endogenous factors, should be extremely abstract to be equally applicable to the many disparate domains of institutional development. At such a level of abstraction, the model may not predict or exclude anything in particular, and therefore may not be of great value. An account of institutional design and development is more likely to come from integrated, probably situation-specific, models that bring together economic constraints and human-specific competencies in particular domains of social interaction.

References

Ainslie, G. (2005). Précis of Breakdown of Will. *Behavioral and Brain Sciences, 28,* 635–673. https://doi.org/10.1017/S0140525X05000117

Alford, J. R., & Hibbing, J. R. (2004). The Origin of Politics: An Evolutionary Theory of Political Behavior. *Perspectives on Politics,* 2 (4), 707–723. https://doi.org/10.1017/s1537592704040460

Anderson, K. G., Kaplan, H. S., Lam, D., & Lancaster, J. (1999). Paternal care by genetic fathers and stepfathers II: Reports by Xhosa high school students. *Evolution & Human Behavior,* 20, 433–451. https://doi.org/10.1016/S1090-5138(99)00022-7

Anderson, K. G., Kaplan, H. S., & Lancaster, J. (1999). Paternal care by genetic fathers and stepfathers I: Reports from Albuquerque men. *Evolution & Human Behavior,* 20, 405–431. https://doi.org/10.1016/S1090-5138(99)00023-9

Balvig, F. (2005). When Law and Order Returned to Denmark. *Journal of Scandinavian Studies in Criminology and Crime Prevention,* 5, 167–187. https://doi.org/10.1080/14043850410010711

Barkow, J., Cosmides, L., & Tooby, J. (1992). *The Adapted Mind: Evolutionary psychology and the Generation of Culture.* New York: Oxford University Press.

Barrett, H. C. (2005). Enzymatic Computation and Cognitive Modularity. *Mind & Language,* 20, 259–287. https://doi.org/10.1111/j.0268-1064.2005.00285.x

Bicchieri, C. (2006). *The Grammar of Society: The Nature and Dynamics of Social Norms.* Cambridge: Cambridge University Press.

Boyer, P. (1998). Cognitive Tracks of Cultural Inheritance: How Evolved Intuitive Ontology Governs Cultural Transmission. *American Anthropologist,* 100, 876–889. https://doi.org/10.1525/aa.1998.100.4.876

Brousseau, E., & Glachant, J.-M. (2008). *New Institutional Economics: A Guidebook.* Cambridge; New York: Cambridge University Press.

Buss, D. M. (1989). Sex Differences in Human Mate Preferences: Evolutionary Hypotheses Tested in 37 Cultures. *Behavioral and Brain Sciences,* 12, 1–49. https://doi.org/10.1017/S0140525X00023992

——. (2000). *The Dangerous Passion: Why Jealousy Is As Necessary As Love and Sex.* New York: Free Press.

——. (Ed.) (2005). *The Handbook of Evolutionary Psychology.* Hoboken, NJ: John Wiley & Sons Inc.

Buss, D. M., & Duntley, J. D. (2008). Adaptations for exploitation. *Group Dynamics: Theory, Research, and Practice,* 12, 53–62. https://doi.org/10.1037/1089-2699.12.1.53

Cardenas, J. C., Stranlund, J., & Willis, C. (2002). Local Environmental Control and Institutional Crowding-Out. *World Development,* 28 (10), 1719–1733. https://doi.org/10.1016/S0305-750X(00)00055-3

Carvalho, J.-P., & Koyama, M. (2010). Instincts and institutions: the rise of the market. In W. N. Butos (Ed.), *The Social Science of Hayek's 'The Sensory Order'* (pp. 285–309). Bingley: Emerald Group Publishing Limited.

Cosmides, L., & Tooby, J. (1994). Origins of domain specificity: The evolution of functional organization. In L. A. Hirschfeld, S. A. Gelman, et al. (Eds.), *Mapping the mind: Domain specificity in cognition and culture.* (pp. 85–116). New York: Cambridge University Press.

——. (2006). Evolutionary psychology, moral heuristics, and the law. In G. Gigerenzer & C. Engel (Eds.), *Heuristics and the law.* (pp. 175–205). Cambridge, MA; Berlin: MIT Press; Dahlem University Press.

——. (Eds.). (2005). *Neurocognitive Adaptations Designed for Social Exchange.* Hoboken, NJ: John Wiley & Sons Inc.

Daly, M., & Wilson, M. (1988). *Homicide.* New York: Aldine.

Darley, J., & Pittman, T. (2003). The Psychology of Compensatory and Retributive Justice. *Personality and Social Psychology Review, 7* (4), 324–336. https://doi.org/10.1207%2FS15327957PSPR0704_05

de Quervain, D. U., Fischbacher, U., Treyer, V., Schellhammer, M., Schnyder, U., Buck, A., & Fehr, E. (2004). The Neural Basis of Altruistic Punishment. *Science, 305,* 1254–1258.

Demorest, R. A., Posner, J. C., Osterhoudt, K. C., & Henretig, F. M. (2004). Poisoning Prevention Education During Emergency Department Visits for Childhood Poisoning. *Pediatric emergency care, 20,* 281.

Dequech, D. (2006). Institutions and Norms in Institutional Economics and Sociology. *Journal of economic issues, 40,* 473.

Dopfer, K. (2005). *The Evolutionary Foundations of Economics.* Cambridge: Cambridge University Press.

Dunbar, R. I. M., Barrett, L., & Lycett, J. (2005). *Evolutionary Psychology: A Beginner's Guide: Human Behaviour, Evolution, and the Mind.* Oxford: Oneworld.

Ellis, B. J. (1993). The evolution of sexual attraction: Evaluative Mechanisms in Women. In J. Barkow, L. Cosmides, & J. Tooby (Eds.), *The Adapted Mind. Evolutionary Psychology and the Generation of Culture* (pp. 267–288). New York: Oxford University Press.

Ellis, B. J., Bates, J. E., Dodge, K. A., Fergusson, D. M., Horwood, L. J., Pettit, G. S., & Woodward, L. (2003). Does father absence place daughters at special risk for early sexual activity and teenage pregnancy? *Child Development, 74,* 801–821.

Enright, R. D. (1984). Distributive justice development: Cross-cultural, contextual, and longitudinal evaluations. *Child Development, 55,* 1737–1751.

Ermer, E., Cosmides, L., & Tooby, J. (Eds.). (2007). *Functional Specialization and the Adaptationist Program.* New York: Guilford Press.

Fehr, E., Schmidt, K. M., Kolm, S.-C., & Ythier, J. M. (2006). The Economics of Fairness, Reciprocity and Altruism—Experimental Evidence and New Theories. In S.-C. Kolm & J. M. Ythier (Eds.), *Handbook of the economics of giving, altruism and reciprocity (Vol 1.) Foundations.* (pp. 615–691). New York: Elsevier Science.

Fessler, D. M. T. (2001). Emotions and cost-benefit assessment: The role of shame and self-esteem in risk taking. In G. Gigerenzer & R. Selten (Eds.), *Bounded rationality: The adaptive toolbox* (pp. 191–214). Cambridge, MA: MIT Press.

Frank, R. H. (1988). *Passions within Reason. The Strategic Role of the Emotions.* New York: Norton.

Garland, D. (1990). *Punishment and Modern Society. A Study in Social Theory.* Oxford: Clarendon Press.

Gellner, E. (1985). *Relativism and the Social Sciences.* Cambridge; New York: Cambridge University Press.

Gigerenzer, G. (2002). *Adaptive Thinking: Rationality in the Real World.* New York; Oxford: Oxford University Press.

Gigerenzer, G., Todd, P. M., & Group, A. B. C. R. (1999). *Simple Heuristics that Make us Smart.* New York: Oxford University Press.

Goody, J. (1986). *The Logic of Writing and the Organization of Society.* Cambridge: Cambridge University Press.

Greene, J. (2005). Cognitive Neuroscience and the Structure of the Moral Mind. In P. Carruthers (Ed.), *The Innate Mind: Structure and Contents* (pp. 338–352). New York: Oxford University Press.

Greif, A. (2006). *Institutions and the Path to the Modern Economy: Lessons from Medieval Trade.* Cambridge; New York: Cambridge University Press.

Gudeman, S. (1986). *Economics as Culture: Models and Metaphors of Livelihood.* London: Routledge & Kegan Paul.

Gürerk, Ö., Irlenbusch, B., & Rockenbach, B. (2006). The Competitive Advantage of Sanctioning Institutions. *Science, 312,* 108–111.

Hagen, E. H., & Hammerstein, P. (2006). Game theory and human evolution: A critique of some recent interpretations of experimental games. *Theoretical population biology, 69,* 339–348.

Haidt, J. (2001). The emotional dog and its rational tail: A social intuitionist approach to moral judgment. *Psychological review, 108,* 814–834.

——. (2007). The new synthesis in moral psychology. *Science, 316,* 998–1002.

Heintz, C. (2007). Institutions as Mechanisms of Cultural Evolution: Prospects of the Epidemiological Approach. *Biological Theory, 2,* 244–249.

Hibbing, J. R., & Alford, J. R. (2004). Accepting Authoritative Decisions: Humans as Wary Cooperators. *American Journal of Political Science*, 48 (1), 62–76. https://doi.org/10.1111/j.0092-5853.2004.00056.x

Hodgson, G. M. (1999). *Evolution and Institutions: On Evolutionary Economics and the Evolution of Economics.* Cheltenham; Northampton, MA: Edward Elgar.

Hoebel, E. A. (1964). *The Law of Primitive Man: A Study in Comparative Legal Dynamics.* Cambridge, MA: Harvard University Press.

Kahneman, D., Slovic, P., & Tversky, A. (Eds.). (1982). *Jugdments under Uncertainty: Heuristics and Biases.* Cambridge: Cambridge University Press.

Kanazawa, S. (2002). Bowling with our imaginary friends. *Evolution & Human Behavior,* 23, 167–168.

Kaplan, H. S., & Gangestad, S. W. (2005). Life History Theory and Evolutionary Psychology. In D. M. Buss (Ed.), *The Handbook of Evolutionary Psychology* (pp. 68–95). Hoboken, NJ: John Wiley & Sons.

Knight, J. (1995). Models, Interpretations and Theories: Constructing Explanations of Institutional Emergence and Change. In J. Knight & I. Sened (Eds.), *Explaining Social Institutions* (pp. 95–120). Ann Arbor, MI: University of Michigan Press.

Knight, J., & North, D. C. (1997). Explaining Economic Change: The Interplay Between Cognition and Institutions. *Legal Theory,* 3, 211–226.

Knight, J., & Sened, I. (Eds.). (1995). *Explaining Social Institutions.* Ann Arbor, MI: University of Michigan Press.

Kohlberg, L. (1981). *The Philosophy of Moral Development: Moral Stages and the Idea of Justice.* San Francisco, CA: Harper & Row.

Kuran, T. (1995). *Private Truths, Public Lies: The Social Consequences of Preference Falsification.* Cambridge, MA: Harvard University Press.

Kurzban, R., & Leary, M. R. (2001). Evolutionary origins of stigmatization: The functions of social exclusion. *Psychological Bulletin,* 127, 187–208.

Kurzban, R., & Neuberg, S. (2005). Managing ingroup and outgroup relationships. In D. M. Buss (Ed.), *The Handbook of Evolutionary Psychology.* (pp. 653–675). Hoboken, NJ: John Wiley & Sons Inc.

Lieberman, D., Tooby, J., & Cosmides, L. (2003). Does morality have a biological basis? An empirical test of the factors governing moral sentiments relating to incest. *Proceedings of the Royal Society of London Series B Biological sciences,* 270, 819–826. https://doi.org/10.1098/rspb.2002.2290

Loewenstein, G., & O'Donoghue, T. (2005). *Animal Spirits. Affective and Deliberative Processes in Economic Behavior.* Carnegie Mellon University.

Macrae, C. N., Bodenhausen, G. V., Milne, A. B., & Calvini, G. (1999). Seeing more than we can know: Visual attention and category activation. *Journal of Experimental Social Psychology,* 35, 590–602.

Maine, H. S. S. (1963). *Ancient Law; Its Connection with the Early History of Society and its Relation to Modern Ideas.* Boston, MA: Beacon Press.

McCabe, K. A., & Smith, V. L. (2001). Goodwill Accounting and the process of exchange. In G. Gigerenzer & R. Selten (Eds.), *Bounded Rationality: The Adaptive Toolbox.* (pp. 319–340). Cambridge, MA: MIT Press.

McClosky, H., & Brill, A. (2003). *Dimensions of Tolerance*. New York: Russell Sage Foundation.

McDermott, R. (2006). Editor's Introduction. *Political Psychology, 27*, 347–358. https://doi.org/10.1111/j.1467-9221.2006.00503.x

Merton, R. K. (1996). *On Social Structure and Science*. Chicago, IL; London: University of Chicago Press.

New, J., Cosmides, L., & Tooby, J. (2007). Category-specific attention for animals reflects ancestral priorities, not expertise. *Proceedings of the National Academy of Sciences of the United States of America, 104*, 16598–16603.

Nichols, S., & Knobe, J. (2008). Moral responsibility and determinism: The cognitive science of folk intuitions. In J. Knobe & S. Nichols (Eds.), *Experimental Philosophy*. (pp. 105–126). New York, NY: Oxford University Press.

Nørager, R. (2009). Why Evolutionary and Cognitive Developmental Psychology? The Importance of Non-Human Primates & Human Infants for Understanding Adult Use of Modern Computerized Technology. In H. Høgh-Olesen, J. Tønnesvang, & P. Bertelsen (Eds.), *Human Characteristics* (pp. 117–149). Newcastle upon Tyne: Cambridge Scholars Publishing.

North, D. C. (1990). *Institutions, Institutional Change, and Economic Performance*. Cambridge; New York: Cambridge University Press.

——. (2005). *Understanding the Process of Economic Change*. Princeton, NJ: Princeton University Press.

Ostrom, E. (1990). *Governing the Commons: The Evolution of Institutions for Collective Action*. Cambridge; New York: Cambridge University Press.

——. (2005). *Understanding Institutional Diversity*. Princeton, NJ: Princeton University Press.

Petersen, M. B. (2010). Distinct Emotions, Distinct Domains: Anger, Anxiety and Perceptions of Intentionality. *The Journal of Politics, 72*, 357–365. https://doi.org/10.1017/S002238160999079X

Petersen, M. B., Sell, A., Tooby, J., & Cosmides, L. (2010). Evolutionary Psychology and Criminal Justice: A Recalibrational Theory of Punishment and Reconciliation. In H. Høgh-Olesen (Ed.), *Human Morality and Sociality* (pp. 72–131). Basingstoke: Palgrave Macmillan.

Pierson, P. (2004). *Politics in Time: History, Institutions and Social Analysis*. Princeton, NJ: Princeton University Press.

Pooley, A. J., & Fiddick, L. A. J. C. U. (2010). Social Referencing 'Mr. Yuk': The Use of Emotion in a Poison Prevention Program. *Journal of Pediatric Psychology* 35 (4), 327–339. https://doi.org/10.1093/jpepsy/jsp070

Posner, E. (2000). *Law and Social Norms*. Cambridge, MA: Harvard University Press.

———. (2007). *Social Norms, Nonlegal Sanctions, and the Law*. Cheltenham; Northampton, MA: Edward Elgar.

Posner, R. A. (1981). *The Economics of Justice*. Cambridge, MA: Harvard University Press.

Price, M. E., Cosmides, L., & Tooby, J. (2002). Punitive sentiment as an anti-free rider psychological device. *Evolution & Human Behavior, 23*, 203–231. https://doi.org/10.1016/S1090-5138(01)00093-9

Quinlan, R. J. (2003). Father absence, parental care, and female reproductive development. *Evolution & Human Behavior, 24*, 376–390. https://doi.org/10.1016/S1090-5138(03)00039-4

Roberts, J. V., Stalans, L. J., Indermaur, D., & Hough, M. (2002). *Penal Populism and Public Opinion: Lessons from Five Countries*. New York: Oxford University Press.

Robinson, P. H., Kurzban, R., & Jones, O. (2007). The Origins of Shared Intuitions of Justice. *Vanderbilt Law Review, 60*, 1633–1688.

Saad, G., & Gill, T. (2014). The Framing Effect when Evaluating Prospective Mates: An Adaptationist Perspective. *Evolution and Human Behavior, 35*, 184–192. https://doi.org/10.1016/j.evolhumbehav.2014.01.002

Schaller, M. (2006). Parasites, Behavioral Defenses, and the Social Psychological Mechanisms Through Which Cultures Are Evoked. *Psychological Inquiry, 17*, 96–137.

Searle, J. R. (1995). *The Construction of Social Reality*. New York: Free Press.

Sidanius, J., & Veniegas, R. C. (2000). Gender and race discrimination: The interactive nature of disadvantage. In S. Oskamp et al. (Eds.), *Reducing Prejudice and Discrimination*. (pp. 47–69). Mahwah, NJ: Lawrence Erlbaum Associates, Inc., Publishers.

Sigelman, C. K., & Waitzman, K. A. (1991). The development of distributive justice orientations: Contextual influences on children's resource allocations. *Child Development, 62*, 1367–1378.

Smith, K., Larimer, C., Littvay, L., & Hibbing, J. R. (2007). Evolutionary Theory and Political Leadership: Why Certain People Do Not Trust Decision Makers. *Journal of Politics, 69*, 285–299. https://doi.org/10.1111/j.1468-2508.2007.00532.x

Sperber, D. (1996). *Explaining Culture: A Naturalistic Approach*. Oxford: Blackwell.

Sugden, R. (1986). *The Economics of Rights, Co-operation and Welfare*. Oxford: Blackwell.

Symons, D. (1979). *The Evolution of Human Sexuality*. New York: Oxford University Press.

Tooby, J., & Cosmides, L. (1992). The psychological foundations of culture. In J. H. Barkow, L. Cosmides, et al. (Eds.), *The Adapted Mind: Evolutionary*

Psychology and the Generation of Culture. (pp. 19–136). New York, NY: Oxford University Press.

Turiel, E. (1994). The development of social-conventional and moral concepts. In P. Bill (Ed.), *Fundamental Research in Moral Development. Moral Development: A Compendium, Vol. 2.* (pp. 255–292). New York: Garland Publishing, Inc.

——. (2002). *The Culture of Morality: Social Development and Social Opposition.* New York: Cambridge University Press.

Tyler, T. R. (2001). A Psychological Perspective on the Legitimacy of Institutions and Authorities. In J. T. Jost & B. Major (Eds.), *The Psychology of Legitimacy* (pp. 416–435). Cambridge: Cambridge University Press.

van Gennep, A. (1909). *Les rites de passage; étude systématique des rites de la porte et du seuil, de l'hospitalité, de l'adoption, de la grossesse et de l'accouchement, de la naissance, de l'enfance, de la puberté, de l'initiation, de l'ordination, du couronnement des fiançailles et du mariage, des funérailles, des saisons, etc.* Paris: É. Nourry.

Van Schaik, C. P., & Van Hooff, J. A. (1983). On the ultimate causes of primate social systems. *Behaviour*, 85, 91–117.

Weber, M. (2002). *The Protestant Ethic and The Spirit of Capitalism,* trans. by P. Baehr and G. C. Wells. Harmondsworth: Penguin Books.

Wilson, M., & Daly, M. (1992). The man who mistook his wife for a chattel. In J. H. Barkow & L. Cosmides (Eds.), *The Adapted Mind: Evolutionary Psychology and the Generation of Culture* (pp. 289–322). London: Oxford University Press.

——. (1998). Lethal and nonlethal violence against wives and the evolutionary psychology of male sexual proprietariness. In R. E. Dobash & R. P. Dobash (Eds.), *Rethinking Violence Against Women* (pp. 199–230). Thousand Oaks, CA: Sage Publications, Inc.

Yamagishi, T. (1992). Group size and the provision of a sanctioning system in a social dilemma. In D. Messick & H. Wilke (Eds.), *Social Dilemmas: Theoretical Issues and Research Findings* (pp. 267–287). Oxford: Pergamon.

3. Why Ritualized Behavior?

Introductory Note

Why do people perform rituals? Over the world and however far we can go in the past, human groups seem to engage in what we would recognize as, well, 'rituals' of some kind or other, even though we may be very unclear about what that term is supposed to convey. Pierre Liénard nudged me to join forces and re-open that question, which used to be central in classical anthropology, together with the additional query, what is the connection (if any) between the collective ceremonies described by anthropologists or historians, and the compulsive behaviors of obsessive patients?

So, why perform rituals? The question of why this (vaguely defined) way of behaving is universal was more often avoided than addressed in anthropology, as quite a few anthropologists have pointed out (Bloch, 1974; Rappaport, 1999). We were told that collective rituals expressed a world-view, or reflected social values or made manifest a social order etc. All such statements raise more questions than they solve. Why would you need a *ritual* to do any of these things?

As for the striking similarities between collective ceremonies and the individual, often pathological rituals observed in obsessive-compulsive disorder (OCD)—the article provides a detailed account of these similarities—the question had been largely abandoned after Sigmund Freud's desultory observation (1948) that religious ritual could be described as collective obsessiveness and obsessiveness as a kind of individual religion... which did not help much.

Our work diverged from previous models and theories of rituals in three distinct ways.

First, Liénard and I agreed that we should try to describe ritualization rather than rituals. That is not a pedantic distinction. Rituals are the

 https://doi.org/10.11647/OBP.0257.04

outcome—the collective or private ceremonies found in most human cultures, the routines of individuals with obsessive-compulsive disorder, as well as the repetitive behaviors of many children. Ritualization is the combination of underlying processes that creates all this, making it natural or even compelling individuals to engage in these behaviors. A great deal of confusion in anthropology stems from a focus on the result, on 'rituals', rather than on the processes that cause them. Anthropologists have for instance wasted much time trying to define the term ritual, to demarcate what is and what is not a ritual, and so forth. This is a bit like spending one's time trying to define what counts as a 'fire' and what does not, rather than describing the physics and chemistry of combustion—for a more recent critique of that unfortunate tendency, see Boyer & Liénard (2020).

Second, Liénard suggested that we should build our account on the basis of the 'security motivation' model proposed by Szetchman & Woody (2004) to account for the neuro-physiology of obsessive-compulsive disorders. Together with previous evolutionary models by Abed & de Pauw (1998), as well as Fiske & Haslam (1997), this neuro-physiological model provided a key to understanding how ordinary actions can become ritualized. Our model is very much a modified version of the Szechtman & Woody account, with a few important twists, as discussed in the paper. (I should point out that the neuro-physiology in the paper is of course partly out of date, although the main points remain valid).

Third, Freud was obviously wrong—most anthropologists would agree with that—but it matters to understand exactly why. Consider people performing a collective ritual, e.g., sacrificing a pig to the ancestors as a way to placate them and ward off witches and devils. The reason why people engage in such behaviors is that they receive messages from other people, their elders for instance, that one should engage in this course of action. The content of these messages is the reason why the ritual actions are reiterated. As we describe in the paper, people will follow a ritual recipe if it is (even marginally) more relevant than alternatives available in their social environment. In our account, people receive a description of the cultural ceremonies that is relevant because it activates, however faintly, cognitive systems that evolved to protect us against potential hazards like contagion and predators. That is sufficient. This is a matter of cultural selection and reconstruction—in the same way as people select some stories among the many stories they hear, and store and reconstruct them, whilst abandoning other variants or other stories, a process of cultural 'epidemiology' described in detail by Dan Sperber (1996) and Sperber & Hirschfeld (2004).

The re-iteration and performance of such rituals does not, in any way, require that the participants suffered from any special anxieties, that rituals could allay mental states, or any other such functionalist assumptions. Liénard made this even clearer in our subsequent paper, focused on cultural rituals and their dynamics (Liénard & Boyer, 2006). Strikingly, that unfounded assumption (that people participate in collective rituals to assuage their anxieties) is so entrenched, that some of the commentators on the original article took it for granted that we must be defending that explanation, despite our (as we saw it) clear assurances to the contrary.

References

Abed, R. T., & de Pauw, K. W. (1998). An evolutionary hypothesis for obsessive compulsive disorder: a psychological immune system? *Behavioural Neurology*, 11, 245–250. https://doi.org/10.1155/1999/657382

Bloch, M. (1974). Symbols, song, dance, and features of articulation : Is religion an extreme form of traditional authority? *European Journal of Sociology*, 15, 55–81.

Boyer, P., & Liénard, P. (2020). Ingredients of 'rituals' and their cognitive underpinnings. *Philosophical Transactions of the Royal Society B*, 375(1805), 20190439. https://doi.org/10.1098/rstb.2019.0439

Fiske, A. P., & Haslam, N. (1997). Is obsessive-compulsive disorder a pathology of the human disposition to perform socially meaningful rituals? Evidence of similar content. *Journal of Nervous & Mental Disease*, 185, 211–222. https://doi.org/10.1097/00005053-199704000-00001

Freud, S. (1948). Zwangsbehandlungen und Religionsübungen. In A. Freud et al. (Eds.), *Gesammelte Werke von Sigmund Freud, chronologisch geordnet* (VII, pp. 107–116). London: Imago Publishing.

Liénard, P., & Boyer, P. (2006). Whence Collective Rituals? A Cultural Selection Model of Ritualized Behavior. *American Anthropologist*, 108, 814–827. https://doi.org/10.1525/aa.2006.108.4.814

Rappaport, R. A. (1999). *Ritual and Religion in the Making of Humanity*. Cambridge; New York: Cambridge University Press.

Sperber, D. (1996). *Explaining Culture: A Naturalistic Approach*. Oxford: Blackwell.

Sperber, D., & Hirschfeld, L. A. (2004). The Cognitive Foundations of Cultural Stability and Diversity. *Trends in Cognitive Sciences*, 8, 40–46. https://doi.org/10.1016/j.tics.2003.11.002

Szechtman, H., & Woody, E. (2004). Obsessive-Compulsive Disorder as a Disturbance of Security Motivation. *Psychological Review*, 111, 111–127. https://doi.org/10.1037/0033-295X.111.1.111

Why Ritualized Behavior?

Precaution Systems and Action Parsing in Developmental, Pathological and Cultural Rituals[1]

with Pierre Liénard[2]

Abstract: Ritualized behavior, intuitively recognizable by its stereotypy, rigidity, repetition, and apparent lack of rational motivation, is found in a variety of life conditions, customs, and everyday practices: in cultural rituals, whether religious or non-religious; in many children's complicated routines; in the pathology of obsessive-compulsive disorders (OCD); in normal adults around certain stages of the life-cycle, birthing in particular. Combining evidence from evolutionary anthropology, neuropsychology and neuroimaging, we propose an explanation of ritualized behavior in terms of an evolved Precaution System geared to the detection of and reaction to inferred threats to fitness. This system, distinct from fear-systems geared to respond to manifest danger, includes a repertoire of clues for potential danger as well as a repertoire of species-typical precautions. In OCD pathology, this system does not supply a negative feedback

1   An earlier version of this chapter was originally published as Boyer, P., & Liénard, P. (2006). Why ritualized behavior? Precaution systems and action parsing in developmental, pathological and cultural rituals. *Behavioral and Brain Sciences, 29,* 595–613. Republished by permission of Cambridge University Press.

2   We are grateful to Leda Cosmides and John Tooby for initial inspiration, and to Dan Fessler, Thomas Lawson, Robert McCauley, Pascale Michelon, Mayumi Okada, Tom Oltmanns, Ilkka Pyysiäinen, Howard Waldow, Dan Wegner, Harvey Whitehouse, and Jeff Zacks, for detailed comments on a draft version of this article.

to the appraisal of potential threats, resulting in doubts about the proper performance of precautions, and repetition of action. Also, anxiety levels focus the attention on low-level gestural units of behavior rather than on the goal-related higher-level units normally used in parsing the action-flow. Normally automatized actions are submitted to cognitive control. This 'swamps' working memory, an effect of which is a temporary relief from intrusions but also their long-term strengthening. Normal activation of this Precaution System explains intrusions and ritual behaviors in normal adults. Gradual calibration of the system occurs through childhood rituals. Cultural mimicry of this system's normal input makes cultural rituals attention-grabbing and compelling. A number of empirical predictions follow from this synthetic model.

1. Ritualized Behavior

In a variety of circumstances, humans produce rituals, intuitively recognizable by their stereotypy, rigidity, repetition, and apparent lack of rational motivation. Behavior of this kind is found in cultural rituals, religious or non-religious; in the complicated routines of many children; in the pathology of obsessive-compulsive disorders; in normal adults around certain stages of the life-cycle, especially during birthing. The common features of these behaviors cry out for explanation.

We build on a variety of prior models to describe a core psychological process that we call action ritualization—which is only a part of individual or cultural rituals, but a crucial part. The occurrence of ritualization depends on the conjunction of two specialized cognitive systems. One is a motivational system geared to the detection of and reaction to particular potential threats to fitness. This 'Hazard-Precaution System' includes a repertoire of clues for potential danger as well as a repertoire of species-typical precautions. The other system might be called 'Action Parsing.' It is concerned with the division of the flow of behavior into meaningful units. In some circumstances, specific interaction between these systems creates ritualized actions. The circumstances are different for individual, pathological, and collective rituals, as we will see. But the core ritualization process explains some of their common properties.

There is no precise definition of 'ritual' in any of the three fields that deal with its typical manifestations. Cultural anthropologists generally accept a very vague definition of the term as scripted, stereotypic forms of collective action (Gluckman, 1975). Ethologists use criteria such as repetition and stereotypy (Payne, 1998). Clinical psychologists' descriptions of OCD pathology, as in the DSM-IV, mention 'ritualistic behaviors' without more precision (American Psychiatric, 1995).

Besides, models of the phenomenon are generally limited to one domain of ritual. There is a large clinical literature about children's OCD but little study of normal childhood ritualization, simply because the latter is not pathological, even though it may be difficult to understand one without the other (Evans, Leckman, Carter, Reznick, et al., 1997). Models of OCD do not usually cover normal episodes of obsessiveness and ritualistic compulsion in the life-cycle although these are probably continuous with the pathology (Mataix-Cols, do Rosario-Campos, & Leckman, 2005). Very few anthropologists have considered the striking similarities between cultural ritualized behavior and individual pathology (Rappaport, 1999). A notable exception is Alan Fiske (Dulaney & Fiske, 1994; Fiske & Haslam, 1997), who re-opened an issue famously framed by Freud a long time ago (Freud, 1928).

Following up on Fiske's pioneering work, discussed in Section 8.1 , as well as neuro-physiological (Szechtman & Woody, 2004) and evolutionary (Abed & de Pauw, 1998) models, we aim to provide a model of the different domains of occurrence of ritualized behavior. We certainly do not mean to underestimate the obvious differences, but we do think that the common features of ritualized actions require an explanation. We aim to provide an integrated model that includes not only a cognitive specification of the behavioral patterns and their elicitation conditions, but also the neural correlates of the behaviors and of their pathological distortion, the developmental patterns involved, and the evolutionary background.

It might seem imprudent to make any general statements about a disparate set that includes pathological and normal manifestations, and individual as well as collective rituals. Note, however, that our aim here is not to account for all these behaviors. Our aim is to account for the psychological salience of a particular feature they share, namely the performance of what we call here 'Ritualized Behavior,' a precisely defined way of organizing a limited range of actions. In the following sections we outline the diverse domains of ritualized behavior before putting forward an integrated neural-developmental-evolutionary model of ritualization.

2. Diverse Domains of Ritualization

2.1 Obsessive-Compulsive Disorder (OCD)

The main features of the pathology of OCD are familiar: intrusive, bothersome thoughts about potential danger, as well as a strong compulsion to engage in stereotyped and repetitive activities with no rational justification. Standard criteria in the DSM-IV include (a) intrusive thoughts that (b) cause distress and (c) are often accompanied by ritualistic behaviors that (d) disturb normal activity and (e) are recognized as irrational by the patient (American Psychiatric, 1995).

Typical obsessions include contamination and contagion (i.e., fear of catching other people's germs, of ingesting contaminated substances, of passing on diseases to others), possible harm to others (e.g., handling kitchen utensils and wounding people), as well as social ostracism following shameful or aggressive acts (thoughts about assaulting others, shouting obscenity, exhibitionism, etc.). This is often combined with 'thought-action fusion'—the assumption that having forebodings of possible misfortunes is tantamount to bringing them about—and an exaggerated feeling of responsibility for others (Salkovskis et al., 2000).

Obsessions are typically accompanied by rituals. Some patients engage in endlessly repeated sequences of washing hands, cleaning tools or utensils (Hodgson & Rachman, 1972). Others repeatedly verify that they properly locked their door, rolled up the car window, or turned off the gas stove (Hodgson & Rachman, 1977). Still others are engaged in constant counting activities or need to group objects in sets of particular numbers, with specific alignments (Radomsky, Rachman, & Hammond, 2001). Although a categorical division between 'checkers,' 'washers,' and 'hoarders' has become popular in descriptions of OCD and as a descriptive clinical tool, there seems to be a large overlap in these categories (Khanna, Kaliaperumal, & Channabasavanna, 1990). A more accurate description would construe 'contamination,' 'insecurity and doubt,' and 'excessive precautions' as dimensions of the syndrome (Mataix-Cols et al., 2005), with each patient presenting a cluster of symptoms distributed along these dimensions (Calamari et al., 2004). Most patients are aware that their obsessions are unreasonable and their rituals pointless (patients' insight used to be a criterion in the DSM) but they also report that neither is easily controlled (Eisen, Phillips, & Rasmussen, 1999).

2.2 Children's Rituals

Most young children engage in ritualistic behaviors in a limited range of situations and at a particular stage of development, starting at age 2 and peaking in middle childhood. This developmental phase is characterized by perfectionism, preoccupation with just-right ordering of objects, attachment to a favorite object (imbued with a special value), concerns about dirt and cleanliness, preferred household routines, action repeated over and over or a specific number of times, rituals for eating, awareness of minute details of one's home, hoarding, and bedtime rituals. (Obviously, most children in most situations also create disorder, at least relative to what adults expect; insistence on 'just so' performance is limited to highly specific contexts.) The themes and the age-range are similar among American and other cultural groups (A. H. Zohar & Felz, 2001). In many children, rituals are connected to anxiety states with specific targets. Among them is the fear of strangers, as well as the possibility of inflicting harm to self or others, possible contamination, attack by strangers or animals. The tendency to engage in rituals is correlated with anxiety or fearful traits (A. H. Zohar & Felz, 2001). Both fears and rituals typically evolve with development, from 'just so' insistence to elaborate rituals (Leonard, Goldberger, Rapoport, Cheslow, & Swedo, 1990). Younger children's ritualistic behaviors are related to prepotent fears such as stranger and separation anxieties, whereas the ritualistic behaviors of older ones are related to more specific and contextual fears such as contamination and social hazard (Evans, Gray, & Leckman, 1999). Some children connect their rituals to supposed effects by magical beliefs in ritual efficacy (Evans, Milanak, Medeiros, & Ross, 2002), but this is by no means necessary or even general.

Although the facts of childhood ritualization are familiar and impressive, there is no definitive account of the functional basis of such behaviors in young children. This is mostly because OCD pathology is seen as discontinuous with the 'normal' routines of childhood, given both the obvious differences in frequency and emotional intensity and the fact that only very few young ritualists become clinically obsessive (Leonard et al., 1990). However, it seems difficult to understand the pathology in the absence of a proper causal model for this highly recurrent, culturally stable part of the normal developmental process (Evans et al., 1997).

2.3 Life-Stage-Relevant Intrusive Thoughts

Specific disturbing thoughts occur in many people at particular phases in the lifetime, notably pregnancy, motherhood, and fatherhood. Senseless, intrusive, unacceptable ideas, thoughts, urges, and images about infants are common among healthy parents of newborns, both fathers and mothers (Abramowitz, Schwartz, Moore, & Luenzmann, 2003). The content of intrusions is related to specific stages of the life-cycle. While new fathers and post-partum mothers report fears about harming the infant, pregnant women report heightened fears about contamination (Abramowitz et al., 2003). They also develop rituals of washing and cleaning related to these intrusions. A common underlying theme is uncertainty and doubt concerning possible harm to the infant. Three-quarters of the new parents surveyed by Abramowitz et al. reported persistent thoughts about accidents, suffocation, and other possible ways of intentionally harming the infant (Abramowitz et al., 2003). The individuals feel responsible for these intrusive thoughts. Development of specific perinatal anxieties may be part of a 'primary parental preoccupation' complex that includes nesting behaviors, repeated checking, thoughts about the infant's perfection, and fantasies about possible threats to its security (Leckman et al., 2004). Rodent models suggest oxytocin as a major modulator of such maternal behaviors (Leckman et al., 2004).

The connection between these non-clinical context-relevant intrusions and OCD is not just a matter of similarity. The onset of OCD in women occurs during pregnancy more than at other life-stages (Maina, Albert,

Bogetto, Vaschetto, & Ravizza, 2000; Neziroglu, Anemone, & Yaryura-Tobias, 1992). Note that the development of intrusions and early rituals into OCD is quite distinct from the evolution of post-partum depression (Williams & Koran, 1997). The former triggers very specific, highly consistent obsessive thoughts as opposed to unfocused or frequently shifting depressive ruminations. OCD onset also results in an urge to act (perform specific rituals) very different from the withdrawal from action observed in post-partum depression (Hagen, 2002). Among OCD patients, pregnancy and postpartum result in more severe symptoms (Labad et al., 2005). Activation of the fronto-striatal networks as a result of infant cries is different in new mothers and controls (Lorberbaum et al., 2002), suggesting functional calibration of the circuitry involved in OCD (see Section 3.1).

2.4 Cultural Rituals

A great variety of social occasions are identified as 'rituals' in the anthropological literature. They range from private ceremonies with few participants, or indeed just one person, to large gatherings, and from single acts to long sequences spread over months or years. The general themes range from worship to protection to aggression. The occasions for ritualized behaviors also vary, based either on contingencies such as illness or misfortune, life-stages like birth, initiation, and death, or recurrent occasions such as seasonal changes. Finally, the connections between rituals and religious concepts are crucial in some cases (e.g., ancestor worship, Islamic prayer), or only peripheral (e.g., anti-witchcraft divination), or just absent (as in 'secular' rituals).

How do we recognize such actions? As Roy Rappaport argued, it seems that we (anthropologists but also lay folk) use a conjunction of specific criteria that a model of ritual should explain (Rappaport, 1979). Here is a slightly modified list of features he emphasized:

1. First, actions are divorced from their usual goals. In cultural rituals, one typically washes instruments or body parts that are already clean, one enters rooms to exit them straightaway, one talks to interlocutors that are manifestly absent. Also, many rituals include actions for which there could not possibly be any clear empirical goal, such as passing a

chicken from hand to hand in a circle, going round a temple seven times, and so forth.

2. Second, cultural rituals are often presented as compulsory, given a particular situation. People are told that a particular ceremony must be performed. More often than not, there is no explanation of why that ritual should be performed given the circumstances. True, a ritual often has a specific overall purpose (e.g., healing a particular person, keeping witches at bay); but the set of sequences that compose the ritual are not connected to this goal in the same way as sub-actions connect to sub-goals in ordinary behavior (Boyer, 1994).

3. Third, in many cultural rituals people create an orderly environment that is quite different from the one of everyday interaction. People line up instead of walking, they dance instead of moving, they wear similar clothes or make-up, they build alignments of rocks or logs, they create elaborate color and shape combinations, and so on. Related to this is the recurrent concern with delimiting a particular space (a sacred circle, a taboo territory) often visually distinct from the other, unmarked space.

It is important to distinguish 'rituals' from ritualization. There may be lots of different reasons why particular kinds of ceremonies are found in human cultures, why they persist, and why they are relatively stable. We discuss these issues elsewhere (Liénard & Boyer, forthcoming). For instance, one may propose plausible evolutionary scenarios for the existence of birth celebrations and of death rituals in most cultural environments. But these scenarios do not explain why these social occasions all include ritualized behavior in the precise sense intended here.

2.5 General Features of Rituals

Behavior in these different domains displays obvious similarities:

1. Compulsion. Given certain circumstances, people feel that it would be dangerous or unsafe or improper not to perform ritualized actions. There is an emotional drive to perform the action, often associated with some anxiety at the thought of not performing it (especially in patients and children) and some relief after performance. Naturally, this varies between domains. Anxiety precedes ritual actions or behavior in many personal and pathological rituals but not always in cultural rituals.

Common to all domains, though, is the important fact that compulsion does not require any explanation. People feel that they must perform the ritual, otherwise. . . [something might happen], but they require no specific representation of what would happen otherwise.

2. Rigidity, adherence to script. People feel that they should perform a ritual in the precise way it was performed before. They strive to achieve a performance that matches their representation of past performances and attach negative emotion to any deviation from that remembered pattern. This is familiar in childhood rituals and OCD but also in the 'traditionalistic' flavor of most cultural rituals (Bloch, 1974). Deviation from the established pattern is intuitively construed as dangerous, although in most cases the participants have or require no explanation of why that is the case.

3. Goal-demotion. Rituals generally include action-sequences selected from ordinary goal-directed behavior. But the context in which they are performed, or the manner of performance, results in 'goal-demotion,' in performance divorced from observable goals. For instance, people tie shoelaces that were tied already; they touch a specific piece of furniture without trying to move it or use it as support; they wash hands many more times than hygiene would require; and so on.

4. Internal repetition and redundancy. Repeated enactments of the same action or gesture, as well as reiterations of the same utterances, are typical of many rituals. A given sequence is executed three or five or ten times. What matters is the exact number. This makes many ritual sequences clearly distinct from everyday action, in which there is either no repetition of identical sequences (e.g., in assembling a musical instrument, one performs a series of unique actions), or each repeated act has a specific outcome (e.g., in weaving), or repetition is cumulative (the egg-whites rise only after a long period of whipping).

5. A restricted range of themes. Many rituals seem to focus around such themes as: pollution and purification, danger and protection, the possible danger of intrusion from other people, the use of particular colors or specific numbers, the construction of an ordered environment (Dulaney & Fiske, 1994). A ritual space or instruments are described as 'pure' or 'safe' (or, on the contrary, as the locus of concentrated 'pollution') or the point of the ritual is to 'purify' people or objects, to 'cleanse' mind or body, and so on. In collective rituals, this concern with

pollution and cleansing is so prevalent that it has been considered a foundation of religious ritual (Douglas, 1982).

Is there a common explanation for these different features of ritualized behavior? Here we will start from pathology and summarize what can be safely concluded from the clinical and neuropsychological evidence. This supports a particular model of action ritualization which we will also extend to developmental rituals in children and adults, before proceeding to the distinct case of cultural rituals.

3. Interpretations of Compulsive Ritualization

3.1 Neuropsychological Modeling

OCD has been interpreted as a specific dysfunction of the basal ganglia (Rapoport, 1990, 1991). To understand how this would result in the specific symptoms, the impairment should be described in terms of the specific functions of a cortical-striato-pallidal-thalamic circuit (CSPT). This network includes projections from many cortical areas (including medial and orbital frontal cortex) into the striatum (caudate and putamen) and back to the cortex via the substantia nigra and thalamus (Rauch et al., 2001; Saxena, Brody, Schwartz, & Baxter, 1998). This has been confirmed by neuro-imaging studies, as OCD is associated with increased activity of the orbitofrontal cortex (OFC) as well as in the striatum, thalamus, and anterior cingulate cortex (ACC) (Saxena et al., 2004; Saxena et al., 1998). Also, the anatomy of the caudate, putamen, and globus pallidus seems to differ between patients and controls (see, e.g., (Giedd, Rapoport, Garvey, Perlmutter, & Swedo, 2000). One generally distinguishes between a 'direct' and an 'indirect' pathway in the CSPT networks (see Fig. 1). The direct pathway links (1) frontal cortices to (2) the striatum, to the globus pallidus (pars interna) and substantia nigra (pars reticulata) to (4) thalamus and (5) cortex. The indirect pathway connects (1) cortex to (2) striatum to (3a) globus pallidus (pars externa) and subthalamic nucleus to (3b) globus pallidus (pars interna) and substantia nigra (pars reticulata) to (4) thalamus to (5) cortex.

The basal ganglia are involved in the formation of habits, motor habits in particular (Rauch et al., 1997). The pattern of projections from

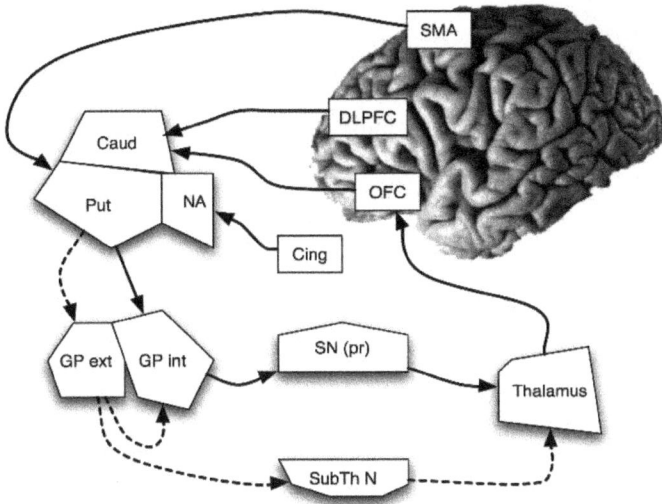

Fig. 1. A summary of some cortico-striatal pathways relevant to OCD. Continuous
line for the 'direct' pathway and dotted line for 'indirect' pathways (both
highly simplified). SMA: Supplementary Motor Area, DLPFC: dorso-lateral
prefrontal cortex, OFC: orbito-frontal cortex, Caud: caudate nucleus, Put:
Putamen, Cing.: Cingulate Cortex, NA: Nucleus Accumbens, GP: globus
pallidus (external and internal), SN(pr): substantia nigra pars reticulata,
SubTh Nuc: Subthalamic nuclei. (Figure by P Boyer, 2006).

the cortex to the striatum suggests that the latter may store summaries
or 'chunks' of motor behavior. This is confirmed by involvement of the
striatum in the learning and production of habitual responses (Graybiel,
1998). Striatal networks may act as coordinators of cortical input and
orchestrators of motor habits.

What specific dysfunction would result in OCD symptoms? In animal
models, modifying dopamine uptake in the striatum results in stereotypic
and repetitive behavior (Canales & Graybiel, 2000; Szechtman, Sulis, &
Eilam, 1998). So an imbalance between various parts of the basal ganglia
system or a modification in the dynamics of cortico-striatal pathways
are probably involved in the condition. Saxena and colleagues identify
the 'indirect' pathway as the locus of impairment. In their model, the
association of globus pallidus (external) and subthalamic nucleus
can be construed as a 'basal ganglia control system' that modulates
the projections to the thalamus and cortices (Saxena et al., 1998). The
indirect pathway consists of inhibitory (GABAergic) projections from
the striatum to the thalamus. To the extent that this pathway becomes

less tonic, it would fail to inhibit habitual motor responses and result in unmotivated, stereotypic routines (Saxena et al., 1998).

Also important is the regulatory role played by the orbitofrontal cortex (OFC) and the anterior cingulate cortex (ACC). Early neuroimaging studies showed differential activation of these regions in OCD patients in situations of symptom provocation (Adler et al.; Rauch et al., 1994). OFC activation makes sense given its role in the selection, control, and inhibition of behavior as demonstrated both by neuroimaging and by lesions of this area (Happaney, Zelazo, & Stuss, 2004; Ogai, Iyo, Mori, & Takei, 2005; Schnider, Treyer, & Buck, 2005). Anterior cingulate activity is also revealing. Ablation of the area has been used in refractory OCD cases (Kim et al., 2003). ACC hyperactivity is not limited to situations of symptom provocation (Ursu, Stenger, Shear, Jones, & Carter, 2003). In an event-related study of error-processing, Fitzgerald and colleagues found increased ACC activity with error-detection in both patients and controls, with significantly higher increases in patients. The amount of ACC activity also correlated with the severity of the patients' compulsive symptoms (Fitzgerald et al., 2005). The anterior cingulate can be described as an error-detection network that activates top-down responses to situations of conflicting information, for example, between expectation and perception in errors, or between discrepant stimuli (Van Veen & Carter, 2002).

All this converges to suggest that OCD may stem from a dysfunction of a neural system involved in the production and inhibition of a particular set of habitual or routinized behaviors. The etiology of the dysfunction includes probable genetic factors (Campbell et al., 1999; J. Zohar, Kennedy, Hollander, & Koran, 2004) as well as infectious conditions (Giedd et al., 2000; Henry, Perlmutter, & Swedo, 1999), although evidence for either cause is tentative. The compulsive nature of the actions seems to result from a failure to inhibit strongly motivated routines initiated in the striatum, either because striatal networks over-respond to cortical inputs, or because their inhibitory effect on thalamic networks is diminished, or both, leading to ritualization. This picture is consistent with the clinical and pharmacological evidence (Kaplan & Hollander, 2003; J. Zohar et al., 2004).

3.2 Cognitive models: General or specific?

Cognitive models provide a bridge from neuropsychological findings to the phenomenology of OCD symptoms. A classical cognitive model describes the condition as a disorder of threat-appraisal and cognitive control (Rachman & Shafran, 1998; Salkovskis, 1985). Patients produce a misguided appraisal of intrusive thoughts, exaggerate the threats present in the environment as well as the extent of their own responsibility for what befalls others, and finally fail to appreciate the measure of safety introduced by normal precautions. In this model, OCD differs from other anxiety conditions (general anxiety disorder, panic) only in that the eliciting stimuli are very specific—a series of intrusive thoughts with recurrent themes (Clark, 1999).

Obsessions and compulsions might then result from a general failure to appreciate levels of danger, to evaluate one's responsibility in external events, and to form an appropriate picture of one's situation. For instance, ritualized repetition may stem from the patient's failure to realize that he or she has actually accomplished the action (Pitman, 1987). There is indeed evidence (though not conclusive) for general memory problems. OCD patients have the right intuitions in both memory for actions and source monitoring (i.e., whether they performed as opposed to imagined performing an action) but they report less confidence in their own intuition (Hermans, Martens, De Cort, Pieters, & Eelen, 2003).

However, there is also definite evidence for domain-specific aspects of OCD. For instance, OCD patients are similar to controls in their recall of neutral objects but are markedly better at recalling dangerous items (Tolin et al., 2001). OCD 'checkers' are impaired in their recall of own actions but less so in recall of other information (Ecker & Engelkamp, 1995). In terms of attention, modified Stroop tasks show that OCD 'washers are more attentive to contamination words than are controls, and OCD patients in general show more interference than controls do from danger-related words (Foa, Ilai, McCarthy, Shoyer, & et al.).

3.3 Security-Motivation

Most cognitive models of OCD are phrased in domain-general terms. An exception is Abed and de Pauw's evolutionary hypothesis about OCD as a disruption of a specific 'psychological immune system'

(Abed & de Pauw, 1998). The hypothesis starts from the observation that the prevalence of OCD would suggest the tail of a phenotypic distribution rather than harmful mutations. According to Abed and de Pauw, obsessional phenomena are an exaggerated version of thought processes selected because they lead to risk-avoidance behavior (in particular through fear or disgust). Central to the hypothesis is the fact that intrusive thoughts, in patients and normal individuals, consist of detailed scenarios of possible danger, an 'Involuntary Risk Scenario Generating System' (Abed & de Pauw, 1998).

A similar evolutionary background motivates Szechtman and Woody's interpretation of the condition in terms of a 'security-motivation' system (Szechtman & Woody, 2004). The model is an attempt to integrate the diverse components of the relevant behaviors (emotion, perception of specific information, typical actions, inhibition or disinhibition of automatic routines) in a motivational system functionally specialized in potential danger.

In contrast to general cognitive impairment models, both Abed and de Pauw's and Szechtman and Woody's models provide a parsimonious account for the specificity of OCD intrusions.

The security system is present in all normal human beings and monitors external signals of particular kinds of potential danger. The neural circuitry involved in both normal and pathological safety motivation can be broken down into three major functional components with excitatory and inhibitory links. An appraisal system handles information that matches input conditions for environmental cues of potential danger. A security motivation system handles the evaluation of these cues. A set of various evolved security-related programs is engaged, depending on the outcome of this motivation assessment, with specific motor and visceral output (see Fig. 2).

As a result of engaging security-related motor-programs (this may consist in visual inspection of one's environment, cleaning, ordering, etc.), the security motivation system produces a specific experience of things being 'just right' which feeds back into the danger appraisal system.

Szechtman and Woody's identification of the neural correlates of these systems extends beyond the cortico-striatal pathways. The appraisal of potential danger involves perceptual and memory information and feeds

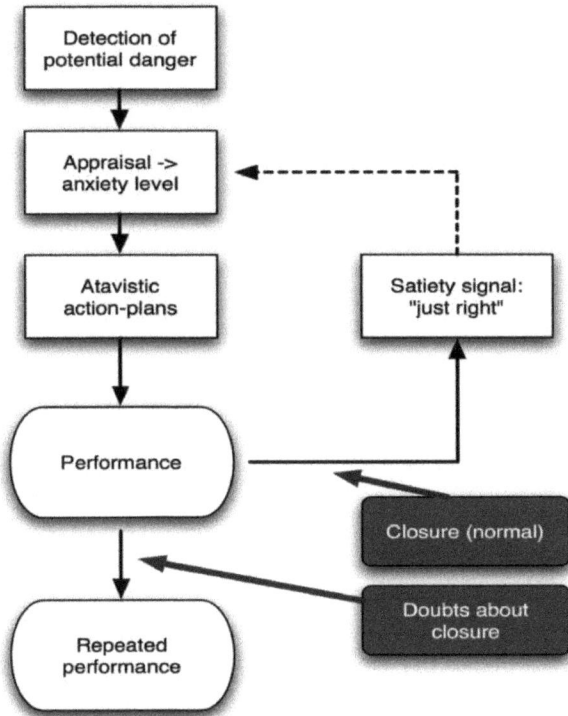

Fig. 2. An interpretation of Szechtman and Woody's (2004) model. Rectangles correspond to distinct systems activated, rounded boxes to behavioral results and call-outs to aspects of the processing. Danger clues are evaluated and action-plans selected, resulting in a 'just right feeling' that sends negative feedback to danger appraisal. This loop is absent or impaired in patients, leading to doubts about performance, which themselves result in repetition and rigid action-plans. (Figure by P Boyer, 2006).

into both orbital cortex and the cortical-striatal pathways. From there, Szechtman and Woody identify two distinct informational loops. One of them, the affect loop, includes most of the 'indirect pathway' structures, producing a specific anxiety. In parallel, a 'security-related programs' loop, connects striatum to the globus pallidus (internal) and ventral thalamus to elicit the performance of stored motor routines. Finally, the normal inhibition of these two loops is provided by brainstem structures after performance of the elicited motor routines. The model states that OCD is the result of a dysfunction in a satiety signal, plausibly generated in brainstem structures, that connects the performance of security related behaviors as inhibitory feedback to a subsystem that generates and sustains security motivation.

3.4 Outstanding Questions

In our view, while current models of compulsion have great descriptive and explanatory value, they still provide an incomplete account of various aspects of the obsessive and compulsive spectrum, especially if we include normal as well as pathological manifestations of ritual dispositions.

A more complete model should account for the following aspects of ritualized behavior:

1. Why these specific themes? The thoughts patients and others report are clearly not random conceptual associations. They center on a few threats that are particularly disturbing. Even this is much too broad a description. People have intrusive thoughts about causing accidents involving their kin, but not complete strangers; they fear contamination more than bone fracture or inflammation; they fear that they may have left the back door open or the oven on, not that their car will be stolen or the fridge will break down.

2. Why these specific actions? Compulsions seem to focus on a narrow set of possible actions. This is clear for contamination compulsions which result in repeated washing and cleaning. The same applies to checking behaviors, limited to visual cues. Not all actions seem likely to become compulsive.

3. Why combine the actions in that way? Many compulsive rituals organize action in a very specific way. For instance, there are many negative rules in compulsions (avoid treading on the lines on the pavement). Also, there are specific rules about the number of iterations (touch this chair three times) or about the order of actions (tie the right shoe before the left one).

4. Why does ritual provide relief? Most clinicians agree on a temporary lowering of anxiety levels after the performance of rituals. The question points to one possible explanation for the compulsive character of the behavior. Could it be that patients intuitively reproduce behaviors that reduce anxiety? But then, what is it about such organization of action that could reduce anxiety?

5. Why does ritual eventually strengthen obsessions? This too is a feature often noted by clinicians (see, e.g., Salkovskis, 1985). Although rituals provide some relief, this is only temporary and the intrusive thoughts quickly come back. Indeed, it would seem that the more rituals one performs, the more focused and bothersome are the intrusive thoughts.

4. Ritualized Action: The Core Process

What follows is a list of the different points of the model which will be explained in the following sections . In our view, ritualization in young children, in normal adults at particular life-stages, and in patients comprises a series of processes in which specific information is acquired or retrieved and specific behavioral plans are engaged:

1. Security-motivation systems are engaged. This may be because of potential danger cues in the environment (described below), information imparted by other people, self-generated thoughts, or intrusions. In any case, these thoughts focus on cues for potential hazards chosen in a small set that we call the Potential Hazard Repertoire.

2. Safety motivation triggers an arousal state in which non-action is intuitively considered dangerous (something must be done) although there need be no clear representation of why that is the case.

2a. This state triggers a non-deliberate, non-controlled search for action-sequences that appear intuitively appropriate. Some cues make some actions seem apposite although the subject generally has no explanation for the intuition (or may only have ex post facto rationalizations). These actions are selected from what we call an Evolutionary Precaution Repertoire.

2b. The arousal triggers a special attentional state that focuses on low-level properties of own actions. The action-flow is parsed in smaller units than is usually the case.

2c. The arousal state may bias the appraisal system in such a way that 'just right' or 'closure' experience is delayed. This triggers doubts about actual or proper performance and reiteration of action-plans.

3. Performance of the actions with attention to low-level parsing [see 2b above] may impose a heavy load on working memory-systems, with two consequences:

3a. The intrusive themes are temporarily pushed away from conscious access, resulting in a short-lived reduction in anxiety level.

3b. The intrusive themes are monitored by automatic, not controlled processes, which should result in higher salience (and renewed intrusion) after performance.

These different steps are summarized in Figure 3 . In what follows we explain the processes engaged in more detail and provide arguments for their presence in most domains of ritualization. An important point

to emphasize is that we do not identify any particular component of
the overall process as being exclusively pathological. In our view, most
reactions to inferred threats engage all these processes. Whether or
not a given action triggers doubt about proper performance, leading
to rigid repetition, that is, ritualization of these reactions, may be a
matter of degree.

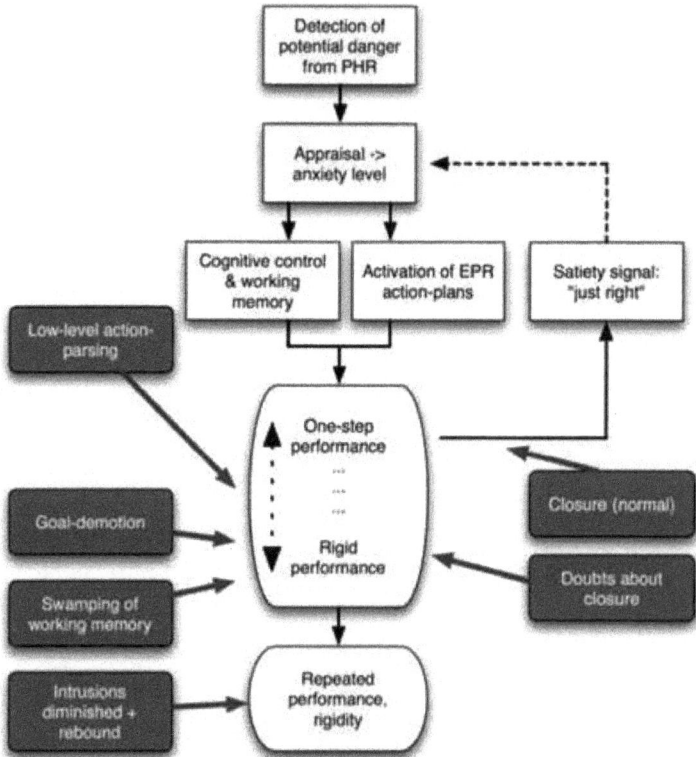

Fig. 3. Summary of our Potential Hazard and Precaution model. Boxes denote
specific processes with corresponding neural systems. Rounded box
describes performance. Dark call-outs describe some of their typical
properties. Clues for danger must suggest hazards from the Potential
Hazard Repertoire. Appraisal of the clues if modulated by anxiety, leading
to activation of plans from Evolutionary Precaution Repertoire and action-
monitoring systems. At the normal end of the spectrum, performance
triggers satiety feelings with a negative feedback to danger appraisal
systems. At the pathological end of the spectrum, doubts about proper
performance lead to repetition and a positive feedback to danger appraisal.
(Figure by P Boyer, 2006).

5. Why These Particular Obsessions and Compulsions?

5.1 Logic of Our Evolutionary Approach

Intrusions and compulsions are bothersome and time-consuming. Not only do they confer no particular adaptive advantage, they seem to be clearly maladaptive in diverting attention and memory resources from valuable goals. However, note that OCD and other disorders of the fronto-striatal circuitry (Tourette's syndrome, ADHD, and schizophrenia) all have some genetic basis, as may be suspected from their prevalence (Bradshaw & Sheppard, 2000) and is tentatively confirmed by gene-loci studies (Arnold, Zai, & Richter, 2004; Grados, Walkup, & Walford, 2003).

To the extent that a specific kind of motivation is involved in the pathology of ritualization (perhaps also in its normal occurrence), it makes sense to wonder why and how humans are endowed with this special focus on particular kinds of hazards. In particular, are such systems the outcome of the evolutionary history of the species? In this case ultimate explanations would help us make sense of the pathology (Nesse, 1998), a strategy used in physiology (Nesse & Williams, 1996), psychiatry (Baron-Cohen, 1997; Cosmides & Tooby, 1999; Stevens & Price, 2000) and neuropsychology (Duchaine, Cosmides, & Tooby, 2001), and, as mentioned earlier, already outlined in some studies of OCD (Abed & de Pauw, 1998).

Providing an evolutionary model requires the following steps: (1) identify the relevant fitness-related problem; (2) identify the knowledge base and computational rules that would be minimally required to solve that problem in ancestral environments; and (Willour et al., 2004) provide experimental evidence for the actual operation of a mental system that meets this computational specification. Once this is accomplished, such a model may allow us to delineate possible pathogenic scenarios that are causally deeper than the vague clusters identified in DSM-IV (Murphy & Stich, 2000).

There are some indications that this approach may be appropriate for anxiety disorders and OCD in particular. First, negative emotions like anxiety or persistent low mood should not be considered as dysfunctional. They may consist in evolved warning systems whose negative rewards steer organisms away from fitness-reducing situations

(Nesse, 1998). Second, the specific thoughts and actions that compose the symptoms may be linked to evolutionary concerns (Leckman, 2003; Mataix-Cols et al., 2005). Third, some of the conditions associated with fronto-striatal impairment may actually result in adaptive phenotypes (Bradshaw & Sheppard, 2000).

5.2 Two Types of Fitness-Threats

We know enough of early primate and early human living conditions to identify broad categories of highly salient danger in our evolutionary past: reproductive risk (e.g., for females, mating with un-nurturing or low-fitness males; for males, cuckoldry or choosing unhealthy females); predation (failing to detect or deter predators); contamination from pathogens (bacteria, viruses, toxins); resource scarcity (e.g., failing to anticipate seasonal changes); social harm (e.g., ostracism, but also reduced cooperation).

From an evolutionary standpoint, we should expect (1) that such recurrent hazards, not more recent ones, would be the target of specific emotions, and (2) that different kinds of hazard require different decision rules. On the first point, it is clear that specific emotions target hazards of great evolutionary ancestry rather than more recent ones, even though the latter may be much more dangerous. Our danger-avoidance systems do not seem to rely on an unprejudiced tabulation of which features of the environment effectively predict harm or misfortune. If this were the case, we would observe in modern conditions many cases of anxieties, fear, or even phobic aversions to electricity, cars, and cigarettes, which cause vastly more deaths than do spiders and rats. But we observe the opposite. Second, it seems that different kinds of fitness-threats do activate different inferential rules. Specific principles inform the gender-specific perception of particular mates as more or less of a waste of reproductive potential (Buss, 1989). Predator-prey interaction is governed by early-developed intuitions that do not apply to other interactions (Barrett, 1999). Recurrent features of disgust reactions suggest a pathogen-minimizing system that adapts to local conditions (Fessler, Arguello, Mekdara, & Macias, 2003; Rozin, Haidt, & McCauley, 1993) or to particular individual circumstances such as pregnancy (Fessler & Navarrete, 2003; Profet, 1993). Problems of resource scarcity are handled by specific foraging strategies (Krebs & Inman, 1994) which can override explicit reasoning (Rode, Cosmides, Hell, & Tooby, 1999). Finally, a host of 'social intelligence' principles support the monitoring of social interaction, from the establishment of friendships and coalitions (Harcourt & de Waal, 1992; Kurzban & Leary, 2001; Tooby & Cosmides, 1996), to dominance (Sidanius & Pratto, 1999) and punishment (Boyd & Richerson, 1985; Kurzban & Leary, 2001).

At this point we must introduce an important distinction between two types of fitness-threatening situations. First, there are cases of manifest threats, cases in which the organism receives signals about the presence of the source of danger: for example, a predator or enemy attack, or seeing one's infant in danger. Situations of this type are handled by specialized and context-specific fear-mechanisms in humans as in other primates (LeDoux, 2003; Maren & Quirk, 2004) and result in aggression, freezing, or flight routines (Blair, 2001; Payne, 1998). Second, there are inferred threats, when the potential danger is probable given certain clues in the environment. For instance, the strange taste of a particular dish may be evidence of rotting; tracks may betray the recent passage of a dangerous predator; a particular person's attitude may indicate that they will not cooperate. Such circumstances typically engage what Abed and de Pauw called an 'Involuntary Risk Scenario Generation.' Naturally, the distinction is a rough one (many situations involve threats for which there are direct and indirect clues). It is also, obviously, species-specific since some situations are a threat to some organisms but not others.

5.3 Potential Danger as a Specific Domain

It may seem odd to hypothesize a domain-specific system whose activation is triggered by such disparate potential inputs as a footprint, a disgusting odor, or the fact that one's infant is out of sight for a moment. How specific is the system if it can encompass such physically different stimuli? But this objection assumes that domain-specific inference systems are tied to a physically specified range of stimuli, which is true for some perceptual systems (e.g., 3D vision) but certainly not for most higher-level functional systems. A human mind can parse linguistic input in just the same way on the basis of auditory, visual, or tactile information. Neuro-cognitive systems specialized in assessing the value of potential mates use information from conversations, from comparison of visual information to some ideal template, from observed interactions between the potential mate and other people, and so forth. Indeed, it would be surprising (and maladaptive) if a particular kind of physical input always triggered a unique inference-system. A man is a man is a man, but a father, a brother, an attacker, and a potential mate should activate different mental systems.

So the autonomy or specificity of a domain-specific system can be inferred, not from focus on a physically specific range of cues, but from specific processing principles, a specific kind of output, a specific learning logic, and—in some cases—a specific pattern of impairment. These are criteria that seem present in the case of the Hazard-Precaution system.

There is indeed some behavioral evidence that humans have specific inference rules for information relative to precautions. Fiddick and colleagues have demonstrated that when considering precautionary rules (e.g., 'if you take oranges on board you will not get scurvy'), subjects pass logical tests for verification of rule-violation that they fail in other contexts (Fiddick, Cosmides, & Tooby, 2000). This is a replication, in another domain, of the performance on rule-verification in the Wason selection task observed when the rules allude to social contracts, however unfamiliar, as opposed to other deontic domains, however familiar (Cosmides, 1989; Fiddick et al., 2000). Although these findings concern explicit judgment more than intuition, they suggest that potential hazard management might require cognitive processing that is quite different from other inferential tasks.

5.4 The Limited Range of Obsessions and Compulsions

To explain the recurrent features of both intrusions and compulsions, our model stipulates two kinds of databases, called Potential Hazard Repertoire and Precaution Repertoire respectively. Intrusions and compulsions have to do with a specific, narrow range of hazards, which, in our view, are best explained as recurrent threats to fitness in ancestral environments.

One reason for defending this hypothesis is that the actions combined in ritual sequences are generally (i) species-specific and (ii) precaution-related. Ritualists do not generally design entirely novel behavioral sequences from scratch. Rather, they combine familiar elements of actions (e.g., washing, cleansing, checking) into novel sequences. This is also manifest in animal models of the condition. The ritualistic behaviors triggered in rats treated with quinpirole (a dopamine agonist) are species-specific, consisting in checking with return to a home-base, similar to those of controls, but stylized, redundant, and time-consuming (Szechtman et al., 1998). Second, these actions are generally relevant ones as a protection against various kinds of fitness-threatening situations (Rapoport & Fiske, 1998). A review of the different dimensions of OCD obsessions but also adult normal intrusions and children's anxieties should illustrate the point.

5.4.1. Contamination. Thoughts about contamination and contagion are too specific to be interpreted as the outcome of a general lowering of the anxiety threshold. They tend to center on invisible agents such as toxins, viruses, and microbes—of obvious evolutionary import. Besides, people's anxious thoughts about contamination focus on modes of contact (touching with the hand, kissing, licking, having sex, sharing food, breathing next to a particular source) that are actually used by pathogen vectors. In patients, the compulsions associated with these thoughts are not arbitrary either. They center on measures such as washing and cleansing, protecting oneself from intrusive material by staying at a distance, avoiding contact, suspending breathing. In ancestral environments, before the discovery of asepsis, these procedures would indeed constitute the only measures to reduce or control contamination.

There is behavioral and cross-cultural evidence that a concern with possible contamination triggers specialized inferential circuitry in humans. For instance, Fessler and colleagues have documented the disproportionate representation of meat among the foods that are 'good to taboo' in many cultures. They connect this to the specific challenges of meat consumption caused by protozoa and other pathogens (Fessler & Navarrete, 2003). In the same way, meat seems to be the chief target of early-pregnancy aversions, a period of dangerous immuno-depression (Fessler, 2002). More generally, many sources of disgust are also sources of contamination: decaying corpses but also rotting substances, feces, spit, and so on.

5.4.2. Symmetry and order in one's environment. Many children and adults are concerned with creating an orderly environment. Children align toys in a particular order, ritual participants need to create elaborately ordered displays, and the same is true of many OCD 'checkers.' These behaviors are often construed, especially in the domain of children's rituals, as the expression of a need for reassurance; as the urge to create a recognizable and therefore reassuring environment.

However, this 'therefore' is question-begging. What is reassuring about a predictable environment? True, predictability implies a reduction in computational load, but that cannot be the reason, as children and ritualists in general devote great amounts of time and cognitive resources creating their orderly world. So there might be other aspects of order and symmetry that motivate cognitive investment. In our view, ordered environments combine two properties that may explain this motivation.

First, alignments and symmetry are such that they make other agents' intrusions clearly visible. Anecdotal (but massive) evidence suggests that children but also various sub-clinical obsessive personality-types get quite upset when 'intruders' such as parents or cleaners disrupt their sequences and alignments. We speculate that the point of the ordering may be precisely to detect such disruptions. Or rather, that the behavior may be a stored action-plan that would have this function in other environments. This is indeed the one explanation of some animals' 'tidying up' routines as an anti-predator strategy (Curio, 1993). So the creation of a non-trivial order that is not immediately detectable by intruders may be a powerful motivation in such compulsions. Note that childhood rituals center on the home environment and in particular on children's own personal space (usually their bedroom).

Second, the specific use of symmetry and conceptual order (alternating colors, corresponding shapes) is diagnostic of uniquely human dispositions to alter the environment. Bowerbirds may be among the few exceptions—and seem to resort to similar ways of making a display salient: pure colors, symmetry, and so on. Indeed, people readily detect such specific alterations—which has been used for millennia as a way of advertising human presence. Cairns are improbable pilings of rocks that no species other than human beings would build. Broken twigs, straight paths, and color markings serve as landmarks for the same reason. What makes this possible is the combination of sophisticated symmetry and pattern-detection capacities in humans (Bornstein & Krinsky, 1985; Bornstein & Stiles-Davis, 1984; Fisher, Ferdinandsen, & Bornstein, 1981) and sophisticated tool-making capacities (Wynn, 1993). This is particularly relevant to children's construction of ordered environments, which may consist of a period of systematic training in the construction of such signals of human presence.

These are bound to remain speculative as there is, to our knowledge, no systematic research on the cognitive and emotional processes involved in ordered displays, particularly in children's strong motivation to produce such environments.

5.4.3. Social offence. Some of the intrusive thoughts of obsessive people center on possible acts that would offend or harm other people, resulting in social exclusion. These fears also represent, in our view, a domain of evolutionary hazard. Given human dependence on conspecifics for all aspects of survival, it is not surprising to find that possible social strife is seen as extremely dangerous. Life in complex societies makes this dependence diffuse and impersonal. By contrast, in ancestral environments people depended on known members of the group. Conflict in such groups threatens each member's access to resources, cooperation, and information (Tooby & DeVore, 1987). In this domain too, it seems that the precautionary measures taken by obsessives are in fact rather appropriate. For instance, one of the features of OCD patients (especially checkers) is a tendency to monitor actions, in particular the minutiae of one's own behavior, well beyond the 'normal' limits. Another common feature is that people choose to avoid social contact lest they insult or assault others, which again is intuitively appropriate as a precautionary device.

5.4.4. Harm to offspring. Intrusive thoughts reported by adults often focus on possible harm to one's own offspring, accompanied by fears of handling tools and utensils in a dangerous way, smothering or dropping the infant, as well as forgetting about the baby and losing it (particularly in stores and other public places). Again, the danger is one of obvious evolutionary significance, as tools and weapons are part of our ancestral past. Also, shifting attention away from one's infant is risky but unavoidable in humans who need to attend to such tasks as foraging or processing food. Again, the compulsive precautions (hyper vigilance, neglect towards other people and social interactions, etc.) would seem appropriate given these hazards.

5.5 The Precaution System Associates Domain-Specific Repertoires

Specific reactions to inferred threats suggest a functional system that we called the Precaution System, whose specific input consists in inferences to non-manifest threat and whose output is selective activation of particular precautions. At both ends of its operation, the postulated system is highly specific. The Precaution System does not respond to all or most actually significant signals of potential danger, but to a limited repertoire of cues. As we said above, humans seem to infer fitness threats, with a specific anxiogenic response, from wounds or rotting carcasses, but not from tobacco smoke or electricity.

The range of action-plans activated is also restricted to a few possible precautions (washing, avoiding contact, etc.) that may or may not be most appropriate given changing circumstances. Note that this model does not account for some sub-varieties of OCD symptomatology. Hoarding, for instance, does not seem to result in ritualized behavior in the precise sense described here. This may be because the underlying processes are different from other OCD dimensions, as is suggested by neuroimaging studies (Calamari et al., 2004; Saxena et al., 2004). In our model, the specificity of cues and responses maps a set of highly recurrent threats in human evolutionary history.

6. Why the Complicated Action?

6.1 Ordinary Action-Parsing

The ritualization process imposes particular constraints on the performance and sequencing of action. This is why the features of ritual should be considered in the context of action representation in general. Human beings attend to each other's behavior and react to it, which means that they must 'parse' other people's and their own behavior in meaningful units (Newtson, 1973). The experimental study of such parsing mechanisms provides a background against which we can understand specific features of ritual.

People identify actions as belonging to particular categories (e.g., putting on one's socks) but also as part of larger sequences (putting on one's socks as part of getting dressed). This 'partonomic' structure is general to action sequences in normal contexts. Small units are parts of larger units and the boundaries between large units tend to coincide with a boundary at a lower level. Zacks and colleagues distinguish between three levels of representation: that of simple gestures (sequences of a few seconds), that of behavioral episodes (an order of longer magnitude, actions like 'getting dressed'), and that of a script (series that can span a much longer time, e.g., 'eating out,' 'giving a talk') (Zacks & Tversky, 2001; Zacks, Tversky, & Iyer, 2001).

In the absence of specific instructions to the contrary, people spontaneously describe and recall behavior in terms of middle-level behavioral units (Zacks & Tversky, 2001; Zacks, Tversky, et al., 2001), that could be called a 'basic level' for event-taxonomies (Rifkin, 1985). Indeed, people can generate far more categories of events at that middle-level than either super- or subordinates (Morris & Murphy, 1990). Mid-level breakpoints also correspond to specific neural activity (Speer, Swallow, & Zacks, 2003; Zacks, Braver, et al., 2001). It is certainly not a coincidence that this is also the level of description at which people typically ascribe goals to behavior. While gestures do not readily reveal intention, and scenes include many different intentions, behavioral episodes typically constitute the realization of a particular goal. Action-parsing develops early in infants and seems to focus on the intentional unit level from that early stage (Baldwin & Baird, 1999; Baldwin, Baird, Saylor, & Clark, 2001).

6.2 Goal-Demotion in Ritualized Action

These studies converge to suggest that spontaneous parsing focuses on middle-level action-units connected to specific goals. It is very difficult for normal humans not to parse action at that level. Indeed, an excessive focus on a low-level, gestural description of behavior, with the attendant imprecision about goals, is characteristic of frontal lobe or schizophrenic patients (Janata & Grafton, 2003; Zalla, Pradat-Diehl, & Sirigu, 2003).

Now this focus on low-level gesture analysis of the action-flow is precisely what happens in cultural and individual rituals. People's attention is typically drawn to the details of performance, the particular direction of a gesture, the specific number of times an action should be performed, and so on. Conversely, the description of ritual action in terms of goals is either not available or in any case irrelevant.

This is what we call 'goal-demotion.' Although there may be a goal for the overall ritual script, there are no obvious sub-goals for its components. In typical patients' rituals or in developmental rituals, there may be an explicit goal. For instance, producing a particular alignment of twigs in a particular order is supposed to ward off intruders; or a sequence of familiar actions, for example, tying one's shoes in a very specific way, will prevent accidents. But the contribution of each part of the script is not connected to particular sub-goals. For some ritual actions it is impossible for the actor to imagine what contribution they would make as they reverse the results achieved through previous actions (e.g., piling up objects and carefully putting them back in a line before piling them up again). More generally, the actions are considered an indispensable part of the script although the subject has no representation of why he or she should be included in it. This contrasts with the standard parsing of action-flow, where the units identified at all levels of partonomic division correspond to specific goals. Indeed, in a typical example of routinized efficient practice, that of blacksmithing techniques, the correspondence between action-units and goals serves to mobilize different units of knowledge as they become relevant to the sub-task at hand (Keller & Keller, 1996). This is emphatically not the case in ritualized behavior, the performance of which seems to be a 'tunnel' in which each action only points to the following one in the prescribed sequence (Bloch, 1974).

6.3 Swamping of Working Memory

There is very little study of the attentional effects of the focus on low-level features of action, combined with high control and hypersensitivity to possible mistakes, during performance of personal rituals. Our model suggests a specific, temporary effect on working memory which would explain some effects of rituals. Working memory is a specific memory system that holds information for a short time and allows updates and transformations of that information (Baddeley, 2000). In typical working memory tasks subjects are asked to repeat a sequence of letters in the right order, repeat in inverse order, repeat the sequence formed by letters while ignoring digits provided in between, or specify which was the third letter before last in a series that ends unexpectedly. In all such tasks, the subject must consider a certain set of information units or chunks at the same time in order to perform the required operations (Baddeley, 2000).

In our view, one of the effects of prescribed, rigidly compulsory action-sequences is a momentary overloading or 'swamping' of working memory, especially if the action sequences are represented at the fine-grain parsing level. This is very much what happens to some patients whose spontaneous action-parsing remains at this same low level of description. As Zalla puts it in her description of frontal lobe patients, 'the weakening of the causal connections between the component actions leads to the decomposition and the fragmentation of the action representation. [...] The increased amount of fragmented information rapidly overloads subjects' working memory capacity' (Zalla, Verlut, Franck, Puzenat, & Sirigu, 2004). A similar point can be made about fragmentation of action in OCD compulsions (Ursu et al., 2003).

Many ritual prescriptions resemble the tasks designed by cognitive psychologists in the study of working memory. They require focused attention on a set of different stimuli and their arrangement. For instance, a requirement to turn round a ritual pole three times clockwise without ever looking down imposes executive control of two tasks at the same time. Also, the frequent combination of a positive prescription ('do x. . .') and a negative one ('. . .while avoiding doing y') would seem to engage working memory and executive control in a way that is not usually present in everyday action flow.

6.4 Core Ritualization is the Opposite of Routinization

In the model proposed here, ritualized acts are very different from other routines. However often an individual may perform a ritualized action, it does not seem to become automatic. On the contrary, it remains constrained by high-level cognitive control. Ritualized actions as described here require high cognitive control because the rules often apply to familiar actions (e.g., walking, talking, preparing food) and turn them into more difficult tasks (e.g., walking without treading on the line). This clashes with a commonsense notion that rituals only include actions that one performs 'routinely' or 'without thinking.' Indeed, it is essential to our model that the component of rituals that we called Ritualized Behavior cannot be automatic.

7. Implications of the Model: Individual Ritual

7.1 Intrusions as Context-Sensitive Adaptive Algorithms

A surprising conclusion from the very few systematic studies of intrusions and mild compulsions in the normal population is that thoughts about potential dangers (contamination, social harm) and some compulsive reactions are not confined to the clinical population. Most normal people seem to experience the same kind of intrusive thoughts as patients do, and to some degree generate the same ritualized action-plans to avoid such dangers (Abramowitz et al., 2003; Rachman & de Silva, 1978). The crucial difference, then, is not in the contents of the thoughts but in their appraisal (Salkovskis, 1985).

The evidence available is insufficient to address the fundamental questions of the distribution, themes, intensity, and effects of intrusions in the normal population. Our model implies that intrusions are generally not dysfunctional. They are the outcome of systems geared to protecting the organism against potential dangers by over-interpreting specific inputs, which would suggest this prediction:

[P1] The position of an individual along fitness-related life-cycle dimensions (young vs. old, male vs. female, nulliparous vs. multiparous, high vs. low status) should predict the frequency, intensity and contents of intrusive thoughts.

So far, we only know that contagion and risk intrusions become highly salient during the perinatal period (Abramowitz et al., 2003; Leckman et al., 2004). This may also be true of other stages in the life-cycle, such as puberty, menarche, and the death of relatives. There is simply no general, population-sample study of thought-intrusions and their correlates. Sampling bias is particularly likely in this domain. Perinatal intrusions get noticed only because pregnancy is a period of higher medical monitoring.

7.2 Spontaneous Optimization and Relief

Why the strange rules and prescriptions in compulsive action? Also, why should such performances induce temporary relief? Many patients explicitly associate their rituals with specific obsessions, stating that performing the ritual is one way of inhibiting or repressing the unwanted thoughts (Salkovskis, 1985). Clinicians' observations and patients' reports converge in suggesting that the relief from unbearable anxiety, though temporary, is palpable. But there is nothing in current cognitive models to explain the fact.

In our view these two questions are related, and the common answer lies in the effects of ritualization on cognitive control and working memory. We suggested earlier that the performance of rituals, accompanied by numerous, specific, attention-demanding prescriptions, has the effect of 'swamping' working memory. We propose that such rituals constitute spontaneous and moderately efficient forms of thought-suppression. The difficulties of thought suppression in everyday life (trying not to recall unpleasant experiences or not to mull over possible future misfortunes) are familiar to everyone. Dan Wegner and colleagues have studied the phenomenon in controlled environments and demonstrated the complex control processes at work in such attempts (Wegner & Erskine, 2003; Wegner & Schneider, 2003). One interesting feature of these experimental studies is that only a few techniques are available to effectively 'push away' unwanted thoughts. They include focusing on emotional information of greater intensity than the target thoughts, or focusing attention on intrinsically difficult tasks like mathematical problems. These are difficult precisely because they recruit working memory to a greater extent than most everyday tasks and cannot be accomplished automatically.

Obviously, compulsive rituals are in many ways different from the phenomena observed in such studies. First, Wegner's subjects generally have no intrinsic motivation to avoid the suppressed thoughts, other than compliance with the experimenter's instructions. By contrast, OCD patients are strongly motivated. Second, the intrusions in patients are far stronger (more difficult to push away from consciousness) than a simple neutral theme suggested by an experimenter. Third, patients have a history of thought-intrusion and thought-avoidance, whereas experimental subjects are genuine beginners in the domain.

Notwithstanding these differences, we think the studies on thought-suppression are important to suggest a possible mechanism for the elaboration and rigidity of ritual prescriptions. In our view, patients with complicated compulsions have spontaneously attained an optimal point in the kind of activity that is so demanding in cognitive control that intrusive thoughts can be, at least for a while, pushed away from consciousness.

This 'trick' exploits certain features of the action-parsing systems reviewed (see Section 6.1). Given that action-parsing processes are engaged when any behavior is witnessed or produced, there are not many tricks that could force attention to focus on the low-level description of action. Among these features is repetition, which results in goal-demotion. Another such gimmick, obviously, is to borrow a sequence from ordinary scripts and perform it in a context that makes goal-ascription impossible: for example, wash objects without using water, pretend to trace an imaginary line, and so on. What results from these 'tricks' is what we called 'goal-demotion' above. Actions are represented without attaching a goal to each behavioral unit, as would be the case in non-ritual contexts.

This has several implications for the organization of compulsive rituals:

[P2] Compulsive actions should be such that they mobilize working memory and require high degree of cognitive control.

We have suggested that this is precisely what complicated prescriptions achieve, in particular when they result in control of usually automatic actions, such as choosing which shoe to tie first, or whether to push the doorbell button with this or that finger.

[P3] Compulsive rituals may be the outcome of a trial-and-error process.

This means that patients more or less deliberately (usually not) try various behaviors with various prescriptive rules until they reach an optimum, that is, the maximal occupation of working memory that is compatible with the intrinsic limits of memory itself. This would carry another consequence:

[P4] The symptoms should become unstable if the actions become routinized.

Working memory is effectively swamped when usually automatic actions are submitted to cognitive control. But even demanding tasks (e.g., tying one's shoes in a particular order that changes with the time of the day) might become partly automatic with time. One would predict that this would result in diminished efficacy and the spontaneous search for different prescriptions, or for more complex sequences. Naturally, this dynamic model does not imply that patients are at any point aware of the effect of prescriptive rules on memory. They may simply come to associate slightly more controlled action to slightly diminished intrusion, which would be enough gradually to lead to the baroque complications of individual rituals. We do not have much comparative clinical evidence concerning the particular contents of obsessive-compulsive rituals, that is, the number of actions, their precise description, their prescribed order, and so on, as opposed to general descriptions such as 'washing' or 'checking.' Nor do we have much in terms of longitudinal studies of ritual elaboration or progression; which is why these remain speculative predictions from the model.

7.3 Ironic Outcomes

Studying normal subjects instructed not to think about a particular item, Wegner showed that thought suppression typically results in a 'rebound'—in higher salience of the unwanted thoughts (Wegner & Schneider, 2003). This, in Wegner's model, is caused by the combination of two distinct processes engaged in thought suppression. While an explicit process directs and monitors the suppression, implicit processes are engaged that detect material associated with the target item (Wegner & Erskine, 2003). Here again, we do not wish to read too much in the parallel between an experimental paradigm and a long-lasting behavior pattern. However, an ironic outcome would seem to follow from the working-memory swamping scenario:

[P5] The precise intrusions that rituals can tone down should become more frequent or more difficult to resist as rituals are frequently practiced.

Although it has not been studied in precise quantitative terms, this ironic rebound does seem characteristic of compulsive rituals (Rachman & de Silva, 1978). The patients who perform more rituals are typically more anxious, and also more bothered by their intrusive thoughts. In other words, the long-term effects of ritual performance are the opposite of its short-term results. Indeed, this may be why an effective cognitive and behavioral therapy for OCD, in particular exposure and reaction prevention (ERP), requires that the patient evoke the dangerous thoughts but restrain the compulsive response (Rachman, Hodgson, & Marks, 1971).

7.4 Developmental Calibration

Our model implies specific claims about the Hazard-Precaution system in children, suggesting that early childhood is a period of calibration of the system. Many cognitive systems require calibration, that is, a change in parameters as a function of specific information picked up in the child's environment (Bjorklund & Pellegrini, 2002). A salient example is the development of food-preferences in young children, with a period of unlimited tolerance followed by 'parameter-setting' when young children reject anything that does not taste familiar (Birch, 1990). Another domain would be predator-prey relations, in which common assumptions are gradually refined in view of local circumstances (Barrett, 1999).

We can make a similar point about the Potential Hazard Repertoire. As we said, the system should handle indirect clues and produce inferences about the potential presence of dangerous substances, predators, and conspecifics. But it immediately appears that the number of possible clues is multiplied by the fact that (a) any one of these dangerous situations could be detected using a large number of possible clues and (b) the situations themselves must have changed a great deal, and changed frequently, during human evolution. Indeed, modern humans have adapted to variable conditions of subsistence in primary forests, grasslands, and dry savannas. They also had to adapt to seasonal changes. Most important, cultural evolution led to rapid cultural change, or 'life in the fast lane' (Boyd & Richerson, 1985). Ecological and cultural change means that old predators are gone but new ones are present; that noxious substances are not found in the same plants or animals; and that social interaction is handled in significantly different ways.

In this way the security system is a learning system, that appears in infants as a disposition to pick up particular kinds of locally relevant information from the natural and social environment, and changes its parameters as a function of that information. This would explain not just why children perform ritualistic behaviors, but also why the phenomenon appears and subsides at particular stages of development and why its typical manifestations evolve from prepotent fears for which there is clear preparedness, to more complex inferred threats like social harm. The system is designed to address a specific question: How to create a secure environment and to provide a series of contextually relevant solutions like washing, cleaning, checking, or modifying one's interaction with other agents? This implies particular directions for development in the kinds of thoughts and compulsions found in childhood. If the system is in calibration during that period, we should observe the following:

[P6] Anxiogenic thoughts should become gradually more specific with development.

[P7] Compulsive reaction should become more specific with development.

In terms of anxiety, a fear of vaguely defined predatory animals should become a fear of particular animals, a fear of strangers should become a fear of particular strangers, and so forth, as the system picks up information from the environment. This applies to compulsions, too. At an early stage, all recipes should be equiprobable. At a later stage, children should acquire locally relevant associations between a particular potential danger and a particular recipe. This also predicts differences in the rituals of older children from different groups. To the extent that different cultural groups live in different conditions, different kinds of dangers would be relevant and different clues significant:

[P8] Fears and compulsions should become more culturally specific as children get older.

We already have some fragmentary evidence that developmental trends in children's fears support these predictions. Fantasies and intrusive thoughts change with development, as mentioned earlier (Evans et al.; Leonard et al.).

7.5 Cultural Similarities and Differences in Pathological Ritual

Our model assumes that there is a Precaution system focused on certain kinds of potential danger. We also suggested that this system undergoes calibration during childhood, given that clues about potential danger change with changing environments. This would imply specific predictions about cross-cultural variations in the condition:

[P9] Anxieties and fears that result in compulsion belong to the narrow range of ancestral potential dangers: contamination, intrusion, social offence, and resource-depletion.

[P10] We should observe important cultural differences in the relative prevalence of symptom clusters (or 'subtypes').

There is very scant comparative anthropological evidence for anxieties or fears, although it seems to suggest something of this kind. In industrialized countries, the notion of electricity and cars as massive killers is virtually absent from the repertoire of phobic and obsessive patients. Also, the few studies of OCD patients in non-Western environments report the familiar obsessive themes of social offence, contagion, and potential danger (Arrindell, de Vlaming, Eisenhardt, van Berkum, & Kwee, 2002; Barker-Collo, 2003; Bertschy & Ahyi, 1991; Sasson et al., 1997) and the prevalence of OCD as a general category is the same in different places (Weissman et al., 1994).

Cultural differences too are suggestive, although there are to date very few (reliable) comparative studies of the condition and most of them only bear on clinical populations (so we have no evidence of what intrusive thoughts are common or exceptional in the population at large). For instance, a study from Bali documents a culture-specific tweaking of the general OCD themes. The patient needs to identify all passers-by in terms of genealogy and status, and reports obsessions about spirits and witches (Lemelson, 2003). Both are culturally specific variants of the social harm and social exposure obsessions, as hierarchy and status are fundamental to social interaction in Balinese society and social strife is expressed through witchcraft accusations (Barth, 1993). In Muslim countries, by contrast, many patients report concerns about pollution and contamination strongly influenced by religious prescriptions on hygiene and purity of thought (Al-Issa, 2000; Mahgoub & Abdel-Hafeiz, 1991; Okasha, Saad, Khalil, el Dawla, & Yehia, 1994). A sample of Bahrain patients showed that the fear of blasphemy was prevalent (about 40% of cases), which may be a local expression of the fear of social harm and potential exclusion (Shooka, Al-Haddad, & Raees, 1998).

This would suggest that an important calibrating factor is the range of cultural messages emphasizing potential danger. In particular, further epidemiological studies of the various dimensions of OCD (contagion, social offence, checking) may be correlated to the intensity of precautionary messages available in the environment of development. While Islam includes many descriptions of possibly impure actions or thoughts, Western children are bombarded with insistent warnings about invisible germs. Whether this results in significantly different normal and pathological intrusions is simply not documented yet.

8. Implications of the Model: Cultural Ritual as Derivative

So far, we have not mentioned one of the most salient and socially important manifestations of ritualized behaviors, namely, collective, culturally sanctioned rituals. We consider that the model presented so far can help us understand why rituals are widespread the world over and why they are compelling—an argument summarized here and presented elsewhere in more ethnographic detail (Liénard & Boyer, 2006).

8.1 A Capacity for Ritual?

We start from the work of Fiske and colleagues. Comparing hundreds of ritual sequences with clinical descriptions of OCD cases, they showed that the same themes recur over and over again in both domains (Dulaney & Fiske, 1994; Fiske & Haslam, 1997). OCD-typical features that also enter into rituals include specific (lucky or unlucky) numbers, use of special colors, repetition of actions, measures to prevent harm, ordering and symmetry, stylized verbal expressions, washing, concern with contagion, and so forth (Fiske & Haslam, 1997).

Fiske and colleagues speculate that there may be a human capacity to perform cultural rituals, that is distorted or hyperactive in pathological individual ritual (Fiske & Haslam, 1997). In Fiske's model, rituals are used to channel individual anxiogenic thoughts and make them bearable by providing a broader cultural context in which they can be shared and make better sense. Fiske and Haslam did not pursue the psychological and cultural implications of this hypothesis. It would provide a simple and elegant way of explaining the similarities in themes and actions between pathological and cultural ritual. Moreover, it would do so by connecting both to evolved, species-specific anxiogenic situations.

However, we consider that cultural rituals may be better explained in a different way, as partly parasitic on the Hazard-detection and Precaution systems described above. Our main reason for preferring this account is that it is more parsimonious. There is no empirical evidence that humans do have a specific capacity for ritual. There are no evolutionary grounds to consider that such a specific capacity would be adaptive (see our discussion of rituals as possible adaptation in Section 9.1.) So this is a costly hypothesis. By contrast, we have seen that there is solid evidence for systems specialized in responses to potential hazard. So if the disposition to perform cultural rituals is a by-product of these systems, we do not need to posit additional mechanisms.

8.2 The Cultural Selection Background

The first assumption in our treatment is that cultural rituals, like other forms of cultural behaviors, should be treated as the outcome of cultural selection (Boyd & Richerson, 1985; Durham, 1991; Sperber, 1985). Representations that we call 'cultural' occur with roughly the same content in other minds among people of a particular group. Indefinitely many factors (local or universal, psychological as well as physical) can in principle contribute to the spread of a particular mental representation. One type of factor of great interest to us is the set of general human dispositions that make certain representations, once they are expressed or conveyed by some people, particularly attention-grabbing or memorable or compelling, leading to their cultural transmission (Sperber, 1994).

We observe that people seem compelled to perform particular ceremonies at particular junctures, and also that they seem compelled to perform them in (what they judge to be) the prescribed way. This is what we need to explain. Now, one way to explain this would be to posit that there must be a particular urge to perform such ceremonies, or that they may fulfill particular needs of the human mind or of human groups. However, there may be another kind of explanation, based on the fact that people who receive information about particular performances already have sets of mental systems designed to respond to particular classes of stimuli. The question becomes: Which mental systems would be activated, such that performing this ceremony in these circumstances would seem compelling?

8.3 Cultural Information, Mimicry, and Cognitive Capture

Cognitive systems can be functionally described in terms of their particular input format, their operating principles, and their output. The input formats of cognitive systems are, in some cases, well known. For instance, the auditory stream provides information about pitch and location, which is then routed to different systems (Romanski et al., 1999). The pitch information is divided into linguistic input and non-linguistic input, transmitted to different parts of the auditory cortex (Liegeois-Chauvel, de Graaf, Laguitton, & Chauvel, 1999). At each step, the transfer from one system to the other depends on the signals' format. This extends to higher cognitive systems.

The range of stimuli or internally generated information that meets the input format of a system is its domain. Now it is important to distinguish between an evolutionary or proper domain of stimuli and an actual domain (Sperber, 1994, 1996). The proper domain includes those objects or situations that played a causal role in giving the particular system a selective advantage. The actual domain includes all objects or situations that trigger activation of the system. In most evolved cognitive systems, the actual domain is larger than the proper domain, giving rise to false alarms. The frog snaps at any small objects whizzing by in its visual field, not just to actual edible insects.

Any system of this kind is vulnerable to capture and mimicry. The terms describe situations in which the system reacts to an input that matches its input format, and is part of its actual domain, yet is not among the classes of stimuli that the system was designed to process, its proper domain. We reserve the term 'mimicry' for the situations in which a particular behavior or physical trait in an organism gains adaptive value by entering the actual domain of another organism's cognitive system. This is what happens in familiar cases, like that of Viceroy butterflies adopting the genuine poison-warning garb of Monarchs without having to manufacture the poison.

A different situation is what we call 'cognitive capture.' Consider a familiar example. Most visual art in humans (from tattooing to painting to architecture) seems strongly biased towards vertically symmetrical displays, while other symmetries are less salient. Vertical symmetry detection capacity appears in infancy (Bornstein & Krinsky, 1985; Fisher et al., 1981), influences pattern recognition in childhood (Bornstein & Stiles-Davis, 1984; Mendelson & Lee, 1981), and has evolved for purposes other than the appreciation of aesthetic displays, most probably for detecting facing predators and healthy mates (Thornhill, 1998). Music too is a good example, as it 'hijacks' certain parts of the auditory cortex and provides auditory super-stimuli (Jerison). Narratives about imagined persons can be, as we say, 'captivating' because they capture our capacities for mind-reading and the explanation of behavior.

This is not mimicry since in the cases mentioned here the organism's Type I error does not benefit another organism. The important point about cognitive capture is that a great deal of human culture is acquired and transmitted because of this inevitable propensity of cognitive systems to 'fire' beyond their proper functional range. Most items of 'culture' in the sense of group-specific sets of norms and concepts depend for their transmission on cognitive capture of this kind (Sperber, 1994).

8.4 Core Ritualization in Cultural Rituals

To understand the cognitive effects of collective rituals, we must describe the kinds of information available to the participants. At first sight, it would seem that most people who participate in most rituals do not have much information at all. People do not generally hold a 'theory' of their own rituals—this is what makes ethnography indispensable and difficult.

However, this is not to say that people participate in a ritual on the basis of mere imitation, peering at their cultural elders and simply performing similar gestures. This would be implausible, given that very little human cultural transmission actually involves such mindless imitation (Sperber, 1996). In this particular case, some behavior activates some mental templates in the mind of observers, and triggers non-random inferences about what is accomplished by the behavior. This, we contend, may be sufficient to explain the cultural success of Ritualized Behavior.

To make comparisons simpler, we follow in our description the outline of action ritualization processes described earlier. The individual reaction to a particular cultural ritual can be functionally described as consisting in the following elements:

People receive specific information about the ritual: a. They are told that a ritual should be performed and are led to infer that non-performance is a dangerous option. For instance, one is told that because of a particular event (someone's illness, a death or a birth, the change of seasons, a war with another group, possible damnation), it is necessary to go through a particular ritual sequence.

b. People also receive information and produce inferences about the kind of danger against which the ritual is supposed to protect the group, for example, 'pollution' by invisible substances, attacks by invisible predators like witches or spirits, threat of disease, possible famine, social strife, and so on. These themes substantially overlap with the Potential Hazard Repertoire.

This triggers a (dampened) activation of Hazard-Precaution system.

People are instructed to participate in the ritual in particular ways. That is, people are generally not allowed to just add to their ritual whatever action they think fit. They are enjoined, more or less explicitly, to follow a particular script. Information about the script has the following properties:

a. Action descriptions include themes that mimic some of the typical outputs of the Hazard-Precaution system: actions such as cleansing, washing, checking.

b. Descriptions of prior conditions, particular taboos, substances to avoid, et cetera, reinforce activation of security motivation system.

c. There is great emphasis on the details of each action, inducing low-level parsing of the action flow during performance, especially because of negative prescriptions.

d. Description induces goal-demotion, by insisting on repetition, redundancy, apparently pointless acts, and so forth.

Performance enacted in these conditions temporarily swamps working memory because of the attentional demands of the tasks.

Performance ironically strengthens the salience of particular themes associated with gestures or situations to avoid during ritual.

These various elements and their putative causal relations are outlined in Figure 4. In the next sections we present some evidence for these various claims and for the psychological and cultural effects of the processes.

8.5 Cognitive Capture in Cultural Rituals

Our model suggests that ritualized actions are culturally successful to the extent that they activate information-processing and motivation systems made manifest in other domains of ritualization. In this sense, cultural rituals result in cognitive capture of the systems described so far, and this is why they can seem attention-demanding and compelling to participants.

Many features of collective rituals activate the Hazard-Precaution system by including cues for potential dangers of the Evolutionary Potential Hazard Repertoire. First, occasions for ritual often allude to clues of possible danger that overlap with the Potential Hazard Repertoire: for example, threats to fitness such as famine or illness, invisible germs or miasma, dangerous invisible pollution present in newborn infants, dead bodies and menstruating women (Bloch & Parry, 1982; Metcalf & Huntington, 1991). Second, details of prescribed performance also include many security-related motifs. As we said previously, many collective rituals include such operations as washing and cleaning, checking and re-checking that a particular state of affairs really obtains, as well as creating a symmetrical or otherwise orderly environment (Dulaney & Fiske, 1994; Fiske & Haslam, 1997), so we will not comment on this any further.

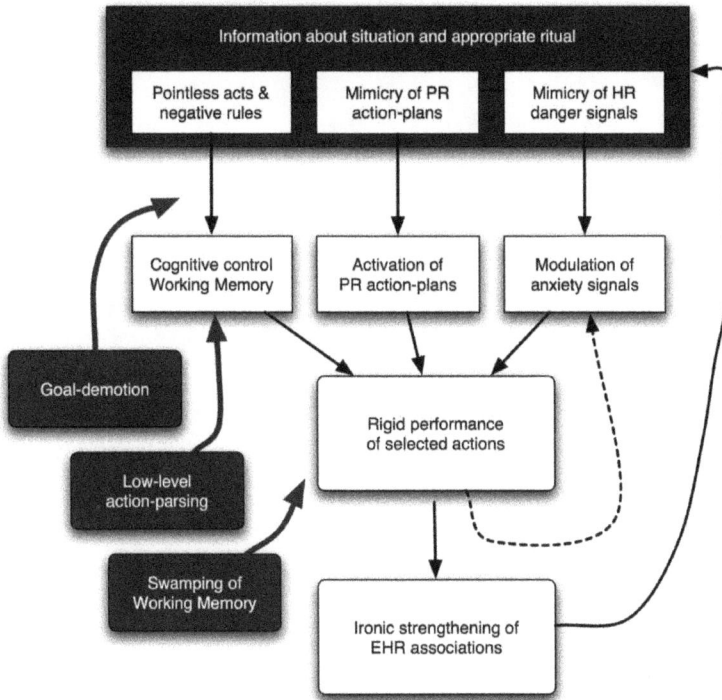

Fig. 4. A simplified model of action ritualization in cultural rituals. Boxes identity different functional systems in the same way as in Fig. 3 . Participants in rituals are provided with two kinds of information, (a) statements about potential danger and (b) scripted recipes for ritual action, that activate the security-motivation systems. Rules for ritual performance result in both goal-demotion and low-level action-parsing with the resulting swamping of working memory. These processes result in highly attention-demanding and compelling performance of rigidly scripted actions. This in turn makes the associations more salient, which should make subsequent messages about ritual more intuitively compelling. (Figure design by P Boyer, 2006).

In our model, precaution systems are activated to the extent that particular themes (e.g., 'this village must be purified') and prescribed actions (e.g., 'wash hands three times in this particular river') trigger activation of evolved Precaution systems. This, however, does not entail that the ritual as a whole should be explicitly and exclusively about these themes. Indeed, there are many ceremonies in which prescribed behavior is only weakly related to these themes, while other themes (e.g., procreation, social exchange, hierarchy) are at the forefront of people's attention. Our claim is only that the ritualization itself is derived from the operation of Precaution and action-parsing systems.

8.6 Ceremonies, Ritualized Action, and Routinization

This model, in our view, at least provides elements that go some way towards an explanation of why ceremonies that include ritualized actions are found in most human groups and are generally stable within traditions. The model also has some implications that make it diverge from received anthropological usage and common intuitions about ritual.

Ritualized actions are not 'rituals.' Ritualized actions as described here are only a subset of what people actually do in what are called 'rituals.' For instance, a ceremony may include a typical example of what we described earlier, such as, a prescription to turn around a cow three times clockwise while avoiding to stare above the horizon and making sure to touch the cow with one's thumb only. But the circumambulation of the cow may be an element of a larger ceremony that also includes singing, dancing, feasting, and all sorts of other behaviors that are not precisely scripted in the sense described here. In other words, ritualized behaviors are certainly not the whole of 'rituals.'

Ritualization is not routinization. The model has the slightly counter-intuitive implication, that ritualized action is described as quite different from routinized behavior, indeed as its opposite. In most ceremonies we expect to find an alternation between phases of ritualized action (high control, attentional focus, explicit emphasis on proper performance) and routinized action (possible automaticity, low attentional demands, lesser emphasis on proper performance).

Cultural ritual is not individual ritual writ large. We said that cultural ritualized actions are 'derivative' and it is important to stress that they are a by-product of the Precaution systems and the action-parsing systems, not of individual ritualized behavior. Given the similarities between individual and cultural forms of ritual, it is of course tempting to take one as a scaled version of the other, as Freud suggested (Freud, 1928). But this is clearly misguided. First, to maintain the parallel, cultural rituals would need to be behaviors that social groups initiate because they perceive certain potential dangers. But groups as a whole do not literally behave or perceive, only their members do. Also, cultural rituals differ from individual ones in the way the information about compelling action is acquired—from other agents and from personal intuition, respectively. Most importantly, what compels performance is entirely different in the two situations. While individual ritualists (especially patients) may feel great anxiety at the prospect of not going through the ritual sequence, participants in a cultural ritual are likely to participate (among other reasons) to the extent that the particular sequence meets a minimal threshold of relevance. The idea of 'scaling' would also predict all sorts of interesting phenomena that are simply not observed; for example, that people who become more religious would tend to become more obsessive, or that OCD patients would tend to be more religious than controls, that children during early childhood should be more interested in religious ritual than at other stages of development, and so on. Although there are connections between certain forms of religious practice and obsessionality (Fallon, Liebowitz, Hollander, Schneier, et al., 1990; Hermesh, Masser-Kavitzky, & Gross-Isseroff, 2003), they fail to support these general conjectures.

9. Conclusions

9.1 Ritualization and Cognitive Adaptations

Our models of individual and cultural ritualization take as a starting point a specific connection between obsessive pathology and security motivation (Mataix-Cols et al., 2005; Szechtman & Woody, 2004) but also a more general set of assumptions about the adaptive character of specialized neuro-cognitive function (Cosmides & Tooby 1994; Duchaine et al., 2001). We have assumed that the Hazard-Precaution system was the outcome of selective pressure for gradually finer-grained inferential detection of and appropriate response to recurrent hazards in ancestral environments. This naturally leads to the question, whether action-ritualization might constitute a cognitive adaptation, in the same way as other domain-specific capacities do (Cosmides & Tooby, 1994). The question should be more specific and bear on either individual or cultural rituals, since the cognitive processes involved are so different.

Let us consider cultural rituals first. In the anthropological literature, there are various hypothetical models of the ways in which participation in collective ceremonial may have conferred adaptive advantage to individuals (Burkert, 1996; Knight, Power, & Mithen, 1998; Rappaport, 1979; Sosis, 2000; Watanabe & Smuts, 1999). This stems from a long anthropological tradition of construing ritual as crucial to social organization and cohesion (Durkheim, 1947; Hocart, 1970; Smith, 1889). We discuss the various hypotheses in more detail elsewhere (Liénard & Boyer, 2006). Suffice it to say that these different models may well explain a disposition to participate in coordinated social action, but not why these common endeavors should include scripted, goal-demoted, redundant scripting of familiar actions.

The question of individual ritualization is more complex. In our model, the activation of the Precaution system normally results in performance of appropriate actions from the Precaution Repertoire— and this, in most circumstances, should produce enough of a closure or satiety experience (Szechtman & Woody, 2004) to preclude reiteration. However, the closure experience probably is the outcome of continuous changes in the relevant circuitry, leading to various degrees of repetitiveness and anxiety about proper performance. So, in our model, it is not the ritualized behavior but the Precaution system itself that constitutes a cognitive-motivational adaptation. It has the hallmarks of such adaptations, such as a specific class of inputs, a specific mode of operation, a particular series of fitness-enhancing consequences, a non-trivial functional design—and, in this particular case, a specific neural implementation as well as specific impairment.

9.2 Phylogeny: Rituals and Displays

What is the connection between human and other animal 'ritual'? We use scare quotes here, as the term is stretched to encompass highly disparate forms of behaviors (Gluckman, 1975). Nevertheless, one should comment on the obvious similarities between human rituals and various forms of animal communication, notably in the context of agonistic and sexual displays where stylized behavior, repetition, and redundancy are clearly present. Is this evidence for the deep phylogenetic ancestry of ritual? In our view, this question suffers from several ambiguities:

First, although we may sometimes follow a 'same effects, same causes' rule of thumb, this is rather misguided if it leads us to confuse observable behaviors with the neuro-cognitive systems that support them (Povinelli, Bering, & Giambrone, 2000). Indeed, even in the limited domain of human rituals, apparently similar behaviors (in patients and in cultural ritual participants) actually stem from very different cognitive processes. This should a fortiori be expected when comparing widely different species.

Second, the question downplays the extent to which certain features of behavior are constrained. Consider OCD patients for instance. They are not motivated by a positive urge to ritualize. Rather, ritualized behavior happens to constitute an optimal response to the anxiety produced by cognitive impairment. Other forms of behavior would not seem appropriate given the anxious concerns; they would not produce temporary relief. So the redundancy, et cetera, in this case stems from the properties of action-parsing and precaution systems in humans. Now consider animal displays. They are strongly constrained too, in this case by the logic of signaling processes. For instance, signals must be clear and distinct enough to preclude ambiguities, which typically results in redundancy (Rowe, 1999). The evolution of attentive receivers requires that signals maintain a relatively high level of accuracy (Bradbury & Vehrencamp, 2000; Silk, Kaldor, & Boyd, 2000) and that the content of the signals be directly related to the fitness dimensions they advertise (Zahavi & Zahavi, 1997). In other words, in both human rituals and animal displays, features like stylization, redundancy, and repetition are the outcome of external constraints, but these seem to be different in the two cases.

This would support the tentative conclusion that the presence of 'ritual' in both cases is a case of behavioral analogy rather than the index of similar capacity and processes. (Obviously, this is not to deny that humans like other animals do engage in stereotypical displays, in situations of courtship or aggression). This is tentative in the sense that we do not know much about the phylogenetic history of ritualization (in the precise sense used here) in the hominin line. The evidence so far simply does not support the notion of a direct evolutionary homology.

9.3 Epilogue

It is a cognitive and evolutionary puzzle that humans perform rituals, given the waste of time and resources involved. We aimed to solve the puzzle by piecing together the evidence from neuroimaging, neuropsychology, clinical psychology, developmental studies, and evolutionary anthropology. Ritualization may be seen as an occasional by-product of specific precaution systems and action-parsing capacities in humans.

This explanation however compels us to discard the common intuition that there is a natural kind of phenomena called 'rituals.' If valid, our model does not explain 'rituals' but a highly specific form of behavior that is found in many of them and occurs for different reasons in the behavior of most normal children and obsessive patients, on the one hand, and in the context of collective rituals, on the other.

Discarding misleading categories of behavior (like 'ritual'—but there are many others) may well be the inevitable consequence and benefit of proposing integrated explanations. Our model is an attempt to bring together neural systems, evolutionary background, behavioral manifestations, and developmental trajectory to the understanding of action-ritualization. We consider this indispensable. True, much work remains to be done to understand the phenomenon. For instance, the cognition of children's ritual is still largely unexplored; the connections between ritual performance and anxiety relief in patients need a proper neurophysiological study; the persuasive power of cultural rituals is not properly explained. But we are confident that all these and other puzzles will be solved by the kind of 'general behavioral science' that transcends fields and discipline boundaries.

References

Abed, R. T., & de Pauw, K. W. (1998). An evolutionary hypothesis for obsessive compulsive disorder: a psychological immune system? *Behavioural Neurology,* 11, 245–250. https://doi.org/10.1155/1999/657382

Abramowitz, J. S., Schwartz, S. A., Moore, K. M., & Luenzmann, K. R. (2003). Obsessive-compulsive symptoms in pregnancy and the puerperium: a review of the literature. *Journal of Anxiety Disorders,* 17, 461–478. https://doi. org/ 10.1016/s0887-6185(02)00206-2

Adler, C. M., McDonough-Ryan, P., Sax, K. W., Holland, S. K., Arndt, S., & Strakowski, S. M. (2000). fMRI of neuronal activation with symptom provocation in unmedicated patients with obsessive compulsive disorder. *Journal of Psychiatric Research,* 34, 317–324. https://doi.org/10.1016/ s0022-3956(00)00022-4

Al-Issa,I.(2000).DoestheMuslimreligionmakeadifferenceinpsychopathology? In I. Al-Issa et al. (Eds.), *Al-Junun: Mental Illness in the Islamic World* (pp. 315–353). Madison, CT: International Universities Press, Inc.

American Psychiatric, A. (1995). *Diagnostic and Statistical Manual of Mental Disorders* (4th ed.). Washington, DC: American Psychiatric Publishing, Inc.

Arnold, P. D., Zai, G., & Richter, M. A. (2004). Genetics of anxiety disorders. *Current Psychiatry Reports,* 6, 243–254. https://doi.org/10.1007/s11920-004-0073-1

Arrindell, W. A., de Vlaming, I. H., Eisenhardt, B. M., van Berkum, D. E., & Kwee, M. G. (2002). Cross-cultural validity of the Yale-Brown Obsessive Compulsive Scale. *Journal of Behavioral Therapy and Experimental Psychiatry,* 33, 159–176. https://doi.org/10.1016/s0005-7916(02)00047-2

Baddeley, A. (2000). Short-term and working memory. In E. Tulving, F. I. M. Craik, et al. (Eds.), *The Oxford Handbook of Memory.* (pp. 77–92). New York,: Oxford University Press.

Baldwin, D. A., & Baird, J. A. (1999). Action analysis: A gateway to intentional inference. In P. Rochat (Ed.), *Early Social Cognition: Understanding Others in the First Months of Life.* (pp. 215–240). Mahwah, NJ: Lawrence Erlbaum Associates, Inc..

Baldwin, D. A., Baird, J. A., Saylor, M. M., & Clark, M. A. (2001). Infants parse dynamic action. *Child Development,* 72, 708–717. https://doi.org/10.1111/1467-8624.00310

Barker-Collo, S. L. (2003). Culture and validity of the Symptom Checklist-90-Revised and Profile of Mood States in a New Zealand student sample. *Cultural Diversity and Ethnic Minority Psychology,* 9, 185–196. https://doi.org/10.1037/1099-9809.9.2.185

Baron-Cohen, S. (1997). *The Maladapted Mind: Classic Readings in Evolutionary Psychopathology.* Hove: Psychology Press.

Barrett, H. C. (1999). *Human Cognitive Adaptations to Predators and Prey.* Doctoral dissertation, University of California, Santa Barbara. University of California, Santa Barbara.

——. (2005). Cognitive Development and the Understanding of Animal Behavior. In B. J. Ellis (Ed.), *Origins of the Social Mind: Evolutionary Psychology and Child Development* (pp. 438–467). New York: Guilford Press.

Barth, F. (1993). *Balinese Worlds.* Chicago, IL: University of Chicago Press.

Bertschy, G., & Ahyi, R. G. (1991). Obsessive-compulsive disorders in Benin: five case reports. *Psychopathology,* 24, 398–401.

Birch, L. L. (1990). The control of food intake by young children: The role of learning. In E. D. Capaldi & T. L. Powley (Eds.), *Taste, Experience, and Feeding* (pp. 116–135): Washington, DC: USical Association.

Bjorklund, D. F., & Pellegrini, A. D. (2002). *The Origins of Human Nature: Evolutionary Developmental Psychology.* Washington, DC: American Psychological Association.

Blair, R. J. R. (2001). Neurocognitive models of aggression, the antisocial personality disorders, and psychopathy. *Journal of Neurology, Neurosurgery & Psychiatry,* 71, 727–731. https://doi.org/10.1136/jnnp.71.6.727

Bloch, M. (1974). Symbols, song, dance, and features of articulation: Is religion an extreme form of traditional authority? *European Journal of Sociology,* 15, 55–81.

Bloch, M., & Parry, J. P. (1982). *Death and the Regeneration of Life.*; New York: Cambridge University Press.

Bornstein, M. H., & Krinsky, S. J. (1985). Perception of symmetry in infancy: The salience of vertical symmetry and the perception of pattern wholes. *Journal of Experimental Child Psychology,* 39, 1–19.

Bornstein, M. H., & Stiles-Davis, J. (1984). Discrimination and memory for symmetry in young children. *Developmental Psychology,* 20, 637–649.

Boyd, R., & Richerson, P. J. (1985). *Culture and the Evolutionary Process.* Chicago, IL: University of Chicago Press.

——. (1992). Punishment allows the evolution of cooperation (or anything else) in sizable groups. *Ethology and Sociobiology,* 13(3), 171–195.

——. (1995). Life in the fast lane: Rapid cultural change and the human evolutionary process. In J. C. Jean-Pierre Changeux (Ed.), *Origins of the Human Brain. Symposia of the Fyssen Foundation.* (pp. 155–169). Oxford: Clarendon Press/Oxford University Press.

Boyer, P. (1994). *The Naturalness of Religious Ideas: A Cognitive Theory of Religion.* Berkeley, CA: University of California Press.

Bradbury, J. W., & Vehrencamp, S. L. (2000). Economic models of animal communication. *Animal Behaviour,* 59, 259–268. https://doi.org/10.1006/anbe.1999.1330

Bradshaw, J. L., & Sheppard, D. M. (2000). The neurodevelopmental frontostriatal disorders: evolutionary adaptiveness and anomalous lateralization. *Brain and Language,* 73, 297–320. https://doi.org/10.1006/brln.2000.2308

Burkert, W. (1996). *Creation of the Sacred: Tracks of Biology in Early Religions.* Cambridge, MA: Harvard University Press.

Buss, D. M. (1989). Sex Differences in Human Mate Preferences: Evolutionary Hypotheses Tested in 37 Cultures. *Behavioral and Brain Sciences,* 12, 1–49. https://doi.org/10.1017/S0140525X00023992

Calamari, J. E., Wiegartz, P. S., Riemann, B. C., Cohen, R. J., Greer, A., Jacobi, D. M., Jahn, S. C., & Carmin, C. (2004). Obsessive-compulsive disorder subtypes: An attempted replication and extension of a symptom-based taxonomy. *Behaviour Research & Therapy*, 42, 647–670. https://doi.org/ 10.1016/S0005-7967(03)00173-6

Campbell, K. M., de Lecea, L., Severynse, D. M., Caron, M. G., McGrath, M. J., Sparber, S. B., Sun, L.-Y., & Burton, F. H. (1999). OCD-like behaviors caused by a neuropotentiating transgene targeted to cortical and limbic D1+ neurons. *Journal of Neuroscience*, 19, 5044–5053.

Canales, J. J., & Graybiel, A. M. (2000). A measure of striatal function predicts motor stereotypy. *Nature Neuroscience*, 3, 377–383. https://doi. org/10.1038/73949

Clark, D. M. (1999). Anxiety disorders: why they persist and how to treat them. *Behavioral Research and Therapy*, 37, 5–27. https://doi.org/10.1016/ s0005-7967(99)00048-0

Cosmides, L. (1989). The logic of social exchange: Has natural selection shaped how humans reason? Studies with the Wason selection task. *Cognition*, 31, 187–276. https://doi.org/10.1016/0010-0277(89)90023-1

Cosmides, L., & Tooby, J. (1994). Origins of domain specificity: The evolution of functional organization. In L. A. Hirschfeld, S. A. Gelman, et al. (Eds.), *Mapping the Mind: Domain Specificity in Cognition and Culture.* (pp. 85–116). New York: Cambridge University Press.

——. (1999). Toward an evolutionary taxonomy of treatable conditions. *Journal of Abnormal Psychology*, 108, 453–464.

Curio, E. (1993). Proximate and Developmental Aspects of Antipredator Behavior. *Advances in the Study of Behavior*, 22, 135–238.

Douglas, M. (1982). *Natural Symbols: Explorations in Cosmology*. New York: Pantheon Books.

Duchaine, B., Cosmides, L., & Tooby, J. (2001). Evolutionary psychology and the brain. *Current Opinion in Neurobiology*, 11, 225–230.

Dulaney, S., & Fiske, A. P. (1994). Cultural rituals and obsessive-compulsive disorder: Is there a common psychological mechanism? *Ethos*, 22, 243–283. https://doi.org/10.1525/eth.1994.22.3.02a00010

Durham, W. H. (1991). *Coevolution. Genes, Cultures and Human Diversity.* Stanford, CA: Stanford University Press.

Durkheim, E. (1947). *The Elementary Forms of the Religious Life*. New York: Collier Books.

Ecker, W., & Engelkamp, J. (1995). Memory for actions in obsessive-compulsive disorder. *Behavioural & Cognitive Psychotherapy*, 23, 349–371. https://doi. org/10.1017/S1352465800016477

Eisen, J. L., Phillips, K., & Rasmussen, S. A. (1999). Obsessions and delusions: The relationship between obsessive-compulsive disorder and the psychotic disorders. *Psychiatric Annals*, 29, 515–522.

Evans, D. W., Gray, F. L., & Leckman, J. F. (1999). The rituals, fears and phobias of young children: insights from development, psychopathology and neurobiology. *Child Psychiatry & Human Development*, 29, 261–276. https://doi.org/10.1023/a:1021392931450

Evans, D. W., Leckman, J. F., Carter, A., Reznick, J. S., et al. (1997). Ritual, habit, and perfectionism: The prevalence and development of compulsive-like behavior in normal young children. *Child Development*, 68, 58–68.

Evans, D. W., Milanak, M. E., Medeiros, B., & Ross, J. L. (2002). Magical beliefs and rituals in young children. *Child Psychiatry & Human Development*, 33, 43–58. https://doi.org/10.1023/A:1016516205827

Fallon, B. A., Liebowitz, M. R., Hollander, E., Schneier, F. R., et al. (1990). The pharmacotherapy of moral or religious scrupulosity. *Journal of Clinical Psychiatry*, 51, 517–521.

Fessler, D. M. T. (2002). Reproductive Immunosuppression and Diet: An Evolutionary Perspective on Pregnancy Sickness and Meat Consumption. *Current Anthropology*, 43, 19–61. https://doi.org/10.1086/324128

Fessler, D. M. T., Arguello, A. P., Mekdara, J. M., & Macias, R. (2003). Disgust sensitivity and meat consumption: A test of an emotivist account of moral vegetarianism. *Appetite*, 41, 31–41. https://doi.org/10.1016/s0195-6663(03)00037-0

Fessler, D. M. T., & Navarrete, C. D. (2003). Meat Is Good to Taboo: Dietary Proscriptions as a Product of the Interaction of Psychological Mechanisms and Social Processes. *Journal of Cognition & Culture*, 3, 1–40. https://doi.org/10.1163/156853703321598563

Fiddick, L., Cosmides, L., & Tooby, J. (2000). No interpretation without representation: The role of domain-specific representations and inferences in the Wason selection task. *Cognition*, 77, 1–79. https://doi.org/10.1016/s0010-0277(00)00085-8

Fisher, C. B., Ferdinandsen, K., & Bornstein, M. H. (1981). The role of symmetry in infant form discrimination. *Child Development*, 52, 457–462.

Fiske, A. P., & Haslam, N. (1997). Is obsessive-compulsive disorder a pathology of the human disposition to perform socially meaningful rituals? Evidence of similar content. *Journal of Nervous & Mental Disease*, 185, 211–222.

Fitzgerald, K. D., Welsh, R. C., Gehring, W. J., Abelson, J. L., Himle, J. A., Liberzon, I., & Taylor, S. F. (2005). Error-related hyperactivity of the anterior cingulate cortex in obsessive-compulsive disorder. *Biological Psychiatry*, 57, 287–294. https://doi.org/10.1016/j.biopsych.2004.10.038

Foa, E. B., Ilai, D., McCarthy, P. R., Shoyer, B., et al. (1993). Information processing in obsessive-compulsive disorder. *Cognitive Therapy & Research*, 17, 173–189.

Freud, S. (1928). *Die Zukunft einer Illusion*. Leipzig: Internationaler Psychoanalytischer Verlag.

Giedd, J. N., Rapoport, J. L., Garvey, M. A., Perlmutter, S., & Swedo, S. E. (2000). MRI assessment of children with obsessive-compulsive disorder or tics associated with streptococcal infection. *American Journal of Psychiatry, 157*, 281–283. https://doi.org/10.1176/appi.ajp.157.2.281

Gluckman, M. (1975). Specificity of social-anthropological studies of ritual. *Mental Health & Society, 2*, 1–17.

Grados, M. A., Walkup, J., & Walford, S. (2003). Genetics of obsessive-compulsive disorders: new findings and challenges. *Brain Development, 25*, 55–61. https://doi.org/10.1016/s0387-7604(03)90010-6

Graybiel, A. M. (1998). The basal ganglia and chunking of action repertoires. *Neurobiology of Learning and Memory, 70*, 119–136. https://doi.org/10.1006/nlme.1998.3843

Hagen, E. H. (2002). Depression as bargaining: The case postpartum. *Evolution & Human Behavior, 23*, 323–336. https://doi.org/10.1016/S1090-5138(01)00102-7

Happaney, K., Zelazo, P. D., & Stuss, D. T. (2004). Development of orbitofrontal function: current themes and future directions. *Brain and Cognition, 55*, 1–10. https://doi.org/10.1016/j.bandc.2004.01.001

Harcourt, A. H., & de Waal, F. B. M. (1992). *Coalitions and Alliances in Humans and Other Animals*. New York: Oxford University Press.

Henry, M. C., Perlmutter, S. J., & Swedo, S. E. (1999). Anorexia, OCD, and streptococcus. *Journal of the American Academy of Child & Adolescent Psychiatry, 38*, 228. https://doi.org/10.1097/00004583-199903000-00002

Hermans, D., Martens, K., De Cort, K., Pieters, G., & Eelen, P. (2003). Reality monitoring and metacognitive beliefs related to cognitive confidence in obsessive-compulsive disorder. *Behaviour Research & Therapy, 41*, 383–401. https://doi.org/10.1016/s0005-7967(02)00015-3

Hermesh, H., Masser-Kavitzky, R., & Gross-Isseroff, R. (2003). Obsessive-compulsive disorder and Jewish religiosity. *Journal of Nervous & Mental Disease, 191*, 201–203. https://doi.org/10.1097/01.nmd.0000055083.60919.09

Hocart, A. M. (1970). *Kings and Councillors; An Essay in the Comparative Anatomy of Human Society*. Chicago, IL: University of Chicago Press.

Hodgson, R. J., & Rachman, S. (1972). The effects of contamination and washing in obsessional patients. *Behaviour Research & Therapy, 10*, 111–117.

——. (1977). Obsessional-compulsive complaints. *Behaviour Research & Therapy, 15*, 389–395.

Janata, P., & Grafton, S. T. (2003). Swinging in the brain: shared neural substrates for behaviors related to sequencing and music. *Nature Neuroscience, 6*, 682–687. https://doi.org/10.1038/nn1081

Jerison, H. (2000). Paleoneurology and the biology of music. In N. L. Wallin, B. Merker, et al. (Eds.), *The Origins of Music.* (pp. 176–196). Cambridge, MA: MIT Press.

Kaplan, A., & Hollander, E. (2003). A review of pharmacologic treatments for obsessive-compulsive disorder. *Psychiatric Services*, 54, 1111–1118. https:// doi.org/10.1176/appi.ps.54.8.1111

Keller, C. M., & Keller, J. D. (1996). *Cognition and Tool Use: The Blacksmith at Work.* New York: Cambridge University Press.

Khanna, S., Kaliaperumal, V. G., & Channabasavanna, S. M. (1990). Clusters of obsessive-compulsive phenomena in obsessive-compulsive disorder. *British Journal of Psychiatry*, 156, 51–54.

Kim, C. H., Chang, J. W., Koo, M.-S., Kim, J. W., Suh, H. S., Park, I. H., & Lee, H. S. (2003). Anterior cingulotomy for refractory obsessive-compulsive disorder. *Acta Psychiatrica Scandinavica*, 107, 283–290. https://doi. org/10.1034/j.1600-0447.2003.00087.x

Knight, C., Power, C., & Mithen, S. (1998). The origins of anthropomorphic thinking. *Journal of the Royal Anthropological Institute*, 4, 129, 129–132.

Krebs, J. R., & Inman, A. J. (1994). Learning and foraging: Individuals, groups, and populations. In L. A. Real et al. (Eds.), *Behavioral Mechanisms in Evolutionary Ecology.* (pp. 46–65). Chicago, IL: The University of Chicago Press.

Kurzban, R., & Leary, M. R. (2001). Evolutionary origins of stigmatization: The functions of social exclusion. *Psychological Bulletin*, 127, 187–208. https://doi. org/10.1037/0033-2909.127.2.187

Labad, J., Menchâon, J. M., Alonso, P., Segaláas, C., Jimâenez, S., & Vallejo, J. (2005). Female reproductive cycle and obsessive-compulsive disorder. *Journal of Clinical Psychiatry*, 66, 428–435. https://doi.org/10.4088/jcp.v66n0404

Leckman, J. F. (2003). Phenomenology of tics and natural history of tic disorders. *Brain & Development*, 25, 24–28. https://doi.org/10.1016/ s0387-7604(03)90004-0

Leckman, J. F., Feldman, R., Swain, J. E., Eicher, V., Thompson, N., & Mayes, L. C. (2004). Primary parental preoccupation: circuits, genes, and the crucial role of the environment. *Journal of Neural Transmission*, 111, 753–771. https://doi. org/10.1007/s00702-003-0067-x

LeDoux, J. (2003). The emotional brain, fear, and the amygdala. *Cellular and Molecular Neurobiology*, 23, 727–738. https://doi.org/10.1023/a:1025048802629

Lemelson, R. B. (2003). Obsessive-compulsive disorder in Bali: the cultural shaping of a neuropsychiatric disorder. *Transcultural Psychiatry*, 40, 377–408. https://doi.org/10.1177/13634615030403004

Leonard, H. L., Goldberger, E. L., Rapoport, J. L., Cheslow, D. L., & Swedo, S. E. (1990). Childhood rituals: normal development or obsessive-compulsive symptoms? *Journal of the American Academy of Child and Adolescent Psychiatry, 29,* 17–23. https://doi.org/10.1097/00004583-199001000-00004

Liegeois-Chauvel, C., de Graaf, J. B., Laguitton, V., & Chauvel, P. (1999). Specialization of left auditory cortex for speech perception in man depends on temporal coding. *Cerebral Cortex, 9,* 484–496.

Liénard, P., & Boyer, P. (2006). Whence Collective Rituals? A Cultural Selection Model of Ritualized Behavior. *American Anthropologist, 108,* 814–827. https://doi.org/10.1525/aa.2006.108.4.814

Lorberbaum, J. P., Newman, J. D., Horwitz, A. R., Dubno, J. R., Lydiard, R. B., Hamner, M. B., Bohning, D. E., George, M. S. (2002). A potential role for thalamocingulate circuitry in human maternal behavior. *Biological Psychiatry, 51,* 431–445. https://doi.org/10.1016/S0006-3223(01)01284-7

Mahgoub, O. M., & Abdel-Hafeiz, H. B. (1991). Pattern of obsessive-compulsive disorder in eastern Saudi Arabia. *British Journal of Psychiatry, 158,* 840–842. https://doi.org/10.1192/bjp.158.6.840

Maina, G., Albert, U., Bogetto, F., Vaschetto, P., & Ravizza, L. (2000). Recent life events and obsessive-compulsive disorder (OCD): The role of pregnancy/delivery. *Psychiatry Research, 89,* 49–58. https://doi.org/10.1016/s0165-1781(99)00090-6

Maren, S., & Quirk, G. J. (2004). Neuronal signalling of fear memory. *Nature Reviews Neuroscience, 5,* 844–852. https://doi.org/10.1038/nrn1535

Mataix-Cols, D., do Rosario-Campos, M. C., & Leckman, J. F. (2005). A multidimensional model of obsessive-compulsive disorder. *The American Journal of Psychiatry, 162,* 228–238. https://doi.org/10.1176/appi.ajp.162.2.228

Mendelson, M. J., & Lee, S. P. (1981). The effects of symmetry and contour on recognition memory in children. *Journal of Experimental Child Psychology, 32,* 373–388.

Metcalf, P., & Huntington, R. (1991). *Celebrations of Death. The Anthropology of Mortuary Ritual.* Cambridge: Cambridge University Press.

Morris, M. W., & Murphy, G. L. (1990). Converging operations on a basic level in event taxonomies. *Memory & Cognition, 18,* 407–418.

Murphy, D., & Stich, S. (2000). Darwin in the Madhouse: Evolutionary Psychology and the Classification of Mental Disorders. In P. Carruthers & A. Chamberlain (Eds.), *Evolution and the Human Mind: Modularity, Language and Meta-Cognition* (pp. 62–92). Cambridge: Cambridge Unversity Press.

Nesse, R. M. (1998). Emotional disorders in evolutionary perspective. *British Journal of Medical Psychology, 71,* 397–415.

Nesse, R. M., & Williams, G. C. (1996). *Evolution and Healing: The New Science of Darwinian Medicine.* London: Phoenix.

Newtson, D. (1973). Attribution and the unit of perception of ongoing behavior. *Journal of Personality and Social Psychology*, 28, 28–38.

Neziroglu, F., Anemone, R., & Yaryura-Tobias, J. A. (1992). Onset of obsessive-compulsive disorder in pregnancy. *American Journal of Psychiatry*, 149, 947–950.

Ogai, M., Iyo, M., Mori, N., & Takei, N. (2005). A right orbitofrontal region and OCD symptoms: a case report. *Acta Psychiatrica Scandinavica*, 111, 74–76; discussion 76–77. https://doi.org/10.1111/j.1600-0447.2004.00395.x

Okasha, A., Saad, A., Khalil, A. H., el Dawla, A. S., & Yehia, N. (1994). Phenomenology of obsessive-compulsive disorder: a transcultural study. *Comprehensive Psychiatry*, 35, 191–197.

Payne, R. J. H. (1998). Gradually escalating fights and displays: The cumulative assessment model. *Animal Behaviour*, 56, 651–662.

Pitman, R. K. (1987). A cybernetic model of obsessive-compulsive psychopathology. *Comprehensive Psychiatry*, 28, 334–343. https://doi.org/10.1016/0010-440X(87)90070-8

Povinelli, D. J., Bering, J. M., & Giambrone, S. (2000). Toward a science of other minds: Escaping the argument by analogy. *Cognitive Science*, 24, 509–541.

Profet, M. (1993). Pregancy sickness as adaptation: A deterrent to maternal ingestion of teratogens. In J. Barkow, L. Cosmides, & J. Tooby (Eds.), *The Adapted Mind. Evolutionary Psychology and the Generation of Culture*. New York: Oxford University Press.

Rachman, S., & de Silva, P. (1978). Abnormal and normal obsessions. *Behaviour Research & Therapy*, 16, 233–248. https://doi.org/10.1016/0005-7967(78)90022-0

Rachman, S., Hodgson, R., & Marks, I. M. (1971). The treatment of chronic obsessive-compulsive neurosis. *Behaviour Research and Therapy*, 9, 237–247. https://doi.org/10.1016/0005-7967(71)90009-x

Rachman, S., & Shafran, R. (1998). Cognitive and behavioral features of obsessive-compulsive disorder. In R. P. Swinson, M. M. Antony, et al. (Eds.), *Obsessive-Compulsive Disorder: Theory, Research, and Treatment* (pp. 51–78): New York: Guilford Press.

Radomsky, A. S., Rachman, S., & Hammond, D. (2001). Memory bias, confidence and responsibility in compulsive checking. *Behaviour Research and Therapy*, 39, 813–822. https://doi.org/10.1016/s0005-7967(00)00079-6

Rapoport, J. L. (1990). Obsessive compulsive disorder and basal ganglia dysfunction. *Psychological Medicine*, 20, 465–469.

——. (1991). Recent advances in obsessive-compulsive disorder. *Neuropsychopharmacology*, 5, 1–10.

Rapoport, J. L., & Fiske, A. (1998). The new biology of obsessive-compulsive disorder: implications for evolutionary psychology. *Perspectives in Biology and Medicine, 41,* 159–175. https://doi.org/10.1353/pbm.1998.0063

Rappaport, R. A. (1979). *Ecology, Meaning and Religion.* Berkeley, CA: North Atlantic Books.

——. (1999). *Ritual and Religion in the Making of Humanity.* Cambridge; New York: Cambridge University Press.

Rauch, S. L., Jenike, M. A., Alpert, N. M., Baer, L., Breiter, H. C., Savage, C. R., & Fischman, A. J. (1994). Regional cerebral blood flow measured during symptom provocation in obsessive-compulsive disorder using oxygen 15-labeled carbon dioxide and positron emission tomography. *Archives of General Psychiatry, 51,* 62–70. https://doi.org/10.1001/archpsyc.1994.03950010062008

Rauch, S. L., Whalen, P. J., Curran, T., Shin, L. M., Coffey, B. J., Savage, C. R., McInerney, S. C., Baer, L. Jenike, M. A. (2001). Probing striato-thalamic function in obsessive-compulsive disorder and Tourette syndrome using neuroimaging methods. *Advances in Neurology, 85,* 207–224.

Rauch, S. L., Whalen, P. J., Savage, C. R., Curran, T., Kendrick, A., Brown, H. D., Bush, G., Breiter, H. C., Rosen, B. R. (1997). Striatal recruitment during an implicit sequence learning task as measured by functional magnetic resonance imaging. *Human Brain Mapping, 5,* 124–132. https://doi.org/10.1002/(SICI)1097-0193(1997)5:2<124::AID-HBM6>3.0.CO;2-5

Rifkin, A. (1985). Evidence for a basic level in event taxonomies. *Memory & Cognition, 13,* 538–556.

Rode, C., Cosmides, L., Hell, W., & Tooby, J. (1999). When and why do people avoid unknown probabilities in decisions under uncertainty? Testing some predictions from optimal foraging theory. *Cognition, 72,* 269–304.

Romanski, L. M., Tian, B., Fritz, J., Mishkin, M., Goldman-Rakic, P. S., & Rauschecker, J. P. (1999). Dual streams of auditory afferents target multiple domains in the primate prefrontal cortex. *Nature Neuroscience, 2,* 1131–1136.

Rowe, C. (1999). Receiver psychology and the evolution of multicomponent signals. *Animal Behaviour, 58,* 921–931.

Rozin, P., Haidt, J., & McCauley, C. R. (1993). Disgust. In M. Lewis & J. M. Haviland (Eds.), *Handbook of Emotions* (pp. 575–595). New York: The Guildford Press.

Salkovskis, P. M. (1985). Obsessional-compulsive problems: a cognitive-behavioural analysis. *Behaviour Research & Therapy, 23,* 571–583. https://doi.org/10.1016/0005-7967(85)90105-6

Salkovskis, P. M., Wroe, A. L., Gledhill, A., Morrison, N., Forrester, E., Richards, C., Reynolds, M., Thorpe, S. (2000). Responsibility attitudes and interpretations are characteristic of obsessive compulsive disorder. *Behaviour Research & Therapy*, 38, 347–372. https://doi.org/10.1016/s0005-7967(99)00071-6

Sasson, Y., Zohar, J., Chopra, M., Lustig, M., Iancu, I., & Hendler, T. (1997). Epidemiology of obsessive-compulsive disorder: a world view. *Journal of Clinical Psychiatry*, 58, 7–10.

Saxena, S., Brody, A. L., Maidment, K. M., Smith, E. C., Zohrabi, N., Katz, E., Baker, S. K., Baxter, L. R., Jr. (2004). Cerebral Glucose Metabolism in Obsessive-Compulsive Hoarding. *American Journal of Psychiatry*, 161, 1038–1048. https://doi.org/10.1176/appi.ajp.161.6.1038

Saxena, S., Brody, A. L., Schwartz, J. M., & Baxter, L. R. (1998). Neuroimaging and frontal-subcortical circuitry in obsessive-compulsive disorder. *British Journal of Psychiatry*, 173, 26–37.

Schnider, A., Treyer, V., & Buck, A. (2005). The human orbitofrontal cortex monitors outcomes even when no reward is at stake. *Neuropsychologia*, 43, 316–323. https://doi.org/10.1016/j.neuropsychologia.2004.07.003

Shooka, A., Al-Haddad, M. K., & Raees, A. (1998). OCD in Bahrain: A phenomenological profile. *International Journal of Social Psychiatry*, 44, 147–154. https://doi.org/10.1177/002076409804400207

Sidanius, J., & Pratto, F. (1999). *Social Dominance. An Intergroup Theory of Social Oppression and Hierarchy*. Cambridge: Cambridge University Press.

Silk, J. B., Kaldor, E., & Boyd, R. (2000). Cheap talk when interests conflict. *Animal Behaviour*, 59, 423–432. https://doi.org/10.1006/anbe.1999.1312

Smith, W. R. (1889). Lectures on the religion of the Semites first series; the fundamental institutions [microform]. New York: Appleton.

Sosis, R. (2000). Religion and intragroup cooperation: Preliminary results of a comparative analysis of utopian communities. *Cross-Cultural Research: The Journal of Comparative Social Science*, 34, 70–87.

Speer, N. K., Swallow, K. M., & Zacks, J. M. (2003). Activation of human motion processing areas during event perception. *Cognitive, Affective & Behavioral Neuroscience*, 3, 335–345. https://doi.org/10.3758/CABN.3.4.335

Sperber, D. (1985). Anthropology and Psychology: Towards an Epidemiology of Representations. *Man*, 20, 73–89. https://doi.org/10.2307/2802222

———. (1994). The modularity of thought and the epidemiology of representations. In L. A. Hirschfeld & S. A. Gelman (Eds.), *Mapping the Mind: Domain-Specificity in Cognition and Culture*. New York: Cambridge University Press.

———. (1996). *Explaining Culture: A Naturalistic Approach*. Oxford: Blackwell.

———. (2000). An objection against memetics. In R. Aunger (Ed.), *Darwinizing Culture. The Status of Memetics as a Science* (pp. 163–173). London: Oxford University Press.

Stevens, A., & Price, J. (2000). *Evolutionary Psychiatry: A New Beginning*. London; Philadelphia: Routledge.

Szechtman, H., Sulis, W., & Eilam, D. (1998). Quinpirole induces compulsive checking behavior in rats: A potential animal model of obsessive-compulsive disorder (OCD). *Behavioral Neuroscience*, 112, 1475–1485.

Szechtman, H., & Woody, E. (2004). Obsessive-Compulsive Disorder as a Disturbance of Security Motivation. *Psychological Review*, 111, 111–127.

Thornhill, R. (1998). Darwinian aesthetics. In C. B. Crawford, D. L. Krebs, et al. (Eds.), *Handbook of Evolutionary Psychology: Ideas, Issues, and Applications.* (pp. 543–572). Mahwah, NJ: Lawrence Erlbaum Associates, Inc.

Tolin, D. F., Abramowitz, J. S., Brigidi, B. D., Amir, N., Street, G. P., & Foa, E. B. (2001). Memory and memory confidence in obsessive-compulsive disorder. *Behaviour Research & Therapy*, 39, 913–927. https://doi.org/10.1016/S0005-7967(00)00064-4

Tooby, J., & Cosmides, L. (1996). Friendship and the banker's paradox: Other pathways to the evolution of adaptations for altruism. In W. G. Runciman, J. M. Smith, et al. (Eds.), *Evolution of Social Behaviour Patterns in Primates and Man.* (pp. 119–143). Oxford: Oxford University Press.

Tooby, J., & DeVore, I. (1987). The reconstruction of hominid behavioral evolution through strategic modeling. In W. Kinzey (Ed.), *Primate Models of Hominid Behavior* (pp. 183–237). New York: SUNY Press.

Ursu, S., Stenger, V. A., Shear, M. K., Jones, M. R., & Carter, C. S. (2003). Overactive action monitoring in obsessive-compulsive disorder: evidence from functional magnetic resonance imaging. *Psychollical Science*, 14, 347–353. https://doi.org/10.1111/1467-9280.24411

Van Veen, V., & Carter, C. S. (2002). The anterior cingulate as a conflict monitor: fMRI and ERP studies. *Physiology & Behavior: The Pittsburgh special issue*, 77, 477–482. https://doi.org/10.1016/s0031-9384(02)00930-7

Watanabe, J. M., & Smuts, B. B. (1999). Explaining religion without explaining it away: Trust, truth, and the evolution of cooperation in Roy A Rappaport's 'The Obvious Aspects of Ritual'. *American Anthropologist*, 101, 98–112.

Wegner, D. M., & Erskine, J. A. K. (2003). Voluntary involuntariness: Thought suppression and the regulation of the experience of will. *Consciousness & Cognition: An International Journal*, 12, 684–694. https://doi.org/10.1016/S1053-8100(03)00054-0

Wegner, D. M., & Schneider, D. J. (2003). The White Bear Story. *Psychological Inquiry*, 14, 326–329. https://doi.org/10.1207/S15327965PLI1403&4_24

Weissman, M. M., Bland, R. C., Canino, G. J., Greenwald, S., Hwu, H. G., Lee, C. K.,Newman, S. C., Oakley-Browne, M. A., Rubio-Stipec, M., Wickramaratne, P. J. (1994). The cross national epidemiology of obsessive compulsive disorder. The Cross National Collaborative Group. *Journal of Clinical Psychiatry*, 55, 5–10.

Williams, K. E., & Koran, L. M. (1997). Obsessive-compulsive disorder in pregnancy, the peurperium, and the premenstruum. *Journal of Clinical Psychiatry*, 58, 330–334.

Willour, V. L., Yao Shugart, Y., Samuels, J., Grados, M., Cullen, B., Bienvenu, O. J., 3rd, . . . Nestadt, G. (2004). Replication study supports evidence for linkage to 9p24 in obsessive-compulsive disorder. *American Journal of Human Genetics*, 75, 508–513. https://doi.org/10.1086/423899

Wynn, T. (1993). Layers of thinking in tool behavior. In K. R. Gibson, T. Ingold, et al. (Eds.), *Tools, Language and Cognition in Human Evolution.* (pp. 389–406). Cambridge: Cambridge University Press.

Zacks, J. M., Braver, T. S., Sheridan, M. A., Donaldson, D. I., Snyder, A. Z., Ollinger, J. M., Buckner, R. L., Raichle, M. E. (2001). Human brain activity time-locked to perceptual event boundaries. *Nature Neuroscience*, 4, 651–655. https://doi.org/10.1038/88486

Zacks, J. M., & Tversky, B. (2001). Event structure in perception and conception. *Psychological Bulletin*, 127, 3–21. https://doi.org/10.1037/0033-2909.127.1.3

Zacks, J. M., Tversky, B., & Iyer, G. (2001). Perceiving, remembering, and communicating structure in events. *Journal of Experimental Psychology: General*, 130, 29–58. https://doi.org/10.1037/0096-3445.130.1.29

Zahavi, A., & Zahavi, A. (1997). *The Handicap Principle: A Missing Piece of Darwin's Puzzle.* New York: Oxford University Press.

Zalla, T., Pradat-Diehl, P., & Sirigu, A. (2003). Perception of action boundaries in patients with frontal lobe damage. *Neuropsychologia*, 41, 1619–1627. https://doi.org/10.1016/S0028-3932(03)00098-8

Zalla, T., Verlut, I., Franck, N., Puzenat, D., & Sirigu, A. (2004). Perception of dynamic action in patients with schizophrenia. *Psychiatry Research*, 128, 39–51. https://doi.org/10.1016/j.psychres.2003.12.026

Zohar, A. H., & Felz, L. (2001). Ritualistic behavior in young children. *Journal of Abnormal Child Psychology: An official publication of the International Society for Research in Child and Adolescent Psychopathology*, 29, 121–128. https://doi.org/10.1023/a:1005231912747

Zohar, J., Kennedy, J. L., Hollander, E., & Koran, L. M. (2004). Serotonin-1D Hypothesis of Obsessive-Compulsive Disorder: An Update. *Journal of Clinical Psychiatry Beyond Refractory Obsessions and Anxiety States: Toward Remission*, 65, 18–21.

4. Social Groups
and Adapted Minds

Introductory Note

Relations between different ethnicities are often fraught with conflict, from mild suspicion to avoidance, discrimination or violent inter-group conflict. In many places, inter-group conflict has consequences for people's well-being, including their health. But why is that the case? In this article, Rengin Firat, Florian van Leeuwen and I tried to propose a general model of inter-group conflict that would explain these well-documented and sometimes paradoxical public health outcomes.

In our view, one cannot properly address questions of inter-group relations without a clear understanding of the ways humans form alliances. In traditional social sciences, people often simply assumed that there are social groups, that people find it self-evident that they 'belong' to a particular collection of individuals, and that people sometimes sacrifice their individual welfare for what they see as the good of the group. Social scientists, like the rest of us, used to find all these phenomena self-evident, simply because they are very familiar.

One advantage of taking an evolutionary standpoint is that the familiar cannot be taken for granted, because it happens to be particular to our species. Sustained alliances between genetically unrelated individuals are rare and limited in scope in most animal species (Dugatkin, 1998). But they are ubiquitous among humans, who can form and maintain alliances both stable and extensive, scaling up from a few individuals to several millions.

How is this possible? A possible, common and often sterile approach is to catalogue those collections of individuals that people identify as

    https://doi.org/10.11647/OBP.0257.06

different 'groups' in their society, and to try to classify kinds of groups. One could sort them, for instance, in terms of size (a street gang vs. an army), permanence (crowds vs. nations), or solidarity (a village vs. a group of commuters) and try to produce a taxonomy of groups based on these observable features. Is that really wrong? In a sense, it is not, since documenting varieties of phenomena is the starting point in any scientific study. But that does not by itself provide us with explanations for the observed similarities and differences.

Alliances between unrelated individual agents are (at least as a goal) mutually beneficial interactions. They dissolve when members do not see participation as favorable to their welfare. That is why the most promising interpretation of group formation and dynamics came from rational choice models (Elster, 1989; Hechter, 1987). These described the way aggregate individual interests could explain group dynamics— the conditions under which each individual may expect to gain from participation in alliances. The one advantage and limitation of these rational choice models is that they assume no complex psychology in the agents, except a set of prior preferences, some perception of the expected benefits from different courses of actions, and of course a motivation to increase their expected benefits. This description of agents, adopted from micro-economics, is often very powerful, especially in the aggregate. But, as many have pointed out, it comes with two limitations. First, it assumes that agents have an accurate perception of the benefits that may result from their behavior, which is a convenient idealization. Second, more important, rational choice models do not (try to) explain why agents have the preferences they have.

Now understanding the origin of preferences, and describing the nature and limits of human capacities, are precisely the main goals of evolutionary psychology, in combination with the models and findings of economics, neuroscience and anthropology. In this perspective, we can put forward precise, testable hypotheses about the kinds of preferences that would have been the object of positive selection in human evolution.

What makes human alliances and groups possible is a set of evolved mechanisms that allow us to see the benefits of coalitions, to detect what alliances are present in our social environment, to monitor who is and who is not committed to the coalitions we join, to signal our own commitment, and so forth. Over the last thirty years, evolutionary scientists have added considerable detail to our understanding of these capacities. For instance, they demonstrated how people are intuitively suspicious of the status of newcomers in a group (Cimino & Delton, 2010), which neuro-physiological systems support coalitional affiliation and rivalry (De Dreu et al., 2011), how people in some countries readily encode 'racial' identities as coalitional rather than merely perceptual (Kurzban et al., 2001; Pietraszewski et al., 2014), how accent is seen as a cue of alliances (Pietraszewski & Schwartz, 2014), and much more. For general surveys of the field, see Boyer (2018, Chapter 1), Pietraszewski (2016), and Tooby & Cosmides (2010).

References

Boyer, P. (2018). *Minds Make Societies. How Cognition Explains the World Humans Create*. New Haven, CT: Yale University Press.

Cimino, A., & Delton, A. W. (2010). On the perception of newcomers: Toward an evolved psychology of intergenerational coalitions. *Human Nature*, 21, 186–202. https://doi.org/10.1007/s12110-010-9088-y

De Dreu, C. K. W., Greer, L. L., Van Kleef, G. A., Shalvi, S., & Handgraaf, M. J. J. (2011). Oxytocin promotes human ethnocentrism. Proceedings of the National *Academy of Sciences*, 108, 1262–1266. https://doi.org/papers2://publication/doi/10.1073/pnas.1015316108

Dugatkin, L. A. (1998). A Model of coalition Formation in Animals. *Proceedings of the Royal Society of London B Biological Sciences*, 265, 2121–2125.

Elster, J. (1989). *Nuts and Bolts for the Social Sciences*. Cambridge; New York: Cambridge University Press.

Hechter, M. (1987). *Principles of Group Solidarity*. Berkeley, CA: University of California Press.

Kurzban, R., Tooby, J., & Cosmides, L. (2001). Can race be erased? Coalitional computation and social categorization. *Proceedings of the National Academy of Sciences of the United States of America*, 98, 15387–15392. https://doi.org/10.1073/pnas.251541498

Pietraszewski, D. (2016). How the mind sees coalitional and group conflict: The evolutionary invariances of n-person conflict dynamics. *Evolution and Human Behavior*, 37, 470–480. https://doi.org/10.1016/j.evolhumbehav.2016.04.006

Pietraszewski, D., Cosmides, L., & Tooby, J. (2014). The Content of Our Cooperation, Not the Color of Our Skin: An Alliance Detection System

Regulates Categorization by Coalition and Race, but Not Sex. *PLoS One*, 9, 1–19. https://doi.org/10.1371/journal.pone.0088534

Pietraszewski, D., & Schwartz, A. (2014). Evidence that accent is a dimension of social categorization, not a byproduct of perceptual salience, familiarity, or ease-of-processing. *Evolution and Human Behavior*, 35, 43–50. https://doi.org/10.1016/j.evolhumbehav.2013.09.006

Tooby, J., & Cosmides, L. (2010). Groups in Mind: The Coalitional Roots of War and Morality. In H. Høgh-Olesen (Ed.), *Human Morality & Sociality: Evolutionary & Comparative Perspectives* (pp. 191–234). New York: Palgrave MacMillan.

Safety, Threat, and Stress in Intergroup Relations

A Coalitional Index Model

with Rengin Firat & Florian van Leeuwen[1]

Contacts between people from different groups engage a variety of human competencies and motivations, from high-level representations of social categories to visceral responses when confronted with strangers, from cognitive appraisal of conflict to a desire to exclude or even attack 'others.' There is a correspondingly diverse set of fields and subfields in psychology and the social sciences focusing on such specific topics as racial prejudice, ingroup bias, ethnic identity, xenophobia, and nationalism. In this article, we propose a model that cuts across boundaries between these different fields to describe and explain fundamental aspects of intergroup relations.

The psychological literature in this domain comprises a vast number of empirical generalizations without an overarching explanatory perspective. This results in many ambiguities and paradoxes. For instance, belonging to a subordinate or stigmatized group is often described as intrinsically stressful, with negative health effects, but living among one's own stigmatized group sometimes has a positive impact on health (Shaw et al., 2012). Or, racism is commonly found to be associated with conservative or authoritarian values, but the supposedly

---

1   An earlier version of this chapter was originally published as Boyer, P., Firat, R., & van Leeuwen, F. (2015). Safety, threat and stress in inter-group relations. A coalitional index model, *Perspectives in Psychological Science* 10(4): 434–450. https://doi.org/10.1177/1745691615583133. Reprinted with permission from Sage Publications.

https://doi.org/10.11647/OBP.0257.07

conservative army is the one setting in the United States where people are most satisfied with interrace relations (Bullock, 2013). Or, people are considered to resent immigrants because they threaten the host population's cultural and symbolic supremacy, but when immigrants assimilate and adopt to the majority's cultural symbols, this triggers even stronger resentment in many people (Guimond, De Oliveira, Kamiesjki, & Sidanius, 2010). Many empirical findings are treated as unrelated phenomena, mostly because they are studied in distinct subfields of the social sciences. Finally, a great deal of the social psychological literature in this domain makes no connection to equally salient processes of intergroup relations studied in anthropology, human evolution, history, and economics.

We propose that many aspects of intergroup relations should be construed as different manifestations of a coalitional psychology. We describe coalitional psychology as a set of evolved mechanisms designed to garner support from conspecifics, organize and maintain alliances, and increase an alliance's chance of success against rival coalitions. In this perspective, the core psychological mechanisms are the same, independent of whether the alliance in question is formed as ethnic (based on perceived similarity and common origin), racial (based on ethnicity combined with phenotypic similarity), regional, or political, and so forth. The point of the proposed paradigm is not to discard or replace extant models or explanations but to illustrate how they can be integrated into a broader framework, which we hope will give rise to new predictions and hypotheses. Consistent with other research in evolutionary psychology (Kurzban & Neuberg, 2005; Navarrete, McDonald, Molina, & Sidanius, 2010; Neuberg, Kenrick, & Schaller, 2010; Tooby & Cosmides, 2010), we argue that whether the coalitional cognitive system is activated, and what information it processes, may provide a parsimonious causal explanation for many representations, attitudes, and behaviors in intergroup relations.

Also, we contend that intergroup relations are strongly influenced by threat-detection mechanisms. Threat detection results in the adjustment of an internal variable, the *coalitional safety index*, an individual's representation of the safety induced by membership in an alliance. The level of this variable is modulated by cues of *coalitional threat* and *support*, for example, cues of decreasing support from one's own group or of increasing menace from rival groups. These threat cues can lead to *coalitional stress*, with standard physiological stress responses.

1. Evolved Cognition Background

1.1 Human Coalitional Psychology

Stable alliances are rare in most animal species (Harcourt & de Waal, 1992). By contrast, cooperation among non-kin toward a common goal in stable alliances is ubiquitous in human social interaction, suggesting a suite of specialized motivations and capacities that appeared during human evolution. Coalitional processes may be found at many different levels of organization, such as political parties, street gangs, office cliques, academic cabals, and bands of close friends, and can include thousands or millions of individuals when ethnic or national categories are construed as coalitions.

Coalitional psychology is a crucial element of the human capacity for collective action, in which a collection of agents cooperate toward a particular (set of) goal(s) that cannot be achieved by any single individual (or only at much greater cost); these agents behave in ways that increase each agent's welfare by making it more likely that the goal is achieved (Hardin, 1982; Myatt & Wallace, 2009). Humans for a long time have required, for their survival and reproduction, extensive support from kin but also from non-kin conspecifics, for example, in hunting (Dubreuil, 2010; Kelly, 1995), parenting (Hrdy, 1999, 2009), trade (Jaeggi & Van Schaik, 2011), and defense against other humans (Gat, 2006; Keeley, 1996). These evolutionary conditions explain why human groups are often stable and competitive. Humans need relatively stable alliances, because many endeavors require a prior assurance that support will be available when needed—warfare is a case in point. Also, human alliances may become rival even in contexts that may not require competition, because social support itself is a rival good. If an alliance builds up offering its members mutual support, it deprives others of that resource, so that one would expect coalitions to emerge as a response to the existence of other coalitions.

Collective action, as described by biologists and economists (Dugatkin, 1998; Medina, 2007; Mesterton-Gibbons & Sherratt, 2007), requires that agents engage in highly specific information processing concerning their own and others' behaviors. For instance, (a) payoffs to other members of the group are considered as gains for self (and, obviously, negative payoffs as losses to self); (b) payoffs for rival alliances are assumed to be zero-sum—the rival group's success is our loss, and vice versa; and (c) other members' commitment to the common goal is crucial to one's own welfare. As a consequence, (a) each member monitors other members' levels of commitment, (b) there is a strong motivation to demonstrate one's commitment to the other members, and (c) there is an inclination to make defection less likely, notably by making it costly.

Participants in coalitional interactions rarely, if ever, represent these principles explicitly. All they are aware of are intuitive preferences, for instance, a desire to punish a renegade, a motivation to engage in risky behaviors for the good of the cause, an interest in whether and how far a specific person can be trusted or the fact that one's enemies' enemies can be strategic allies. Such motives and cognitions may seem self-evident to both actors and observers, and the necessary complex computations are not available to conscious inspection (Kurzban & Neuberg, 2005).

To say that there is a coalitional psychology, distinct from other mental system, does not entail that there is a demarcation between coalitions and non-coalitions in social life. First, coalitional psychology can be activated in relation to very different types of groupings—some may be based on a common category or origin (e.g., gender, ethnicity, nation) and others not (e.g., office cliques). Second, activation of coalitional psychology is in many cases contextual—an agent may treat a certain category as coalitional (e.g., the young against the old, Blacks versus Whites) in some situations but not in others. Third, one may treat a collection of agents as coalitional, while one's partners do not. The coalitional construal is in the eye of the beholder and need not align with others' construals.

When one's representations of a social category activate coalitional psychology, one (implicitly or explicitly) assumes that people belonging to that category have a greater stake in each other's welfare than they have in that of outsiders; one also assumes that they are committed to the common goal, that is, prepared to suffer some costs to advance the overall position of the alliance. This background of assumptions may shape people's representations of group interactions in terms of common goals, potential cooperation, and indirect or direct reciprocity—the features that most explicitly influence group-oriented behavior (Balliet, Wu, & De Dreu, 2014).

1.2 Coalitional Psychology in Context: Threat-Detection Systems

Important aspects of human coalitional psychology should be understood in the context of threat detection. Natural selection results in systems that attend to recurrent danger cues in environments of evolution and guide appropriate responses (Boyer & Bergstrom, 2011; Boyer & Lienard, 2006). Survival and reproductive success require not just avoiding present danger (e.g., a predator present) but also detecting potential fitness threats (e.g., footprints indicating predator presence). Evidence from ethology, neurophysiology, and experimental psychology shows that present and potential hazards elicit different reactions and orchestrate distinct neural circuitry (Blanchard, Griebel, Pobbe, & Blanchard, 2011; Woody & Szechtman, 2011). Research on threat detection has described two features of animal threat-detection systems that are likely relevant for humans' coalitional psychology.

First, safety and threat are not two sides of the same coin (Szechtman & Woody, 2004). Threats can be inferred from the actual presence of particular cues in the environment (e.g., the smell of a predator), but the absence of predators is not usually indicated by any perceptible property of the environment. The absence of evidence is not evidence for absence. Indeed, most complex animals do not immediately infer safety from the removal of threat cues (Dielenberg & McGregor, 1999). Rather, animals' return to a baseline level of perceived security seems to be internally generated, mostly through performance of precautionary routines (Woody & Szechtman, 2011).

Second, the costs and benefits of inferring safety and threat are often asymmetrical (Haselton & Buss, 2000; Haselton & Funder, 2006; Haselton & Nettle, 2006). Individuals usually face a trade-off between false alarms (e.g., inferring the presence of a predator, when none is present) and misses (e.g., failing to infer the presence of a predator, when one is present), where false alarms are much less costly than misses. Therefore, error management models predict that many features of social psychology are characterized by displaying false alarms—that is, by erring on the side of caution. More generally, such models explain why cues that indicate a potential reduction of safety tend to have a stronger impact on attention and motivation than cues that indicate increased safety (Baumeister, Bratslavsky, Finkenauer, & Vohs, 2001; Rozin & Royzman, 2001).

2. The Model

2.1 The Coalitional Safety Index is an Internal Regulatory Variable

We propose that various cues concerning potential social threats and social support are summed up as an internal regulatory variable, a *coalitional safety index*, the level of which is adjusted in each individual from situation to situation. Formally, this variable is similar to other regulatory variables proposed in the biological psychology and physiology (Tooby, Cosmides, Sell, Lieberman, & Sznycer, 2008), such as indexes for hunger or thirst (Loewenstein, 1996), overall security (McGregor, Adamec, Canteras, Blanchard, & Blanchard, 2005; Szechtman & Woody, 2004), and kinship (Lieberman, Tooby, & Cosmides, 2007). Such an index (a) integrates information from many other cognitive systems and sums them in a single value, which (b) has effects throughout the organism, such as allocating cognitive resources, modifying goal priorities, and triggering emotional and physiological reactions, and (c) predictably affects behavior (Tooby et al., 2008). Given human dependence on social support, we expect human cognitive systems to provide efficient monitoring of the availability of coalitional help. Indeed, the evidence shows that people automatically attend to alliance-relevant information in their social environment. For instance, they look for cues of reliability in potential partners by monitoring their behavior (Bacharach & Gambetta, 2001) or their faces (van't Wout & Sanfey, 2008); they seek information about others, for example, through gossip (Dunbar, 1996; Hess & Hagen, 2006; Wert & Salovey, 2004); they automatically monitor alliances among others, even among outsiders (Pietraszewski, Cosmides, & Tooby, 2014)and they carefully evaluate the status of ongoing friendship ties (DeScioli & Kurzban, 2009; Tooby & Cosmides, 1996)

2.2 Coalitional Threat

Coalitional psychological systems, as well as delivering a representation of the social environment as composed of competing alliances, also produce inferences of danger (i.e., information likely to activate appropriate emotional systems and engage specific danger-related physiological response). Other alliances can be seen as threats both to the person (e.g., losing one's job, being attacked) and to his or her group (losing influence, power, cultural pre-eminence, and so on; (Rosenstein, 2008).

People should be able to detect both within and between-alliance threat cues. Cues suggesting that coalitional support is diminishing or absent should result in reduced levels of coalitional safety in people within an alliance (Pratto & John, 1991). Such cues include information pointing out that one's coalition partners do not consider one an actual member of the alliance, that they do not consider one sufficiently committed and trustworthy, or that they are less committed to the coalition than oneself. In situations that allow for potential physical conflict, we would expect people to be sensitive to other coalitions' number, cohesiveness, and aggressiveness, as each of these factors is relevant to the level of safety provided by one's own group (see, e.g., Schaller & Abeysinghe, 2006).

Coalitional threat cues would trigger a strong motivation to engage in a variety of behaviors to avoid the threat and return to a higher level of coalitional safety, for example, by sending clearer commitment signals, by cultivating homogeneity in the group, by avoiding members of other alliances, and by competing with or fighting against members of rival coalitions.

Threat-detection systems do not just raise a general alarm level in the face of generic danger. They typically respond in highly specific ways, in social as well as other domains. Other groups may be associated with economic or territorial competition but also with potential physical violence or with pathogen transmission (Schaller, 2006). Neuberg and colleagues have shown that these diverse kinds of threat representations trigger distinct, appropriate emotional responses and precautionary behaviors (Cottrell & Neuberg, 2005; Schaller & Neuberg, 2012). However, on a physiological level, qualitatively different threats may evoke fairly uniform stress responses.

2.3 Coalitional Stress

Mammals have evolved two neurophysiological responses to direct challenges (Gunnar & Quevedo, 2007). One response is immediate (i.e., within seconds) and involves the fight-or-flight response; the other is a slower, more durable response (i.e., within minutes or hours) that organizes longer-term changes of behavior. The fast reactions are orchestrated by the sympathetic-adrenal medullary system, associated with activation of the sympathetic nervous system, and expressed through release of epinephrine. The slower response involves activation of the hypothalamic-pituitary-adrenal system, is associated with parasympathetic activation, and results in the release of glucocorticoids (cortisol in humans). Repeated activation of these responses results in chronic stress, with important consequences for health and well-being (Sapolsky, 2007).

A crucial part of our model is that the detection of coalitional threat cues in one's social environment triggers a stress response. Repeated exposure to such cues may lead to chronic stress, which in turn yields negative health consequences. Therefore, to the extent that many individuals in a specific social category are exposed to similar coalitional threats, we should expect these effects to translate into differences in health outcomes at the level of social groups.

2.4 Specific Computations

In the model proposed here, many aspects of intergroup psychology are construed as domain specific, geared to the management of coalitions. This stands in contrast to some classical models of social affiliation in terms of broad, domain-general processes, such as stereotyping, preference for familiarity, motives for distinct identity, or desires for self-esteem (see 'Integrating Classical Frameworks' later in this article). We propose that specialized cognitive systems orient attention to specific information relevant for computing coalitional safety and threat. In the course of everyday life, people are constantly sampling their social environment and automatically making inferences about properties of that environment. For instance, perception of the numbers of immigrants in one's country is heavily influenced by the number of visibly 'foreign' individuals encountered (Center, 2006). For the purpose of making inferences about coalitional safety and threat, we expect coalitional psychology to focus on such information as the number of individuals in one's coalitions, the number of individuals in other perceived coalitions, changes in those numbers, the perceived aggressiveness of these coalitions, their cohesiveness, and their respective members' commitment, strength, and so on. The model predicts that these inferences regarding coalitional safety and threat result not in unspecified positive or negative affective states but in domain-specific affective states that motivate a limited set of courses of action, appropriate for coalitional purposes.

We summarize the model in Figure 1. Below we survey a number of well-known aspects of intergroup relations and describe how they can be understood in terms of cues that increase or decrease the coalitional safety index.

3. Intergroup Encounters as Threat Cues

We start with the individual impact of intergroup encounters. In the short survey that follows, we emphasize how a coalitional appraisal system integrates various cues and as a result adjusts the coalitional safety index.

3.1 Association between 'Outgroups' and Danger

The literature on the association between outgroups and danger is vast but essentially convergent, suggesting that this relationship is implicit and largely automatic, resulting in an 'avoidance' rather than 'approach' motivation (Paladino & Castelli, 2008). For example, when primed with faces of Black men, American subjects expect weapons rather than tools (Payne, 2001; Payne, Lambert, & Jacoby, 2002). People categorized as potential enemies seem physically stronger than controls (Fessler & Holbrook, 2013), whereas being in the company of friends

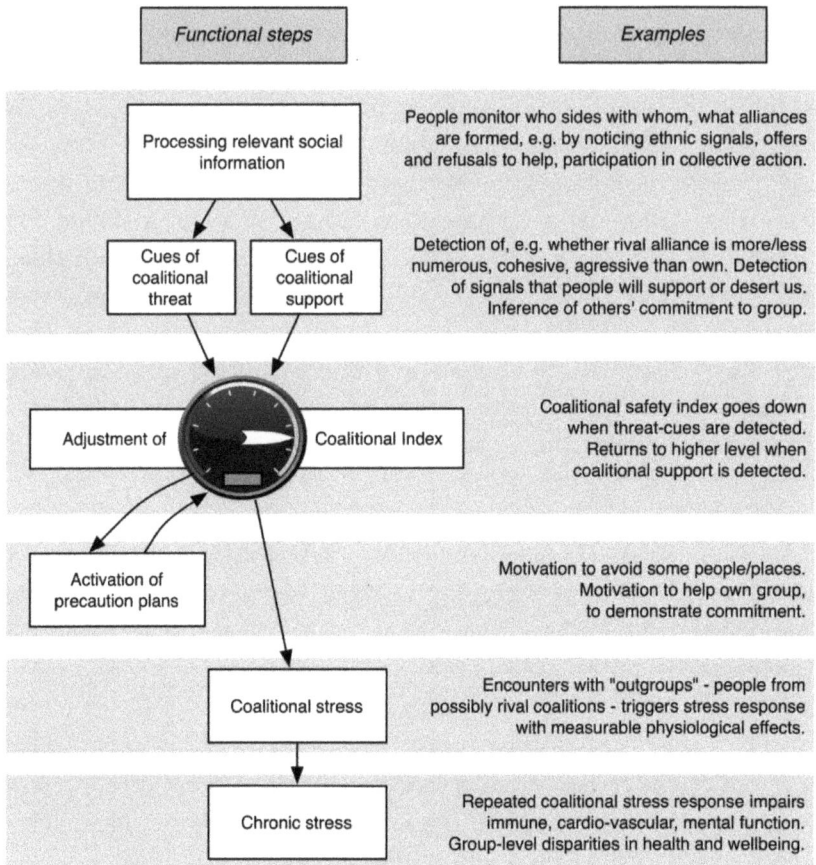

Fig. 1. Schematic representation of functional processes involved in the adjustment of the coalitional safety index (left) and examples of such processes (right). The model describes how attention to social information, for instance, about people's behaviors indicating affiliation, leads to inferences of social threat and social support. These inferences modulate the coalitional safety index, which has two main consequences. First, it changes motivations concerning action plans, for instance, an effort to remain within one's group, to avoid others, or to boost solidarity in one's own group. Second, lowering the coalitional safety index triggers a stress response, which can have adverse long-term consequences. (Figure design by P Boyer. 2015).

makes potential enemies seem physically smaller (Fessler & Holbrook, 2013). Fear is more easily attributed to out-group than ingroup faces (Navarrete et al., 2009), even when participants were assigned to minimal groups—artificial groups construed for the purpose of the experiment based on an arbitrary criterion (Navarrete et al., 2012). Encounters with outgroups are experienced as uncertain and demanding (Blascovich, Mendes, Hunter, Lickel, & Kowai-Bell, 2001), often create a specific form of 'intergroup anxiety' (Stephan & Stephan, 1985), and are associated with an increase in behaviors like blinking and fidgeting (Fazio, Jackson, Dunton, & Williams, 2008). Neuroimaging studies have also demonstrated specific fear-circuitry activation in response to stimuli depicting outgroups (Hart et al., 2000). Why are outgroups implicitly and often explicitly perceived as potential danger? This association is often explained in terms of shared stereotypes about social categories. In this view, encounters between Blacks and Whites in the United States, for example, are stressful because of a White stereotype of Blacks as violent and a Black expectation of White racism. However, it is not parsimonious to explain each case of difficult intergroup contact in terms of specific cultural stereotypes, as they occur even with minimal groups for which there are no stereotypes and more generally because the phenomenon is ubiquitous and thus demands a general explanation. Indeed, most people in most cultures known to history and anthropology have expected intergroup relations to be fraught with danger or at least some measure of hostility (Gat, 2006; Keeley, 1996). The notion of 'others' as threatening is an essential component of the ethnocentric prejudice generally observed in human societies (LeVine & Campbell, 1972).

3.2 Categories Tacitly Construed as Coalitions: Race in the United States

In our model, what drives people's intuitions about members of some social category as potential danger is not (just) information about characteristics of that category but the specific inference that members of that category are a coalition, that they are striving to achieve common goals against other alliances, including their own.

Consider interracial encounters in the United States. Usually, race is automatically encoded by American participants, regardless of protocols and task demands. However, 'race' is unlikely to be part of our evolved conceptual repertoire, because encounters with people of visibly different ancestry are a recent phenomenon in terms of evolutionary history (Cosmides, Tooby, & Kurzban, 2003). These encounters did not occur regularly before efficient modes of long-range transportation were invented. Excluding a long-evolved adaptation to interracial encounters, one possible interpretation of automatic race encoding is that it is simply a byproduct of general perceptual biases. A more plausible alternative is that race, in the United States, is a proxy for coalitional affiliation. To demonstrate that, Kurzban, Tooby, and Cosmides (2001) used a memory-confusion paradigm in which they presented participants with different target faces, together with text suggesting that two coalitions were involved in a conflict. Each of the suggested alliances crossed racial categories. As predicted, this manipulation resulted in significantly less accurate memory for race than in conditions without such coalitional cues (Kurzban et al., 2001), showing that retrieving coalitional affiliation interfered with race but not with other distinctive features like gender. In other words, current coalitional concerns and external cues can easily interfere with encoding or retrieval of racial categories, because they activate the same cognitive systems (Pietraszewski, 2009). The automatic encoding of racial categories, then, is not a simple matter of perceptual cues but requires a conceptual elaboration of these cues as a proxy for coalitional rivalry, which is a specific consequence of the U.S. social history (Cosmides et al., 2003). This coalitional interpretation also makes sense of other empirical results concerning Black–White encounters. For instance, automatic race encoding is stronger when perceiving lower-class Blacks than when perceiving middle-class Blacks (Weeks & Lupfer, 2004), presumably because lower-class Blacks are seen as more hostile than middle-class Blacks by most research participants. Also, gathering participants into mixed-race minimal groups interferes with the familiar phenomenon of racial ingroup bias (Van Bavel & Cunningham, 2009).

3.3 Intergroup Encounters and the Stress Response

As outgroups are associated with hazard, encounters with them trigger physiological processes appropriate in the face of potential danger, a process that is crucial to understanding the cognitive effects of intergroup relations (Blascovich et al., 2001; Page-Gould, Mendoza-Denton, & Tropp, 2008). Specific cardiovascular responses may result from unexpected and limited physical contact with an unfamiliar outgroup (Vrana & Rollock, 1998) or from imposed dyadic interaction with outgroup members (Littleford, Wright, & Sayoc-Parial, 2005). Such cardiovascular reactions are modulated by cognitive appraisal of the situation. For instance, White participants' physiological reactions during dyadic interaction are modulated by the self-description of Black interaction partners (confederates) as advantaged or disadvantaged (Mendes, Blascovich, Lickel, & Hunter, 2002). Also, uncertainty about another's attitudes and intentions is a major contributor to the physiological response. In one study, responses of both Black and White participants to negative evaluations depended on the race of the evaluator and triggered threat reactions only when the evaluator was of the same race. Positive evaluations tended not to trigger threat reactions, except when they contradicted stereotypes. Whites may expect positive evaluations from both Whites and Blacks, and Blacks may expect positive evaluations from Blacks. But Black participants likely expected negative evaluations from Whites and responded to 'suspicious' positive evaluations by Whites with an increased threat response (Mendes, Major, McCoy, & Blascovich, 2008). Such responses are also observed as reactions to merely anticipated interracial encounters, as measured in both cardiovascular responses (Sawyer, Major, Casad, Townsend, & Mendes, 2012) and subjective ratings of health (Page-Gould, Mendoza-Denton, & Mendes, 2014).

These effects of intergroup contact are best understood in terms of an intuitive appraisal of the resources available to each partner (Blascovich et al., 2001). Cognitive, emotional, and physiological responses to intergroup encounters engage both a primary appraisal (to evaluate potential danger) and a secondary appraisal of one's own resources, leading to a coping versus stress polarity, which in turn results in either engagement or antagonizing behaviors (Trawalter, Richeson, & Shelton, 2009).

Stress is a response to situations appraised as incompatible with an organism's goals (Lazarus, 1984). So understanding stress responses requires that we identify the appraisal system involved (Smith & Kirby, 2011). We propose that the coalitional safety index constitutes precisely such an appraisal. Stress responses would make little functional sense if people were confronted only with instances of stereotypes. For instance, the fact that one's partner in an experimental dyad comes from a group reputed to be incompetent should not impair one's own performance or result in a specific cardiovascular response. By contrast, if that encounter is implicitly framed as potential danger, the response is clearly functional.

4. Coalitional Stress and Health

We should expect repeated exposure to stressors, in the coalitional domain as elsewhere, to result in chronic stress with observable physical and mental health consequences.

4.1 Minority–Majority Health Disparities

The world over, immigrants and minorities suffer from worse health than host or majority populations (D. R. Williams, 2012). In many cases, obviously, immigration is confounded with oppression, poverty, or trauma from exile. However, the pattern also obtains in settled immigrant communities, such as Latinos in the United States (Osypuk, Bates, & Acevedo-Garcia, 2010) or South Asians in Britain (Carpenter & Brockington, 1980). Such negative impact of emigration on health sometimes leads to the 'immigrant paradox' whereby foreign-born members of these groups fare better than those born in the host country (Alegría et al., 2008). Health disparities between immigrant and host populations can be observed in virtually all modern industrial societies with large migrant groups (Bak-Klimek, Karatzias, Elliott, & Maclean, 2014; Noymer & Lee, 2013)

A similar disparity is observed between low-status social categories and the rest of the population. For instance, racial-minority members in the United States get sick more often, die at younger ages, and have more hypertension and lower levels of subjective well-being than Whites (Geronimus, Bound, Waidmann, Hillemeier, & Burns, 1996; D. R. Williams, 2012). Though there are exceptions to this pattern (Morales, Lara, Kington, Valdez, & Escarce, 2002), it seems that in general, native ethnic and racial minorities fare worse on various health outcomes and rate their well-being lower than non-minorities.

Part of this disparity stems from economic conditions, such as access to nutrition, type of work, and access to healthcare (Lynch, 2000). However, the differences persist even after controlling for these factors, suggesting that discrimination as such has a general deteriorating effect on health (Mays, Cochran, & Barnes, 2007; Pascoe & Smart Richman, 2009). The poor health outcomes for minorities and stigmatized groups may result from a range of social processes, including categorization, hierarchical ranking of groups, and perceived levels of achievement or competence (Major, Mendes, & Dovidio, 2013).

Stress is generally recognized as the crucial causal link between discrimination and health (Major et al., 2013; D. R. Williams & Mohammed, 2009). Perceived discrimination tends to elevate physiological stress responses such as blood pressure, cardiovascular reactivity, and heart rate (Brondolo, Rieppi, Kelly, & Gerin, 2003; Guyll, Matthews, & Bromberger, 2001; Utsey & Hook, 2007). Epidemiological studies support this stress-based explanation for Blacks in the United States (Clark, 2000; Clark, Anderson, Clark, & Williams, 1999) and for ethnic minorities more generally (McEwen, 2004; McEwen & Stellar, 1993). Even merely anticipated discrimination can produce stress (Karlsen & Nazroo, 2004). That discrimination causes stress explains why the greatest health disparities between minority and majority groups is found in conditions typically brought about or worsened by chronic stress, such as obesity, heart disease, and hypertension (Geronimus et al., 1996).

A similar process may be responsible for deteriorated health among immigrants, as 'acculturation stress' accumulates in individuals confronted with new values or norms (C. L. Williams & Berry, 1991). The connection between acculturation and stress has been observed among Asian immigrants in the United States (Chung & Epstein, 2014), Latino students (Cano, Castillo, Castro, de Dios, & Roncancio, 2014), and older adults (Kwag, Jang, & Chiriboga, 2012). Indeed, newly arrived Latino immigrants in the United States enjoy a health advantage (in terms of adverse effects of chronic stress) over the rest of the Hispanic population, which decreases with each decade spent in the United States (Kaestner, Pearson, Keene, & Geronimus, 2009).

In a survey of health disparities, Major and colleagues reviewed a variety of factors (stereotype threat, excessive vigilance, memories of injustice, attributional ambiguity, and many more), all of which are documented as contributing to stress responses (Major et al., 2013). In summary, there is overwhelming evidence that, in many different ways, the experience of minority or immigrant individuals includes a frequent occurrence of stress-inducing episodes, more so than for host or majority populations (Contrada et al., 2000, 2001).

4.2 Ethnic Density Effects

There is an interesting exception to general health disparities between majority and minority groups: the *ethnic density* effect. This effect refers to the situation when immigrants or members of minorities who live among other members of their group fare better than those who live among the majority population. This effect is counterintuitive, as immigrant or minority neighborhoods are generally poorer, less pleasant, and afford less access to health resources.

Ethnic or group density effects were first observed in the domain of mental health (Bosqui, Hoy, & Shannon, 2014; Halpern, 1993; Shaw et al., 2012). For instance, British Asian immigrants in more homogeneous environments have a lower incidence of psychoses (Boydell et al., 2001; Das-Munshi et al., 2012; Das-Munshi, Becares, Dewey, Stansfeld, & Prince, 2010) and other pathologies like self-harm (Neeleman, Wilson-Jones, & Wessely, 2001). In the United States, the effects of acculturation on depression are modulated by group density among Latinos (Kwag et al., 2012).

Ethnic density also influences general health outcomes (Becares & Nazroo, 2013; Pickett & Wilkinson, 2008). For example, birth weight among U.S. Latinos is higher in mostly Latino neighborhoods (Osypuk et al., 2010); Black mortality from cardiovascular conditions is higher in more mixed neighborhoods in New York (Fang, Madhavan, Bosworth, & Alderman, 1998).

There is no consensus explanation for such density effects and surprisingly little systematic hypothesis testing about its causes (Shaw et al., 2012). Density may correlate with better social integration—that is, each individual has more and better social ties in homogeneous places (Pickett & Wilkinson, 2008). However, it is not clear that social capital mediates the density effect (Becares & Nazroo, 2013). An alternative is that ethnic density provides 'buffering' against the social psychological effects of discrimination (Becares & Nazroo, 2013). Living in an ethnically homogeneous place may decrease the psychological weight of stigma (Pickett & Wilkinson, 2008). Assuming that this is the case, we still have no precise functional description of the processes whereby stigma or, conversely, protection from stigma would result in specific health outcomes.

4.3 Coalitional Interpretation

A proper explanation of the effects of intergroup relations on health should account for both the overall disparity between groups and the interaction with ethnic homogeneity. Explanations in terms of societal phenomena like stigmas or shared stereotypes may not provide a sufficiently specific description of the psychological and physiological processes involved.

We propose that the coalitional safety index is affected by a variety of threat cues, including the absence of individuals willing to extend support, decreases in number of such individuals, the presence of members of rival groups, their number, an increase in their number, their perceived level of hostility, and their perceived capacity to inflict harm. In other words, the perception of coalitional safety is influenced not just by activated beliefs about one's own and other groups but also by inferring probable states of the world from such features as relative numbers, frequencies of encounters, and tenor of interaction.

The daily experiences of minorities or immigrants, on the one hand, and majority or host populations, on the other, diverge on these elementary metrics. First, even assuming an equal level of perceived danger in all intergroup encounters and all else being equal, minority individuals are bound to encounter majority individuals more frequently than vice versa. Second, in these encounters, minority members are more likely than majority individuals to appraise the situation as one of weaker coalitional position. For minority individuals, each encounter with majority members potentially constitutes a threat cue, in that it reminds the minority person that he or she is a member of a less numerous and probably weaker group. So even in terms of low-level properties of the social environment, the natural sampling described above should result in a higher frequency of stressors (i.e., a higher number of situations in which the coalitional safety index is down-regulated, if only momentarily).

Such an information-processing account also explains the ethnic density effect. Living in ethnically homogeneous neighborhoods changes the base rates of encounters with same- and rival-coalition members, thus reducing the number of stressors. One would expect that the cumulative, chronic stress effect is therefore smaller for minority individuals living in homogenous neighborhoods. Our interpretation predicts that this beneficial effect of homogeneous neighborhoods may be diminished if an individual does not perceive the frequent own-ethnicity encounters as interactions with coalitional allies. Indeed, people of very low status in their communities do not benefit from ethnic homogeneity (Ayers et al., 2009; Cano et al., 2014; Chae, Park, & Kang, 2014).

5. Integrating Classical Frameworks

Beyond providing explanations for consequences of intergroup contacts, the coalitional model may also help us integrate some standard perspectives on intergroup relations. Specifically, we consider here distance and con-tact approaches, social identity perspectives, and finally social dominance theory.

5.1 Intergroup Contact and its Paradoxes

We argue that some aspects of intergroup relations should be explained in terms of the psychological processes involved in individual encounters with outgroups. That is also the starting point of the various hypotheses put for-ward in the 'contact' tradition (Dovidio, Gaertner, & Kawakami, 2003), which aims to reduce the prevalence of negative stereotypes and attitudes about outgroups by increasing the frequency and quality of encounters with outgroup members (Thomas F. Pettigrew & Linda R. Tropp, 2006).

However, generalizing this association between more contact and more positive relations would be clearly difficult. Places of high outgroup fear and rejection, like the antebellum South in the United States or apartheid South Africa, were also places of intense, daily contact and deep familiarity between dominant and dominated individuals. That is why the contact literature emphasizes that increased intergroup contact diminishes prejudice only if the persons concerned are equal in status, have common goals, are not in competition, and the contact is sanctioned by authority (Pettigrew, 1997; Thomas F Pettigrew & Linda R Tropp, 2006).

These conditions for beneficial contact show that the benefits depend on coalitional cooperation, which would raise the coalitional safety index in the individuals in contact. People from different social categories may find that categories matter little when they are equal partners in a joint collective action.

A case in point is the U.S. military, which started integrating all its units in 1948. Decades later, U.S. military personnel report levels of satisfaction with intergroup personal relations far above those of civilians (Bullock, 2013). Shortly after the start of the integration process, the units with higher numbers of minority (Black) soldiers reported greater satisfaction than others with interracial relations (Moskos, 1966). This increased satisfaction in heterogeneous units would seem to support the contact hypothesis. But note that the military is a very special social environment, as it constitutes in many ways a situation of coalitional affiliation. Military units are explicitly described as alliances against enemies. In small units like platoons, the specific coalitional dynamic of race is replaced with another one, in which individuals of all categories engage in a high-stakes collective action. Consistent with this interpretation, the beneficial outcomes of army integration change with contexts. Although prejudice is lowest in combat units in times of combat and in dangerous places, it tends to increase in times of peace and in civilian life, when the individuals of different ethnicities are no longer members of the same coalition (Bullock, 2013).

Conversely, the coalitional perspective makes sense of the fact that contact does not reduce prejudice or rejection in situations in which individuals from different categories cannot engage in mutually advantageous collective action, because of institutional or other barriers, as was the case for Blacks and Afrikaners in South Africa (Korf & Malan, 2002). More generally, coalitional dynamics explain why, in contrast to the original formulations of contact theories, intense or frequent intergroup contact can be detrimental. As in the context of health outcomes, intergroup encounters are stressors before they are construed as situations of collective action.

5.2 Limits of Social Identity Interpretations

Safety and threat dimensions of intergroup contact are addressed only indirectly in the framework of social identity theory, self-categorization theory, or what could be called more generally the social identity approach (Hornsey, 2008). Developed on the basis of minimal groups studies in the 1970s and 1980s (Tajfel & Turner, 1986), this approach has been applied to group polarization, group solidarity and cohesiveness, stereotyping, crowd violence and rioting, social influence, conformity, and power. A starting point of this framework is that people are motivated to engage in intergroup competition and other strategies in order to protect and/or promote a positive and secure self-concept (Brewer, 1979). Self-esteem or maintenance of a coherent sense of self are postulated as primary drives, which, combined with comparative assessment, lead people to hold representations of their own and other groups (stereotypes) with associated valence (attitudes) (Hornsey, 2008).

One clear limit of social identity approach lies in justifying these general conjectures. That is, even though intergroup attitudes may be connected to self-concepts, it is not clear why maintaining a positive or 'secure' self-concept would be a fundamental human motivation and through what evolutionary process this could have become a general human need. Moreover, the notion of people choosing among a variety of available identities in the service of maintaining a self-concept is clearly confined to some modern mass societies. It would be irrelevant in places where identity is assigned by genealogy, like most societies in human history.

Even as a descriptive framework, social identity theory has difficulties integrating some common aspects of intergroup relations. A good example is that of immigrant assimilation. From the standpoint of social identity theory, immigrants' adoption to the host population's cultural norms should be seen by members of the latter population as clearly positive, as it reinforces the assumption that these norms are superior. However, that is far from being the case. Studies carried out in the United States, Sweden, and France observed two divergent paths. Some individuals were hostile to cultural differentiation and therefore to immigrants holding on to cultural and ethnic markers. By contrast, others were hostile to immigrants' assimilation, which they saw as a menace. These attitudes correlate with different personality orientations. High authoritarianism predicts the rejection of cultural differentiation. High preference for hierarchical intergroup relations predicts rejection of assimilation (Guimond et al., 2010; Thomsen, Green, & Sidanius, 2008). These two variables account for the two contrary attitudes to assimilation, and neither of them is influenced by the need for a positive and coherent self-concept.

More generally, the connection (in a limited number of modern Western societies) between identity and self-esteem may be more economically interpreted as an effect of fundamental psychological processes. People are motivated to join groups, build them, and maintain them because of the safety and support provided by membership. They are motivated to describe their group as superior because (among other things) this signals to other members their commitment to the group. Safety and signaling motivations are established by independent evidence and have a long evolutionary history. They provide a more parsimonious explanation than self-esteem motives for intergroup dynamics.

5.3 Social Dominance Orientation and Coalitional Investment

Research on social dominance theory (Sidanius & Pratto, 1999) has anticipated some of the hypotheses presented here. Social dominance theory also starts from the observation that most intergroup relations are competitive and emphasizes that humans readily construe hierarchical intergroup relations on arbitrary bases (i.e., not based on age or sex). Also convergent with the coalitional perspective, social dominance theory implies that stereotypes and attitudes are the effect rather than the cause of discriminatory behaviors. As Guimond et al. put it, '[social dominance] theory conceptualizes prejudice as a form of hierarchy-enhancing legitimizing myth, an ideology that justifies intergroup inequality' (Guimond et al., 2010). Such a conceptualization of prejudice is consistent with the notion that stereotypes are explanations rather than descriptions of the social environment (McGarty, Yzerbyt, & Spears, 2002; Yzerbyt, Rocher, & Schadron, 1997). In our perspective, stereotypes are tools used to explicate and communicate to others the contents of one's intuitive expectations about other individuals, for example, that they are in some alliance and constitute a potential danger.

Regarding the psychological variables involved, social dominance theory postulates the personality variable of social dominance orientation (SDO), measuring the extent to which people are motivated to preserve and reinforce the subordination of some social groups (Pratto, Sidanius, Stallworth, & Malle, 1994; Sidanius, Pratto, & Bobo, 1994). The SDO measure predicts a number of attitudes and motivations associated with intergroup differentiation and contact (Guimond et al., 2010; Pratto et al., 1994; Sidanius et al., 1994; Thomsen et al., 2008).

We propose to interpret SDO as one of the stable personality factors contributing to the coalitional safety index. SDO may be a measure of (a) the extent to which individuals construe a particular category as a collective action they are part of, so that they perceive their welfare as dependent on the welfare of the group; and (b) the extent to which they are willing to invest in defending coalitional interests, which would in turn motivate them to preserve group boundaries. Returning to the example discussed above, this may provide an explanation for the association between high SDO and rejection of assimilation. Immigrants' assimilation constitutes a threat because it dilutes the benefits of membership in a dominant group and because it makes member identification more difficult (uncertainty about affiliation increases transaction costs in collective action and creates opportunities for free riding). Blurring of the boundaries between national categories would be perceived as costly and therefore rejected most strongly by those who have construed national categories as coalitions and have invested heavily in this coalition.

6. Implications

We have argued that the coalitional safety index model provides an integrated and parsimonious understanding of safety, threat, and stress in intergroup relations. The model also suggests directions for further investigation.

6.1 Coalitional Cues: Microprocesses of Social Sampling

In the social science literature, people are often described as experiencing social phenomena as large societal entities. For instance, immigrants are said to be directly affected by the host population's xenophobia. Models of 'racism as stressor' simply assume that negative stereotypes and attitudes toward one's own group will trigger stress responses (Lewis-Coles & Constantine, 2006). The connections are clear but lack an explanation. The coalitional perspective provides such an explanation, as indices of racism, negative attitudes, and so forth are construed as reminders of one's coalitional vulnerability. So, for example, it is not racism as such that is stressful but the easy inference from putative racism to one's reduced safety.

Our model emphasizes the microprocesses involved in computing one's coalitional safety index and suggests specific hypotheses about these processes. A system that computes coalitional safety should attend to various cues of the safety provided by one's own coalition and the threat posed by rival coalitions. As mentioned above, such microprocesses may provide a causal understanding of observed connections between anticipated discrimination and stress, minority status and stress, and ethnic density and relative immunity from stress.

We would expect that people's reactions to an immigrant group might be affected by general information about that group's size but also by the frequency of actual encounters with immigrant individuals. The model also predicts that people should attend to the cohesiveness of coalitions, whether members of a coalition act in concert toward a common goal, which may result in lower coalitional safety when one infers one's own coalition to be weaker (or in higher coalitional safety when one infers one's own coalition to be stronger). Cohesiveness cannot really be observed; it must be inferred, for instance, from the similarity (in dress, speech, behavior) of the coalition members.

In short, the coalitional perspective suggests that further exploration of intergroup dynamics should pay special attention to the cognitive processes whereby people automatically sample their social environment and infer underlying properties on the basis of that sampling. This research program would benefit from cognitive psychology findings and models concerning intuitive statistics, 'fast and frugal heuristics,' and other aspects of ecological rationality (Gigerenzer, 2007).

6.2 Gender Differences

Human dispositions and capacities are shaped by what worked toward reproductive success, on average, in evolutionary conditions. This provides a starting point for investigating and explaining gender differences in coalitional psychology.

In standard social psychological models, there is little reason to expect, and generally no explicit predictions of, differences between men and women regarding inter-group processes. By contrast, an evolutionary perspective predicts profound sex differences, as already emphasized in social dominance theory (Sidanius et al., 1994). Through most of human evolution, groups were patrilocal, as men stayed and women moved between groups (Pasternak, Ember, & Ember, 1997; Seielstad, Minch, & Cavalli-Sforza, 1998). Women had to establish support networks with non-kin (Taylor et al., 2000), while men needed to bolster alliances between kin groups to compete with other coalitions (Kaplan, Hill, Lancaster, & Hurtado, 2000), most clearly in tribal warfare, an almost exclusively male (Gat, 2006; Keeley, 1996). As predicted, different patterns of socialization can be found cross-culturally from early childhood (Geary, 2003).

As a consequence, we may expect men to be more motivated than women to see interindividual relations in terms of rival coalitions and more motivated than women to engage in violent coalitional strife; both men and women should be biased toward representing coalitional enemies as typically male. Some psychological evidence supports these conjectures. For instance, after threat priming, men are more likely than women to activate concepts of groups and coalitions (Bugental & Beaulieu, 2009). Women cooperate within a group regardless of competition with rival groups, while rivalry makes men more cooperative inside the group (van Vugt, Cremer, & Janssen, 2007). Men are implicitly biased to see men more than women as enemies (Plant, Goplen, & Kunstman, 2011). In both genders, the association of anticipated harm with a male's face is more difficult to extinguish than the association with a female face (Navarrete et al., 2009).

Sex differences in coalitional psychology may also account for the effects described by Sidanius and colleagues in terms of a *subordinate male target* hypothesis. According to this hypothesis, which is supported by many empirical studies, adult men of the dominated group are the focus of more intense discrimination than women (Sidanius & Pratto, 1999). One possible explanation for this phenomenon is in terms of the potential reproductive value of subordinate women, which would palliate discriminatory attitudes toward women (Sidanius & Pratto, 1999). Further developments of social dominance models point to a simpler and broader explanation, that men are the target because group rivalry recruits mental systems that evolved in the context of tribal warfare, in which males are more likely than females to be aggressors (McDonald, Navarrete, & Van Vugt, 2012; Navarrete et al., 2010; Yuki & Yokota, 2009).

6.3 Coalitional Effects beyond Minorities

The literature reviewed above describes the poor health outcomes of subordinate groups (controlling for confounding socioeconomic variables) as an effect of prejudice, stereotype, or discrimination. The coalitional model by contrast emphasizes the number of encounters with individuals of a rival coalition, especially if these rival coalitions are perceived as stronger, more numerous, increasing in number, or more cohesive than one's own. A prejudice model would not predict that members of majorities experience a negative health impact when an ethnic minority in their neighborhood increases in number or visibility. By contrast, the coalitional perspective predicts that increasingly frequent encounters with people of a rival coalition (the minority), especially when the minority is apparently cohesive (e.g., inferred from displays of common markers, a distinct unfamiliar language, and so on), would increase the number of stress responses in majority individuals.

Note that such negative effects on majority individuals have already been observed in another domain, that of trust. In studies by Putnam and others, generalized social trust (the extent to which one thinks one can trust others in one's social environment) decreases with greater ethnic diversity (Putnam, 2000, 2007). Further studies have shown that this effect depends on the frequency of encounters at the level of small neighborhoods (Dinesen & Sønderskov, 2012). Our coalitional stress model would predict that this may have effects on health as well. There is some evidence in that direction—for example, Whites who live in more homogeneous neighborhoods have better health in New York (Fang et al., 1998) and fewer psychiatric admissions in Chicago (Halpern, 1993). But the data are really sparse, and only largescale surveys could overcome the obvious confounds created by the overall inequality between majority and minorities, as well as potentially harmful effects of majority individuals' own prejudices.

7. Conclusion

The proposed model stipulates that an internal regulatory variable, the coalitional safety index, corresponds to an individual's perceived coalitional security. The index reflects the extent to which he or she can depend on others in the competition against other alliances. It is down-regulated by specific threat cues of reduced support from one's own coalition or increased menace from a rival coalition, which trigger motivations for appropriate precautionary behaviors. Repeated perceptions of such threat cues may cause chronic stress, with negative health consequences.

This perspective allows for the explanation of a great variety of phenomena described in the social psychology of intergroup relations, such as stereotyping, racism, ethnocentrism, stress, and health disparities, in terms of a suite of capacities and motivations shaped by natural selection. The evolved human coalitional psychology is described as a set of universal systems that take as their input specific information about the social environment and activate appropriate motivations to maximize coalitional safety. Interactions between such systems and highly variable social conditions result in culturally and historically specific representations of the social world, which motivate equally specific attitudes and behaviors.

References:

Alegría, M., Canino, G., Shrout, P. E., Woo, M., Duan, N., Vila, D., Torres, M., Chen, C.-N., & Meng, X.-L. (2008). Prevalence of mental illness in immigrant and non-immigrant U.S. Latino groups. *The American Journal of Psychiatry*, 165, 359–369. https://doi.org/10.1176/appi.ajp.2007.07040704

Ayers, J. W., Hofstetter, C. R., Usita, P., Irvin, V. L., Kang, S., & Hovell, M. F. (2009). Sorting out the competing effects of acculturation, immigrant stress, and social support on depression: A report on Korean women in California. *Journal of Nervous and Mental Disease*, 197, 742–747. https://doi.org/10.1097/NMD.0b013e3181b96e9e

Bacharach, M., & Gambetta, D. (2001). Trust in Signs. In K. S. Cook (Ed.), *Trust in Society* (pp. 148–184). New York: Russell Sage Foundation.

Bak-Klimek, A., Karatzias, T., Elliott, L., & Maclean, R. (2014). The determinants of well-being among international economic immigrants: A systematic literature review and meta-analysis. *Applied Research in Quality of Life*, 10, 161–188. https://doi.org/10.1007/s11482-013-9297-8

Balliet, D., Wu, J., & De Dreu, C. K. W. (2014). Ingroup favoritism in cooperation: A meta-analysis. *Psychological Bulletin*, 140, 1556–1581.

Baumeister, R. F., Bratslavsky, E., Finkenauer, C., & Vohs, K. D. (2001). Bad is stronger than good. *Review of General Psychology*, 5, 323–370. https://doi.org/10.1037/1089-2680.5.4.323

Becares, L., & Nazroo, J. (2013). Social capital, ethnic density and mental health among ethnic minority people in England: A mixed-methods study. *Ethnicity & Health*, 18, 544–562. https://doi.org/10.1080/13557858.2013.828831

Blanchard, D. C., Griebel, G., Pobbe, R., & Blanchard, R. J. (2011). Risk assessment as an evolved threat detection and analysis process. *Neuroscience and Biobehavioral Reviews*, 35, 991–998. https://doi.org/10.1016/j.neubiorev.2010.10.016

Blascovich, J., Mendes, W. B., Hunter, S. B., Lickel, B., & Kowai-Bell, N. (2001). Perceiver threat in social interactions with stigmatized others. *Journal of Personality and Social Psychology*, 80, 253–267. https://doi.org/10.1037//0022-3514.80.2.253

Bosqui, T. J., Hoy, K., & Shannon, C. (2014). A systematic review and meta-analysis of the ethnic density effect in psychotic disorders. *Social Psychiatry and Psychiatric Epidemiology*, 49, 519–529. https://doi.org/10.1007/s00127-013-0773-0

Boydell, J., van Os, J., McKenzie, K., Allardyce, J., Goel, R., McCreadie, R. G., & Murray, R. M. (2001). Incidence of schizophrenia in ethnic minorities in London: ecological study into interactions with environment. *BMJ (Clinical Research Ed.)*, 323, 1336–1338. https://doi.org/10.1136/bmj.323.7325.1336

Boyer, P., & Bergstrom, B. (2011). Threat-Detection in Child Development: An Evolutionary Perspective. *Neuroscience & Biobehavioral Reviews*, 35, 1034–1041. https://doi.org/10.1016/j.neubiorev.2010.08.010

Boyer, P., & Lienard, P. (2006). Why ritualized behavior? Precaution systems and action parsing in developmental, pathological and cultural rituals. *Behavioral and Brain Sciences*, 29, 595–613. https://doi.org/10.1017/s0140525x06009332

Brewer, M. B. (1979). In-group bias in the minimal intergroup situation: A cognitive-motivational analysis. *Psychological Bulletin*, 86, 307–324.

Brondolo, E., Rieppi, R., Kelly, K. P., & Gerin, W. (2003). Perceived racism and blood pressure: A review of the literature and conceptual and methodological critique. *Annals of Behavioral Medicine*, 25, 55–65. https://doi.org/10.1207/S15324796ABM2501_08

Bugental, D. B., & Beaulieu, D. A. (2009). Sex differences in response to coalitional threat. *Evolution and Human Behavior*, 30, 238–243. https://doi.org/10.1016/j.evolhumbehav.2009.02.002

Bullock, D. (2013). *The Contact Hypothesis and Racial Diversity in the United States Military*. Doctoral disseration, Texas Woman's University [Dissertation Number: AAI3550788].

Cano, M. Á., Castillo, L. G., Castro, Y., de Dios, M. A., & Roncancio, A. M. (2014). Acculturative stress and depressive symptomatology among Mexican and Mexican American students in the U.S.: Examining associations with cultural incongruity and intragroup marginalization. *International Journal for the Advancement of Counselling*, 36, 136–149. https://doi.org/10.1007/s10447-013-9196-6

Carpenter, L., & Brockington, I. F. (1980). A study of mental illness in Asians, West Indians, and Africans living in Manchester. *The British Journal of Psychiatry*, 137, 201–205.

Pew Research Center (2006). *America's Immigration Quandary*. Washington, DC, Pew Research Center for the People & the Press.

Chae, S.-M., Park, J. W., & Kang, H. S. (2014). Relationships of acculturative stress, depression, and social support to health-related quality of life in Vietnamese immigrant women in South Korea. *Journal of Transcultural Nursing*, 25, 137–144. https://doi.org/10.1177/1043659613515714

Chung, H., & Epstein, N. B. (2014). Perceived racial discrimination, acculturative stress, and psychological distress among asian immigrants: The moderating effects of support and interpersonal strain from a partner. *International Journal of Intercultural Relations*, 42, 129–139. https://doi.org/10.1016/j.ijintrel.2014.04.003

Clark, R. (2000). Perceptions of interethnic group racism predict increased vascular reactivity to a laboratory challenge in college women. *Annals of Behavioral Medicine*, 22, 214–222.

Clark, R., Anderson, N. B., Clark, V. R., & Williams, D. R. (1999). Racism as a stressor for African Americans: A biopsychosocial model. *American Psychologist*, 54, 805–816. https://doi.org/10.1037/0003-066x.54.10.805

Contrada, R. J., Ashmore, R. D., Gary, M. L., Coups, E., Egeth, J. D., Sewell, A., Ewell, K., Goyal, T. M., Chasse, V. (2000). Ethnicity-related sources of stress and their effects on well-being. *Current Directions in Psychological Science*, 9, 136–139. https://doi.org/10.1111/1467-8721.00078

———. (2001). Measures of ethnicity-related stress: Psychometric properties, ethnic group differences, and associations with well-being. *Journal of Applied Social Psychology*, 31, 1775–1820. https://doi.org/10.1111/j.1559-1816.2001.tb00205.x

Cosmides, L., Tooby, J., & Kurzban, R. (2003). Perceptions of race. *Trends in Cognitive Sciences*, 7, 173–179. https://doi.org/10.1016/s1364-6613(03)00057-3

Cottrell, C. A., & Neuberg, S. L. (2005). Different Emotional Reactions to Different Groups: A Sociofunctional Threat-Based Approach to 'Prejudice'. *Journal of Personality and Social Psychology*, 88, 770–789. https://doi.org/10.1037/0022-3514.88.5.770

Das-Munshi, J., Bécares, L., Boydell, J. E., Dewey, M. E., Morgan, C., Stansfeld, S. A., & Prince, M. J. (2012). Ethnic density as a buffer for psychotic experiences: Findings from a national survey (EMPIRIC). *The British Journal of Psychiatry*, 201, 282–290. https://doi.org/10.1192/bjp.bp.111.102376

Das-Munshi, J., Becares, L., Dewey, M. E., Stansfeld, S. A., & Prince, M. J. (2010). Understanding the effect of ethnic density on mental health: Multi-level investigation of survey data from England. *BMJ: British Medical Journal*, 341, 1–9. https://doi.org/10.1136/bmj.c5367

DeScioli, P., & Kurzban, R. (2009). The Alliance Hypothesis for Human Friendship. *PLoS One*, 4. https://doi.org/10.1371/journal.pone.0005802

Dielenberg, R. A., & McGregor, I. S. (1999). Habituation of the hiding response to cat odor in rats (Rattus Norvegicus). *Journal of Comparative Psychology*, 113, 376–387. https://doi.org/10.1037/0735-7036.113.4.376

Dinesen, P. T., & Sønderskov, K. M. (2012). Trust in a Time of Increasing Diversity: On the Relationship between Ethnic Heterogeneity and Social Trust in Denmark from 1979 until Today. *Scandinavian Political Studies*, 35, 273–294. https://doi.org/10.1111/j.1467-9477.2012.00289.x

Dovidio, J. F., Gaertner, S. L., & Kawakami, K. (2003). Intergroup contact: The past, present, and the future. *Group Processes & Intergroup Relations*, 6, 5–20. https://doi.org/10.1177/1368430203006001009

Dubreuil, B. (2010). Paleolithic public goods games: why human culture and cooperation did not evolve in one step. *Biology & Philosophy*, 25, 53–73. https://doi.org/10.1007/s10539-009-9177-7

Dugatkin, L. A. (1998). A model of coalition formation in animals. *Proceedings of the Royal Society London B Biological Sciences, 265,* 2121–2125.

Dunbar, R. I. (1996). Groups, Gossip, and the Evolution of Language. In *New Aspects of Human Ethology* (pp. 77–89). Boston, MA: Springer.

Fang, J., Madhavan, S., Bosworth, W., & Alderman, M. H. (1998). Residential segregation and mortality in New York City. *Social Science & Medicine, 47,* 469–476.

Fazio, R. H., Jackson, J. R., Dunton, B. C., & Williams, C. J. (2008). Variability in automatic activation as an unobtrusive measure of racial attitudes: A bona fide pipeline? In R. H. Fazio & R. E. Petty (Eds.), *Attitudes: Their Structure, Function, and Consequences.* (pp. 85–108). New York: Psychology Press.

Fessler, D. M. T., & Holbrook, C. (2013). Friends Shrink Foes: The Presence of Comrades Decreases the Envisioned Physical Formidability of an Opponent. *Psychological Science.* https://doi.org/papers2://publication/doi/10.1177/0956797612461508

Gat, A. (2006). *War in Human Civilization.* New York: Oxford University Press.

Geary, D. C. (2003). Evolution and development of boys' social behavior. *Developmental review, 23,* 444–470. https://doi.org/10.1016/j.dr.2003.08.001

Geronimus, A. T., Bound, J., Waidmann, T. A., Hillemeier, M. M., & Burns, P. B. (1996). Excess mortality among blacks and whites in the United States. *The New England Journal Of Medicine, 335,* 1552–1558.

Gigerenzer, G. (2007). *Gut Feelings: The Intelligence of the Unconscious.* New York: Viking.

Guimond, S., De Oliveira, P., Kamiesjki, R., & Sidanius, J. (2010). The trouble with assimilation: Social dominance and the emergence of hostility against immigrants. *International Journal of Intercultural Relations, 34,* 642–650. https://doi.org/10.1016/j.ijintrel.2010.01.002

Gunnar, M., & Quevedo, K. (2007). The Neurobiology of Stress and Development. *Annual Review of Psychology, 58,* 145–173. https://doi.org/10.1146/annurev.psych.58.110405.085605

Guyll, M., Matthews, K. A., & Bromberger, J. T. (2001). Discrimination and unfair treatment: Relatioship to cardiovascular reactivity among African American and European American women. *Helath Psychology, 20,* 315–325. https://doi.org/10.1037/0278-6133.20.5.315

Halpern, D. (1993). Minorities and mental health. *Social Science & Medicine, 36,* 597–607.

Harcourt, A. H., & de Waal, F. B. M. (1992). *Coalitions and Alliances in Humans and Other Animals.* New York: Oxford University Press.

Hardin, R. (1982). *Collective action.* Baltimore, MD: The Johns Hopkins University Press.

Hart, A. J., Whalen, P. J., Shin, L. M., McInerney, S. C., Fischer, H., & Rauch, S. L. (2000). Differential response in the human amygdala to racial outgroup vs ingroup face stimuli. *NeuroReport: For Rapid Communication of Neuroscience Research*, 11, 2351–2355. http://links.lww.com/WNR/A4

Haselton, M. G., & Buss, D. M. (2000). Error management theory: A new perspective on biases in cross-sex mind reading. *Journal of Personality and Social Psychology*, 78, 81–91. https://doi.org/10.1037//0022-3514.78.1.81

Haselton, M. G., & Funder, D. C. (2006). The Evolution of Accuracy and Bias in Social Judgment. In M. Schaller, J. A. Simpson, & D. T. Kenrick (Eds.), *Evolution and Social Psychology.* (pp. 15–37). Madison, CT: Psychosocial Press.

Haselton, M. G., & Nettle, D. (2006). The paranoid optimist: an integrative evolutionary model of cognitive biases. *Personality & Social Psychology Review*, 10, 47–66. https://doi.org/10.1207/s15327957pspr1001_3

Hess, N. H., & Hagen, E. H. (2006). Psychological Adaptations for Assessing Gossip Veracity. *Human Nature*, 17, 337–354. https://doi.org/10.1007/s12110-006-1013-z

Hornsey, M. J. (2008). Social Identity Theory and Self-categorization Theory: A Historical Review. *Social and Personality Psychology Compass*, 2, 204–222. https://doi.org/papers2://publication/doi/10.1111/j.1751-9004.2007.00066.x

Hrdy, S. B. (1999). *Mother nature: A History of Mothers, Infants, and Natural Selection.* New York: Pantheon Books.

——. (2009). *Mothers and Others: The Evolutionary Origins of Mutual Understanding.* Cambridge, MA: Belknap Press of Harvard University Press.

Jaeggi, A. V., & Van Schaik, C. P. (2011). The evolution of food sharing in primates. *Behavioral Ecology and Sociobiology*, 65, 2125–2140. https://doi.org/10.1007/s00265-011-1221-3

Kaestner, R., Pearson, J. A., Keene, D., & Geronimus, A. T. (2009). Stress, allostatic load, and health of Mexican immigrants. *Social Science Quarterly*, 90, 1089–1111. https://doi.org/10.1111/j.1540-6237.2009.00648.x

Kaplan, H. S., Hill, K., Lancaster, J., & Hurtado, A. (2000). A theory of human life history evolution: diet, intelligence, and longevity. *Evolutionary Anthropology*, 9, 156–185.

Karlsen, S., & Nazroo, J. Y. (2004). Fear of racism and health. *Journal of Epidemiology and Community Health*, 58, 1017–1018.

Keeley, L. H. (1996). *War before Civilization.* New York: Oxford University Press.

Kelly, R. L. (1995). *The Foraging Spectrum: Diversity in Hunter-Gatherer Lifeways.* Washington, DC: Smithsonian Institution Press.

Korf, L., & Malan, J. (2002). Threat to ethnic identity: The experience of White Afrikaans-speaking participants in postapartheid South Africa. *The Journal of Social Psychology*, 142, 149–169. https://doi.org/10.1080/00224540209603892

Kurzban, R., & Neuberg, S. (2005). Managing ingroup and outgroup relationships. In D. M. Buss (Ed.), *The Handbook of Evolutionary Psychology.* (pp. 653–675). Hoboken, NJ: John Wiley & Sons Inc.

Kurzban, R., Tooby, J., & Cosmides, L. (2001). Can race be erased? Coalitional computation and social categorization. *Proceedings of the National Academy of Sciences of the United States of America*, 98, 15387–15392. https://doi.org/10.1073/pnas.251541498

Kwag, K. H., Jang, Y., & Chiriboga, D. A. (2012). Acculturation and depressive symptoms in Hispanic older adults: Does perceived ethnic density moderate their relationship? *Journal of Immigrant and Minority Health*, 14, 1107–1111. https://doi.org/10.1007/s10903-011-9569-z

Lazarus, R. S. F. S. (1984). *Stress, Appraisal, and Coping.* New York: Springer Pub. Co.

LeVine, R. A., & Campbell, D. T. (1972). *Ethnocentrism.* New York: John Wiley.

Lewis-Coles, M. A., & Constantine, M. G. (2006). Racism-related stress, Africultural coping, and religious problem-solving among African Americans. *Cultural Diversity and Ethnic Minority Psychology*, 12, 433–443. https://doi.org/10.1037/1099-9809.12.3.433

Lieberman, D., Tooby, J., & Cosmides, L. (2007). The architecture of human kin detection. *Nature*, 445, 5. https://doi.org/10.1038/nature05510

Littleford, L. N., Wright, M. O. D., & Sayoc-Parial, M. (2005). White Students' Intergroup Anxiety During Same-Race and Interracial Interactions: A Multimethod Approach. *Basic and Applied Social Psychology*, 27, 85–94. https://doi.org/10.1207/s15324834basp2701_9

Loewenstein, G. (1996). Out of control: Visceral influences on behavior. *Organizational Behavior and Human Decision Processes*, 65, 272–292.

Lynch, J. W. (2000). Income inequality and mortality: importance to health of individual income, psychosocial environment, or material conditions. *British Medical Journal*, 320, 1200–1204.

Major, B., Mendes, W. B., & Dovidio, J. F. (2013). Intergroup relations and health disparities: A social psychological perspective. *Health Psychology*, 32, 514–524. https://doi.org/10.1037/a0030358

Mays, V. M., Cochran, S. D., & Barnes, N. W. (2007). Race, Race-Based Discrimination, and Health Outcomes Among African Americans. *Annual Review of Psychology*, 58, 201–225. https://doi.org/10.1146/annurev.psych.57.102904.190212

McDonald, M., Navarrete, C. D., & van Vugt, M. (2012). Evolution and the psychology of intergroup conflict: the male warrior hypothesis. *Philosophical Transactions of the Royal Society B*, 367, 670–679. https://doi.org/10.1098/rstb.2011.0301

McEwen, B. S. (2004). Protection and damage from acute and chronic stress: allostasis and allostatic overload and relevance to the pathophysiology of psychiatric disorders. *Annals Of The New York Academy Of Sciences*, 1032, 1–7. https://doi.org/10.1196/annals.1314.001

McEwen, B. S., & Stellar, E. (1993). Stress and the individual. Mechanisms leading to disease. *Archives Of Internal Medicine*, 153, 2093–2101.

McGarty, C., Yzerbyt, V. Y., & Spears, R. (2002). *Stereotypes as Explanations: The Formation of Meaningful Beliefs about Social Groups*. New York: Cambridge University Press.

McGregor, I. S., Adamec, R., Canteras, N. S., Blanchard, R. J., & Blanchard, D. C. (2005). Defensive behavior. *Neuroscience and Biobehavioral Reviews*, 29, 1121–1122. https://doi.org/10.1016/j.neubiorev.2005.05.004

Medina, L. F. (2007). *A Unified Theory of Collective Action and Social Change*. Ann Arbor, MI: University of Michigan Press.

Mendes, W. B., Blascovich, J., Lickel, B., & Hunter, S. (2002). Challenge and threat during social interaction with white and black men. *Personality and Social Psychology Bulletin*, 28, 939–952. https://doi.org/10.1177/01467202028007007

Mendes, W. B., Major, B., McCoy, S., & Blascovich, J. (2008). How attributional ambiguity shapes physiological and emotional responses to social rejection and acceptance. *Journal of Personality and Social Psychology*, 94, 278–291. https://doi.org/10.1037/0022-3514.94.2.278

Mesterton-Gibbons, M., & Sherratt, T. N. (2007). Coalition formation: A game-theoretic analysis. *Behavioral Ecology*, 18, 277–286. https://doi.org/10.1093/beheco/arl084

Morales, L. S., Lara, M., Kington, R. S., Valdez, R. O., & Escarce, J. J. (2002). Socioeconomic, cultural, and behavioral factors affecting Hispanic health outcomes. *Journal of Health Care for the Poor and Underserved*, 13(4), 477. https://doi.org/10.1177/104920802237532

Moskos, C. C., Jr. (1966). Racial integration in the armed forces. *American Journal of Sociology*, 72, 132–148.

Myatt, D. P., & Wallace, C. (2009). Evolution, Teamwork and Collective Action: Production Targets in the Private Provision of Public Goods. *Economic Journal*, 119, 61–90. https://doi.org/10.1111/j.1468-0297.2008.02206.x

Navarrete, C. D., McDonald, M., Asher, B., Kerr, N. L., Yokota, K., Olsson, A., & Sidanius, J. (2012). Fear is readily associated with an out-group face in a minimal group context. *Evolution and Human Behavior*, 22, 590–593. https://doi.org/10.1016/j.evolhumbehav.2012.02.007

Navarrete, C. D., McDonald, M. M., Molina, L. E., & Sidanius, J. (2010). Prejudice at the nexus of race and gender: An outgroup male target hypothesis. *Journal of Personality and Social Psychology*, 98, 933–945. https://doi.org/10.1037/a0017931

Navarrete, C. D., Olsson, A., Ho, A. K., Mendes, W. B., Thomsen, L., & Sidanius, J. (2009). Fear extinction to an out-group face: The role of target gender. *Psychological Science, 20*, 155–158. https://doi.org/10.1111/j.1467-9280.2009.02273.x

Neeleman, J., Wilson-Jones, C., & Wessely, S. (2001). Ethnic density and deliberate self harm; a small area study in south east London. *Journal of Epidemiology and Community Health, 55*, 85–90. https://doi.org/10.1136/jech.55.2.85

Neuberg, S. L., Kenrick, D. T., & Schaller, M. (2010). Evolutionary social psychology. In S. T. Fiske, D. T. Gilbert, & G. Lindzey (Eds.), *Handbook of Social Psychology, Vol 2 (5th ed.)*. (pp. 761–796). Hoboken, NJ: John Wiley & Sons Inc.

Noymer, A., & Lee, R. (2013). Immigrant health around the world: Evidence from the World Values Survey. *Journal of Immigrant and Minority Health, 15*, 614–623. https://doi.org/10.1007/s10903-012-9637-z

Osypuk, T. L., Bates, L. M., & Acevedo-Garcia, D. (2010). Another Mexican birthweight paradox? The role of residential enclaves and neighborhood poverty in the birthweight of Mexican-origin infants. *Social Science & Medicine, 70*, 550–560. https://doi.org/10.1016/j.socscimed.2009.10.034

Page-Gould, E., Mendoza-Denton, R., & Tropp, L. R. (2008). With a little help from my cross-group friend: Reducing anxiety in intergroup contexts through cross-group friendship. *Journal of Personality and Social Psychology, 95*, 1080–1094. https://doi.org/10.1037/0022-3514.95.5.1080

Page-Gould, E., Mendoza-Denton, R., & Mendes, W. B. (2014). Stress and coping in interracial contexts: The influence of race-based rejection sensitivity and cross-group friendship in daily experiences of health. *Journal of Social Issues, 70*, 256–278. https://doi.org/10.1111/josi.12059

Paladino, M.-P., & Castelli, L. (2008). On the immediate consequences of intergroup categorization: Activation of approach and avoidance motor behavior toward ingroup and outgroup members. *Personality and Social Psychology Bulletin, 34*, 755–768. https://doi.org/10.1177/0146167208315155

Pascoe, E. A., & Smart Richman, L. (2009). Perceived discrimination and health: A meta-analytic review. *Psychological Bulletin, 135*, 531–554. https://doi.org/10.1037/a0016059.supp

Pasternak, B., Ember, C. R., & Ember, M. (1997). *Sex, Gender and Kinship: A Cross-Cultural Perspective*. Upper Saddle River, NJ: Prentice-Hall.

Payne, B. K. (2001). Prejudice and perception: The role of automatic and controlled processes in misperceiving a weapon. *Journal of Personality and Social Psychology, 81*, 181–192. https://doi.org/10.1037/0022-3514.81.2.181

Payne, B. K., Lambert, A. J., & Jacoby, L. L. (2002). Best laid plans: Effects of goals on accessibility bias and cognitive control in race-based misperceptions of weapons. *Journal of Experimental Social Psychology, 38*, 384–396. https://doi.org/10.1016/s0022-1031(02)00006-9

Pettigrew, T. F. (1997). Generalized intergroup contact effects on prejudice. *Personality and Social Psychology Bulletin,* 23(2), 173–185.

Pettigrew, T. F., & Tropp, L. R. (2006). A meta-analytic test of intergroup contact theory. *Journal of Personality and Social Psychology,* 90, 751–783.

Pickett, K. E., & Wilkinson, R. G. (2008). People like us: Ethnic group density effects on health. *Ethnicity & Health,* 13, 321–334. https://doi.org/10.1080/13557850701882928

Pietraszewski, D. (2009). *Erasing race with cooperation: Evidence that race is a consequence of coalitional inferences.* Doctoral dissertation, UC Santa Barbara [Dissertation Number: AAI3379503].

Pietraszewski, D., Cosmides, L., & Tooby, J. (2014). The Content of Our Cooperation, Not the Color of Our Skin: An Alliance Detection System Regulates Categorization by Coalition and Race, but Not Sex. *PLoS One,* 9, 1–19. https://doi.org/10.1371/journal.pone.0088534

Plant, E. A., Goplen, J., & Kunstman, J. W. (2011). Selective responses to threat: The roles of race and gender in decisions to shoot. *Personality and Social Psychology Bulletin,* 37, 1274–1281. https://doi.org/10.1177/0146167211408617

Pratto, F., & John, O. P. (1991). Automatic vigilance: The attention-grabbing power of negative social information. *Journal of Personality & Social Psychology,* 61, 380–391. https://doi.org/10.1037/0022-3514.61.3.380

Pratto, F., Sidanius, J., Stallworth, L. M., & Malle, B. F. (1994). Social dominance orientation: A personality variable predicting social and political attitudes. *Journal of Personality and Social Psychology,* 67(4), 741. https://doi.org/10.1037/0022-3514.67.4.741

Putnam, R. D. (2000). *Bowling Alone: The Collapse and Revival of American Community.* New York: Simon & Schuster.

———. (2007). E Pluribus Unum: Diversity and Community in the Twenty-first Century The 2006 Johan Skytte Prize Lecture. *Scandinavian Political Studies,* 30, 137–174. https://doi.org/10.1111/j.1467-9477.2007.00176.x

Rosenstein, J. E. (2008). Individual threat, group threat, and racial policy: Exploring the relationship between threat and racial attitudes. *Social Science Research,* 37, 1130–1146. https://doi.org/10.1016/j.ssresearch.2008.04.001

Rozin, P., & Royzman, E. B. (2001). Negativity bias, negativity dominance, and contagion. *Personality and Social Psychology Review,* 5, 296–320. https://doi.org/10.1207/S15327957PSPR0504_2

Sapolsky, R. M. (2007). Stress, Stress-Related Disease, and Emotional Regulation. In J. J. Gross (Ed.), *Handbook of Emotion Regulation.* (pp. 606–615). New York: Guilford Press.

Sawyer, P. J., Major, B., Casad, B. J., Townsend, S. S. M., & Mendes, W. B. (2012). Discrimination and the stress response: Psychological and physiological consequences of anticipating prejudice in interethnic interactions.

American Journal of Public Health, 102, 1020–1026. https://doi.org/10.2105/AJPH.2011.300620

Schaller, M. (2006). Parasites, Behavioral Defenses, and the Social Psychological Mechanisms Through Which Cultures Are Evoked. *Psychological Inquiry*, 17, 96–137. https://doi.org/10.1207/s15327965pli1702_2

Schaller, M., & Abeysinghe, A. M. N. D. (2006). Geographical Frame of Reference and Dangerous Intergroup Attitudes: A Double-Minority Study in Sri Lanka. *Political Psychology*, 27, 615–631. https://doi.org/10.1111/j.1467-9221.2006.00521.x

Schaller, M., & Neuberg, S. L. (2012). Danger, Disease, and the Nature of Prejudice(s). In M. O. James & P. Z. Mark (Eds.), *Advances in Experimental Social Psychology* (Vol. Volume 46, pp. 1–54): Academic Press. https://doi.org/10.1016/B978-0-12-394281-4.00001-5

Seielstad, M. T., Minch, E., & Cavalli-Sforza, L. L. (1998). Genetic evidence for a higher female migration rate in humans. *Nature Genetics*, 20, 278–280. https://doi.org/10.1038/3088

Shaw, R. J., Atkin, K., Bécares, L., Albor, C. B., Stafford, M., Kiernan, K. E., Nazroo, J. Y., Wilkinson, R. G., & Pickett, K. E. (2012). Impact of ethnic density on adult mental disorders: Narrative review. *The British Journal of Psychiatry*, 201, 11–19. https://doi.org/10.1192/bjp.bp.110.083675

Sidanius, J., & Pratto, F. (1999). *Social Dominance. An Intergroup Theory of Social Oppression and Hierarchy*. Cambridge: Cambridge University Press.

Sidanius, J., Pratto, F., & Bobo, L. (1994). Social dominance orientation and the political psychology of gender: A case of invariance? *Journal of Personality & Social Psychology*, 67, 998–1011.

Smith, C. A., & Kirby, L. D. (2011). The role of appraisal and emotion in coping and adaptation. In R. J. Contrada & A. Baum (Eds.), *The Handbook of Stress Science: Biology, Psychology and Health* (pp. 195–208). New York: Springer.

Stephan, W. G., & Stephan, C. W. (1985). Intergroup anxiety. *Journal of Social Issues*, 41(3), 157–175.

Szechtman, H., & Woody, E. (2004). Obsessive-Compulsive Disorder as a Disturbance of Security Motivation. *Psychological Review*, 111, 111–127. https://doi.org/10.1037/0033-295X.111.1.111

Tajfel, H., & Turner, J. C. (1986). The social identity theory of inter-group behavior. In S. Worchel & W. G. Austin (Eds.), *Psychology of Intergroup Relations* (pp. 33–47). Chcago, IL: Nelson-Hall.

Taylor, S. E., Cousino Klein, L., Lewis, B. P., Gruenewald, T. L., Gurung, R. A. R., & Updegraff, J. A. (2000). Biobehavioral responses to stress in females: Tend-and-befriend, not fight-or-flight. *Psychological Review*, 411–429. https://doi.org/10.1037/0033-295x.107.3.411

Thomsen, L., Green, E. G. T., & Sidanius, J. (2008). We will hunt them down: How social dominance orientation and right-wing authoritarianism fuel ethnic persecution of immigrants in fundamentally different ways. *Journal of Experimental Social Psychology*, 44, 1455–1464. https://doi.org/10.1016/j.jesp.2008.06.011

Tooby, J., & Cosmides, L. (1996). Friendship and the banker's paradox: Other pathways to the evolution of adaptations for altruism. In W. G. Runciman, J. M. Smith, et al. (Eds.), *Evolution of Social Behaviour Patterns in Primates and Man.* (pp. 119–143). Oxford: Oxford University Press.

———. (2010). Groups in Mind: The Coalitional Roots of War and Morality. In H. Høgh-Olesen (Ed.), *Human Morality & Sociality: Evolutionary & Comparative Perspectives* (pp. 191–234). New York: Palgrave MacMillan.

Tooby, J., Cosmides, L., Sell, A., Lieberman, D., & Sznycer, D. (2008). Internal regulatory variables and the design of human motivation: A computational and evolutionary approach. In A. J. Elliot (Ed.), *Handbook of Approach and Avoidance Motivation.* (pp. 251–271). New York: Psychology Press.

Trawalter, S., Richeson, J. A., & Shelton, J. N. (2009). Predicting behavior during interracial interactions: A stress and coping approach. *Personality and Social Psychology Review*, 13, 243–268. https://doi.org/10.1177/1088868309345850

Utsey, S. O., & Hook, J. N. (2007). Heart rate variability as a physiological moderator of the relationship between race-related stress and psychological distress in African Americans. *Cultural Diversity and Ethnic Minority Psychology*, 13, 250–253. https://doi.org/10.1037/1099-9809.13.3.250

van't Wout, M., & Sanfey, A. G. (2008). Friend or foe: The effect of implicit trustworthiness judgments in social decision-making. *Cognition*, 108, 796–803. https://doi.org/10.1016/j.cognition.2008.07.002

Van Bavel, J. J., & Cunningham, W. A. (2009). Self-categorization with a novel mixed-race group moderates automatic social and racial biases. *Personality and Social Psychology Bulletin*, 35, 321–335. https://doi.org/10.1177/0146167208327743

van Vugt, M., Cremer, D. D., & Janssen, D. P. (2007). Gender Differences in Cooperation and Competition: The Male-Warrior Hypothesis. *Psychological Science*, 18, 19–23. https://doi.org/10.1111/j.1467-9280.2007.01842.x

Vrana, S. R., & Rollock, D. (1998). Physiological response to a minimal social encounter: Effects of gender, ethnicity, and social context. *Psychophysiology*, 35, 462–469.

Weeks, M., & Lupfer, M. B. (2004). Complicating Race: The Relationship Between Prejudice, Race, and Social Class Categorizations. *Personality and Social Psychology Bulletin*, 30, 972–984. https://doi.org/10.1177/0146167204264751

Wert, S. R., & Salovey, P. (2004). A Social Comparison Account of Gossip. *Review of General Psychology*, 8, 122–137. https://doi.org/10.1037/1089-2680.8.2.122

Williams, C. L., & Berry, J. W. (1991). Primary prevention of acculturative stress among refugees: Application of psychological theory and practice. *American Psychologist*, 46, 632–641. https://doi.org/10.1037/0003-066x.46.6.632

Williams, D. R. (2012). Miles to go before we sleep: Racial inequities in health. *Journal of Health and Social Behavior*, 53, 279–295. https://doi.org/10.1177/0022146512455804

Williams, D. R., & Mohammed, S. A. (2009). Discrimination and racial disparities in health: Evidence and needed research. *Journal of Behavioral Medicine*, 32, 20–47. https://doi.org/10.1007/s10865-008-9185-0

Woody, E., & Szechtman, H. (2011). Adaptation to potential threat: the evolution, neurobiology, and psychopathology. *Neuroscience and Biobehavioral Reviews*, 35, 1019–1033. https://doi.org/10.1016/j.neubiorev.2010.08.003

Yuki, M., & Yokota, K. (2009). The primal warrior: Outgroup threat priming enhances intergroup discrimination in men but not women. *Journal of Experimental Social Psychology*, 45, 271–274. https://doi.org/10.1016/j.jesp.2008.08.018

Yzerbyt, V., Rocher, S., & Schadron, G. (1997). Stereotypes as explanations: A subjective essentialistic view of group perception. In R. Spears, P. J. Oakes, N. Ellemers, & S. A. Haslam (Eds.), *The Social Psychology of Stereotyping and Group Life*. (pp. 20–50). Malden: Blackwell Publishing.

5. How People Think about the Economy

Introductory Note

People have views about the economy, about such things as unemployment, trade, taxation, etc. Where do these opinions come from? Explaining that would certainly count as an example of 'useful' anthropology or political science, considering that most political programs are based on some particular vision of the way a modern economy works, and how it could be made better.

Michael Petersen and I were interested in explaining how people acquire these representations of the economy and, as a result, favor this or that political program.

Our aim was to explain economic ideologies, something that economists are not terribly interested in. Economists generally stop at pointing out that these ideologies are often based on erroneous assumptions, e.g., that labor is what creates value, that trade benefits one party at the expense of the other, that regulations have the intended effects, etc. But why would people reason on the basis of these misleading notions? We are often told that this happens because people are uneducated, or cognitively limited, or they just accept what is 'in their culture', or what fits their interests, or what politicians tell them. But none of these explanations are satisfactory, as we explain in the article.

We considered the hypothesis that economic ideologies are compelling and persistent in modern societies, because of their 'fit' with our evolved dispositions. How is our genetic evolution relevant to our views on international trade and income taxes? Obviously, such

 https://doi.org/10.11647/OBP.0257.08

issues were unknown in our environment of evolution, when we were (mostly) living in small bands of nomadic foragers. But that, in a way, is just the point. Our evolutionary heritage includes not just cognitive systems for understanding the natural world, but also capacities for managing life in groups—in particular, for cooperation and collective action, in which we pool efforts to obtain mutually beneficial outcomes. Over the last thirty years, evolutionary biologists, psychologists and economists have proposed and tested ever more refined models of the way cooperation occurs between humans, and of the psychological capacities and motivations that underpin the exceptional level of cooperation among humans—see summaries in André & Baumard (2011), Boyd & Richerson (2006), Cosmides & Tooby (2015).

This evolved cooperation psychology is part of our adaptations. It governs our reactions to information we receive, concerning the allocation of resources between partners, when we interact with others, share or trade with them. And—this was our starting point in this article—it may also explain our reactions to messages (from news organizations, political agents) concerning such mass-level phenomena as inflation, trade or unemployment.

This should illustrate how evolutionary models and findings are very much relevant to modern, mass-scale societies. A persistent misunderstanding, on the part of those unfamiliar with the field is that such models only apply to technologically simple societies, and that modern patterns of production, consumption, and communication create conditions so special that evolved preferences and capacities become less relevant. But that is just not the case. For instance, Michael Petersen pioneered an evolutionary perspective that promised to account for important features of mass-politics in modern societies (Petersen, 2012a; 2015). Consumption, too, is best understood in terms of evolved motivations (Saad, 2012), and even recent developments of electronic communication, including webpages, social media, etc., illustrate typically human capacities and motivations (Acerbi, 2019).

So, our evolved psychology influences the way we think of the immensely complex set of interactions that constitute an economy—and our representations of the economy in turn make particular political programs attractive. Our article only considered the first causal link, from evolved psychology to economic ideologies.

Speculating further, one might wonder which political programs would best fit our evolved psychology. If we followed our Stone Age intuitions and preferences, what would we choose as our economic policy? Others have wondered about that, and addressed the question with a great deal of sophistication, in particular Paul Rubin and Peter Singer. Rubin emphasizes that trade, being a cooperative interaction that benefits both parties, is an outgrowth of our cooperation psychology—and also notices that much cooperation in humans is based on partner-choice, on the possibility of selecting good partners and rejecting others. These dispositions would favor the free exchange of goods or services, away from the diktats of a chief, a king or a state (2002). Singer places much more emphasis on our capacities for sharing and mutual help and on the evolutionary basis for fairness and moral intuitions. These would favor generous welfare policies, when modern conditions create disadvantages or inequalities (2000). Both are right, in the sense that our cooperation psychology does respond to these two distinct sets of motivations, for mutually beneficial voluntary trade and for social support as a palliative to misfortune (Boyer, 2018, pp. 163–202). Indeed, Michael Petersen's experimental studies show that, regardless of their political affiliation, people can approve or disapprove of particular policy proposals, depending on which of these cognitive systems the material activates (Petersen, 2012b).

References

Acerbi, A. (2019). *Cultural Evolution in the Digital Age.* Oxford: Oxford University Press.

André, J.-B., & Baumard, N. (2011). The evolution of fairness in a biological market. *Evolution,* 650, 1447–1456. https://doi.org/10.1111/j.1558-5646.2011.01232.x

Boyd, R., & Richerson, P. J. (2006). Solving the Puzzle of Human Cooperation. In S. C. Levinson & P. Jaisson (Eds.), *Evolution and Culture* (pp. 105–132). Cambridge, MA: MIT Press.

Boyer, P. (2018). *Minds Make Societies. How Cognition Explains the World Humans Create.* New Haven, CT: Yale University Press.

Cosmides, L., & Tooby, J. (2015). Adaptations for reasoning about social exchange. In D. Buss (Ed.), *The Handbook of Evolutionary Psychology, Second edition.* (II, pp. 625–668). Hoboken, NJ: John Wiley & Sons.

Petersen, M. B. (2012a). The evolutionary psychology of mass politics. In S. C. Roberts (Ed.), *Applied Evolutionary Psychology.* (pp. 115–130). New York: Oxford University Press.

——. (2012b). Social Welfare as Small-Scale Help: Evolutionary Psychology and the Deservingness Heuristic. *American Journal of Political Science,* 56, 1–16. https://doi.org/10.1111/j.1540-5907.2011.00545.x

——. (2015). Evolutionary political psychology: On the origin and structure of heuristics and biases in politics. *Political Psychology,* 36, 45–78. https://doi. org/10.1111/pops.12237

Rubin, P. H. (2002). *Darwinian politics : the evolutionary origin of freedom.* New Brunswick, NJ: Rutgers University Press.

Saad, G. (2012). *The Evolutionary Bases of Consumption.* Oxford : Taylor & Francis.

Singer, P. (2000). *A Darwinian Left: Politics, Evolution, and Cooperation.* New Haven, CT: Yale University Press.

Folk-Economic Beliefs

An Evolutionary Cognitive Model[1]

with Michael Bang Petersen[2]

Abstract: The domain of 'folk-economics' consists in explicit beliefs about the economy held by laypeople, untrained in economics, about such topics as, for example, the causes of the wealth of nations, the benefits or drawbacks of markets and international trade, the effects of regulation, the origins of inequality, the connection between work and wages, the economic consequences of immigration, or the possible causes of unemployment. These beliefs are crucial in forming people's political beliefs and in shaping their reception of different policies. Yet, they often conflict with elementary principles of economic theory and are often described as the consequences of ignorance, irrationality, or specific biases. As we will argue, these past perspectives fail to predict the particular contents of popular folk-economic beliefs and, as a result, there is no systematic study of the cognitive factors involved in their emergence and cultural success. Here we propose that the cultural success of particular beliefs about the economy is predictable if we consider the influence of specialized, largely automatic inference systems that evolved as adaptations

1   An earlier version of this chapter was originally published as Boyer, P., & Petersen, M. B. (2017). Folk-Economic Beliefs: An Evolutionary Cognitive Model. *Behavioral and Brain Sciences*, 41, 1–51. https://doi.org/10.1017/S0140525X17001960. Republished with permission from Cambridge University Press.

2   Acknowledgements: We are grateful to Nicolas Baumard, Martin Bisgaard, Timothy Blaine, Thom Scott-Phillips, Don Ross, Paul Rubin, and four anonymous reviewers for thoughtful and detailed comments on a previous version.

https://doi.org/10.11647/OBP.0257.09

to ancestral human small-scale sociality. These systems, for which there is independent evidence, include free-rider detection, fairness-based partner choice, ownership intuitions, coalitional psychology, and more. Information about modern mass-market conditions activates these specific inference systems, resulting in particular intuitions, for example, that impersonal transactions are dangerous or that international trade is a zero-sum game. These intuitions in turn make specific policy proposals more likely than others to become intuitively compelling, and, as a consequence, exert a crucial influence on political choices.

1. The Domain of Folk-Economic Beliefs

1.1 What Folk-Economic Beliefs Are

The term folk-economic beliefs denotes a large domain of explicit, widespread beliefs, to do with economic and policy issues, held by individuals without systematic training in economic theory. These beliefs include mental representations of economic topics as diverse as tariffs, rents, prices, unemployment, and welfare or immigration policies, as well as mental models of interactions between different economic processes, for example, inflation and unemployment.

Our perspective on the origins and forms of folk-economics is based on two major assumptions. First, we argue that folk-notions of the economy should not be described solely in terms of deviations from normative economic theory. That has, unfortunately, been the common approach to the subject. Folk-views are generally described as the outcome of 'biases,' 'fallacies,' or straightforward ignorance. But describing how human cognition fails to work according to some norm of rationality tells us little

about how it actually works. Second, we propose to make sense of folk-economic beliefs by considering the environment in which many, if not most, human cognitive mechanisms evolved.

The study of folk-economic beliefs should be distinguished from other domains of investigation. Microeconomics addresses actual choices of agents in conditions of scarcity, independently of whatever mental representations trigger these behaviors in actual individuals, and also of the representations they may form of their behavior upon reflection. Another field, behavioral economics often uses experimental designs as a way to elucidate tacit motivations and capacities that direct economic choices in contexts where experimenters can manipulate incentives and information flow between agents (Plott, 1974). Finally, neuro-economics elucidates the brain systems involved in appraising utility and making economic decisions (Camerer et al., 2007; Loewenstein et al., 2008).

The scope of a study of folk-economics is quite different from these three fields (see Figure 1). It focuses on people's deliberate, explicit beliefs concerning economic facts and processes, for example, that foreign prosperity is good or bad for one's own nation, that welfare programs are necessary or redundant, that minimal wages help or hurt the poor, and that rent controls make prices go down or up, and so forth.

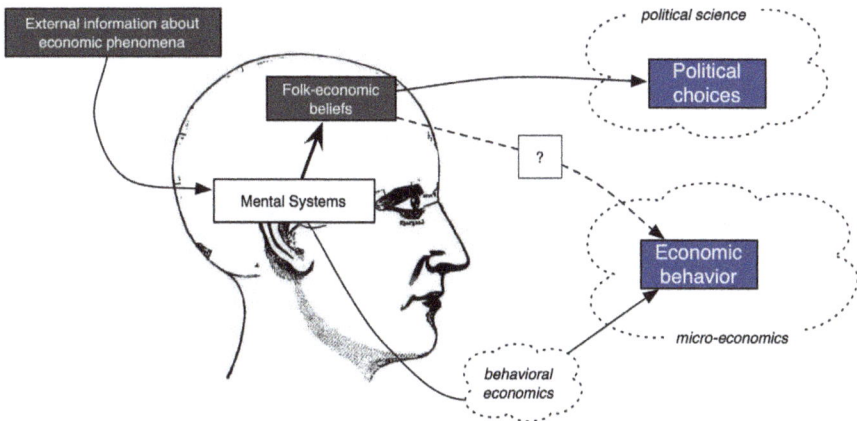

Fig. 1. A summary of the systems and representations involved in forming folk-economic beliefs. External information about economic matters triggers activation of specific mental systems, which results in both economic behavior and explicit folk-economic beliefs. The latter's effects on behavior cannot be assumed. Different fields, represented as clouds, focus on different parts of these processes. The model presented here is about the causal arrow linking specific mental systems to the occurrence of folk-economic beliefs in people's minds. (Figure by P Boyer. 2017)

One should not assume that folk-economic beliefs (henceforth FEBs) have direct and coherent effects on actual economic behaviors. Many FEBs are about macroeconomic processes—for example, the level of unemployment, or the need for foreign trade, or the need for a nation to balance its budget—that are unrelated to people's everyday transactions.

Also, even FEBs that do bear on micro-economic realities, for example, on 'fair' prices or wages, may remain insulated from the psychological processes that drive actual economic behavior, as we explain below, which is why people may recommend specific policy outcomes and behave in ways that contradict that choice (Smith, 2007).

Figure 1 summarizes the different domains of thought and behavior and the research programs involved.

1.2 Why Folk-Economic Beliefs (FEBs) Matter

Understanding FEBs is of crucial importance, even if they do not govern people's economic behavior, because they play a critical role in political choices. Perceptions of macro-economic developments influence how favorably people view the government and how they cast their votes (Nannestad & Paldam, 1994). The translation of inflation, unemployment, and income dynamics into political choices is mediated by people's beliefs about the economy, for example, whether rising unemployment is affected by government policy (Peffley, 1984; Rudolph, 2003a, 2003b). Similarly, economic beliefs underpin people's answers to such questions as: Is it a good idea to increase welfare benefits, impose tariffs on imports, cap rent increases, or institute minimum wages? Folk-economic beliefs constitute a largely unexplored background against which most information about policy is acquired, processed, and communicated among nonprofessionals (Rubin, 2003).

1.3 A Different Approach to the Study of Folk-Economic Beliefs

It is a matter of common knowledge that most people, including the educated public in modern democratic societies, do not think like economists (Smith, 2007, pp. 147–166). It is, for instance, a familiar finding that people are overinfluenced by consideration of sunk costs (Magalhães & Geoffrey White, 2016) or fail to consider opportunity costs (Hazlitt, 2010) in evaluating possible courses of action. More important for social and political debates, people often also express views on economic processes that seem misguided, if not downright fallacious, to most professional economists. There is a growing literature documenting this divergence (see, e.g., Blinder & Krueger, 2004; Caplan,

2006; Haferkamp et al., 2009; Hirshleifer, 2008; Rubin, 2003; Sowell, 2011; Wood, 2002; Worstall). However, there is still very little research on why such beliefs appear, and why they are so widespread.

We argue that many folk-views on the economy are strongly influenced by the operation of non-conscious inference systems that were shaped by natural selection during our unique evolutionary history, to provide intuitive solutions to such recurrent adaptive problems as maintaining fairness in exchange, cultivating reiterated social interaction, building efficient and stable coalitions, or adjudicating issues of ownership, all within small-scale groups of foragers.

The inference systems we describe further on are not specified as ad hoc explanations for folk-economic beliefs. All of these systems have been independently documented by evolutionary biologists, psychologists, and anthropologists who focus on such issues as the evolution of exchange and trade, its form in the small-scale societies in which humans evolved, and its consequences for psychological dispositions and preferences that can be observed in experimental studies on individuals in modern societies; for an overview, see Buss (2015). So, we are not proposing a new description or interpretation of the human evolved psychology of exchange, but rather, using prior findings to illuminate the emergence of folk-economic beliefs in modern contexts.

1.4 Models of Folk-Economic Beliefs Are Not Normative

The model described here is emphatically not a normative proposal. That is, we do not intend to suggest that there is a right way to consider economic processes, and to evaluate folk-economic beliefs in terms of their validity or coherence. This deserves mention, for two reasons.

First, as discussed below, most descriptions of these beliefs, in the literature, were originally motivated by the realization that people do not think like economists, and that they often commit what trained economists would describe as fallacies. By contrast, we argue that this is not a promising way of approaching cultural beliefs in this domain, as the validity (or lack thereof) of these beliefs do not explain their spread.

Second, because FEBs are politically consequential, readers may wonder whether studying them is by itself a political project. That would be the case if, for instance, widespread beliefs were contrasted with a supposedly true picture of the economy, and if that picture was associated with a particular kind of political project. But we suspect (and to a certain degree, the evidence confirms) that individuals of all kinds of political persuasions are equally likely to entertain beliefs that are, in some sense, misguided or incoherent.

Indeed, one could argue that the epistemic value of FEBs is largely orthogonal to their political import. That is, the economy is not a political end in itself but a political means to ends that are essentially contested. In principle, even completely misguided FEBs might give rise to outcomes that are, by some other standards, 'good' or 'just,' at least as far as some specific social group is concerned.

Our more general point is that we believe that the question of whether FEBs are correct or incorrect is orthogonal to the importance of studying them. Few individuals receive formal training in economics and, hence, if they happen to hold correct beliefs, this is as much in need of an explanation as when they generate incorrect ones.

2. Some Folk-Economic Beliefs and Possible Explanations

Evidence for folk-economic beliefs is still scattered and unsystematic. Some FEBs are widespread and well-documented, either through surveys of attitudes such as the General Social Survey (2011), or by more-specific, smaller-scale investigations such as the Kaiser Foundation's 'Survey of Americans and Economists on the Economy' (Kaiser Foundation, 1996). Others are less systematically documented, being inferred from the platforms and common phraseology of political operators, as well as from common journalistic discourse (Wood, 2002; Worstall).

2.1 Examples of Folk-Economic Beliefs

In the following, we present a few examples of widespread beliefs about the economy, selected for their potential influence on political choice. Given that such beliefs are often expressed in vague or emotional terms (e.g., 'markets are bad for society,' 'trade will make us poorer and others richer'), what we propose here are, by necessity, reconstructions of possible beliefs as implied by people's explicit statements or questionnaire responses.

FEB 1. International trade is zero-sum, has negative effects. The notion is expressed in many forms in everyday conversations and in political discourse, and it was also a recurrent theme in early political economy (Hainmueller & Hiscox, 2007). This belief may take many forms. For instance, trade is said to create unemployment at home because foreigners instead of locals are making the things we need (Wood, 2002, pp. 53–55). Also, it is claimed that a nation should always try to export more goods than it imports (Worstall, pp. 29–32). This belief is often associated with the assumption that the wealth of nations is the outcome of a zero-sum game. As a consequence, the assumption that foreigners profit from trade entails that 'we' are losing out. Consistent with this assumption, many people believe (against possible comparative advantage) that trade cannot be beneficial if 'we' import goods that we could manufacture ourselves (Baron & Kemp, 2004, p. 567). After the 2008 recession, many Americans interpreted increased unemployment as an effect of international trade and feared that continued trade would worsen their conditions (Mansfield et al., 2019).

FEB 2. Immigrants 'steal' jobs. Beliefs about the negative economic impact of immigration lie at the center of many policy debates. It is a consistent finding among political scientists that immigration, especially of low-skilled immigrants, is viewed as threatening (Hainmueller & Hiscox, 2010), and a common formulation is that immigrants 'take our jobs' (Simon & Lynch, 1999). This view is associated with the assumption that there is a fixed quantity of jobs to share among people (Wood, 2002, p. 23; Worstall, 2014, p. 75).

FEB 3. Immigrants abuse the welfare system. Another belief, almost diametrically opposite but equally widespread, is that immigrants are a fiscal burden on the welfare system, using up common resources (Sniderman et al., 2014). So, immigrants are intuitively viewed as free-riding both on the jobs 'we' created and the welfare systems 'we' paid for (Alesina & Glaeser, 2004). Given these beliefs, co-occurrences of immigration and fiscal stress can be viewed as causally linked, with important consequences in terms of both policy opinions and of holding immigration-friendly politicians accountable on Election Day.

FEB 4. Necessary social welfare programs are abused by scroungers. Welfare programs, for example, unemployment benefits, are the object of apparently opposing economic beliefs (Aarøe & Petersen, 2014; Alesina & Glaeser, 2004). Experimental studies show the coexistence of those contrary beliefs within individuals. On the one hand, welfare programs are viewed as desirable insurance schemes against unavoidable, essentially random misfortune. On the other hand, unemployment benefits are widely viewed as encouraging laziness and a culture of dependency (Aarøe & Petersen, 2014; Kameda et al., 2002).

FEB 5. <u>Markets have a negative social impact</u>. Rubin (2014) coined the term emporiophobia for the generally negative attitude towards markets observed in many modern societies and documented in many surveys. The belief is that markets as such produce negative outcomes for most participants. Surveys offer evidence that many people, against economists, see markets not as the encounter of buyers and sellers who mutually benefit from trade, but as a place of struggle between partners with unequal bargaining power. The anti-market attitude may also contribute to the rejection of market solutions for the allocation of 'sacred' goods, like organs or children in need of adoption. Many people seem to consider more arbitrary allocations (lotteries, first come first served) as not just fairer than auctions, but also probably more efficient (Alan Page Fiske & Tetlock, 1997; Tetlock et al., 2000)

FEB 6. <u>The profit motive is detrimental to general welfare</u>. The profit motive is seen as an attempt to extract more from transactions than would be warranted by 'fair' pricing. That is why there is a tendency to see private firms as less 'caring' than non-profits, and therefore more likely to create negative externalities (Bhattacharjee et al., 2017). One version of this belief is that there is a special class of 'excessive' profit that differs from the regular or fair allocation of profit to businesses (Wood, 2002, pp. 10–12). Related to this assumption is the notion that regulation is required to limit the excesses of profit-driven businesses (Hirshleifer, 2008). In general, then, the belief seems to be that if most economic actors act on the basis of maximizing their profits, non-economic social domains will be negatively affected, for example, by externalities such as pollution, or more generally through a decrease in solidarity, social trust, and so forth. Contra Adam Smith, the notion that private self-regard creates general welfare seems to be unintuitive (Rubin, 2003).

FEB 7. <u>Labor is the source of value</u>. This is the assumption that the amount of labor necessary to produce a good is an essential (or the only) factor that determines its 'value,' a (generally undefined) quantity that is not necessarily expressed by market price. This assumption is not often expressed in such general terms, but the proposition is implicit in many widespread beliefs about labor and wages (Wood, 2002, pp. 175–178; Worstall, pp. 15–17). It is also present in opinions on the unfairness of low wages for hard or unpleasant jobs, especially those involving hard physical labor.

FEB 8. <u>Price-regulation has the intended effects</u>. The belief is that regulation generally does what it is supposed to do, as government policy can direct the economy towards desired results (Hirshleifer, 2008); (Wood, 2002, p. 77). For example, in the United States, many cities imposed rent-control in the 1960s—and such measures were a major item in politicians' platforms (Dreier, 1999)—with the goal of creating an ample supply of cheap housing; see Schipper (2015) for similar processes in Israel. The FEB here is that such regulation efforts will work as intended, for example, that rents will stay low after the imposition of rent-control, or that minimum wages can affect wages without affecting the demand for labor (some people even think that the latter measure could boost employment rates (Haferkamp et al., 2009, p. 533). More broadly, regulation is often seen as an efficient way to protect people against undesirable market dynamics. Chinese respondents, for instance, believe that China was spared the worst effects of the 2008 downturn by its government regulations (Yuen & Greene, 2011).

This is only a short list of widespread folk-beliefs about the economy. Because there is very little study of such cultural beliefs as of yet, we have scant evidence for the relative cultural spread of each of these FEBs, and of possible associations between them and various social or cultural variables. The beliefs in question may well vary between social classes, cultures, age-groups, and so on. One aim of this article is to demonstrate the importance and theoretical interest of this domain of cultural beliefs and motivate more detailed empirical research in the domain.

2.2 Common Explanations: Ignorance, Self-Interest, Biases

There are three main ways of explaining the divergence between laypeople's and economists' views: in terms of ignorance, in terms of self-interest, or as the outcome of specific biases that affect people's perception of economic facts.

2.2.1. <u>Lack of economic knowledge or training</u>. The ignorance hypothesis simply assumes that non-normative views stem from a lack of relevant information, similar to the widespread ignorance in the political domain, long lamented by political scientists (Converse, 1964). It is certainly true that most laypeople are unaware of many fundamental principles of economic analysis. For instance, if people knew some rudiments of price theory, they would not be surprised that useful water is much cheaper than useless diamonds. If they knew about comparative advantage, they might see international trade in a different way (Haferkamp et al., 2009). However, this interpretation has one major defect—it predicts that people's common views will be non-normative, but it does not predict that they will be non-normative in any particular way. Not knowing about a domain would predict random, vague, or nonexistent opinions, as in popular conceptions of quantum mechanics, rather than the specific set of beliefs observed (Caplan, 2008, pp. 9–11).

2.2.2. <u>Self-interested beliefs</u>. If beliefs are not random, that may be because they are influenced by people's perception of their interests. In this view, people adopt beliefs that would justify more resources being apportioned to them and less to their enemies or competitors (Dahl & Ransom, 1999). One difficulty with this interpretation is that it accounts for only some of the beliefs described above. It can explain, for example, how industrial workers in the United States might feel they will lose out if their jobs move to China, and therefore consider that protectionism is overall a good thing. But beliefs are sometimes less clearly connected to self-interest. For instance, many people feel that markets are bad, even though larger, more competitive markets provide them with cheaper goods, which is clearly in their interest. So, self-interest is at best an incomplete explanation, and in general is not a straightforward predictor of economic beliefs, or indeed of political choices (Caplan, 2008; Green & Shapiro, 1994). It should be noted that one type of interest that does seem to explain some variation in FEBs is partisan interests. During economic downturns, for example, people are much more likely to ascribe the government responsibility if they identify with the opposition party than with the government party (Martin Bisgaard, 2015; M Bisgaard & Slothuus, 2018). However, although partisanship provides a motivation to reach certain conclusions (e.g., 'the government is responsible for this economic downturn' or 'the government is not responsible for this downturn'), the question still remains as to how people generate the particular beliefs about the workings of the economy that allow them to reach their desired conclusion.

2.2.3. Cognitive biases. Finally, another alternative to the knowledge gap is to consider that people's views are the outcome of specific biases. The term denotes tacit patterns of reasoning that orient people towards a limited set of conclusions from the evidence. There is a vast psychological literature for reasoning biases (Gilovich et al., 2002). For example, the 'confirmation bias' is the tendency to notice and remember instances of the hypotheses we hold and to ignore other cases as noise, with the result that prior assumptions seem ever more strongly confirmed.

In the domain of beliefs about the economy, Bryan Caplan, for instance, identified an anti-foreign bias (what is good for foreigners is bad for us), an anti-market bias (inability to see how markets would turn private greed into a social good), a make-work bias (if people work more, there will be more wealth), and a pessimistic bias (economies are heading towards less prosperity) (Caplan, 2008). In a similar way, Haferkamp et al. argue that the divergence between economists' and laypeople's views does not reduce to self-interest or ignorance, but rather results from multiple biases, like the well-documented status-quo bias and omission bias (doing something detrimental is worse than not doing something beneficial) (Haferkamp et al., 2009, p. 530). Finally, people's selection of economic beliefs often reflects own-side partisan bias (Martin Bisgaard, 2015).

2.3 Proximate and Ultimate Factors

Models based on identifying particular cognitive 'biases' have the merit of taking seriously the fact that the emergence of these beliefs may lie in the way information about the economy is processed in human minds, which is certainly the right starting point. However, we propose that the study of folk-economic beliefs should move beyond a description on terms of fallacies and biases. One major problem with bias-oriented accounts of cognitive phenomena is that a bias is often simply a re-description of the empirical phenomenon under investigation (Gigerenzer, 1991; Gigerenzer et al., 1999). For example, when it is observed that people attend more to more recent and vivid information, this is explained by an 'availability heuristic' that simply stipulates that people attend more to more recent information. In a sense, this is fine; after all, science requires the systematization of observations about the world. But explanations require causal models as well.

Within the biological sciences, researchers distinguish between 'proximate' and 'ultimate' explanations, where proximate explanations describe how a biological system works and ultimate ones explain why the system exists (Buss et al., 1998; T. C. Scott-Phillips et al., 2011). Bias-based models are largely equivalent to proximate explanations. To develop a scientific understanding of folk-economic beliefs, we need to attend also to the level of ultimate explanations, not just because doing so provides a more complete understanding, but also because we will then be able to develop more precise predictions about the psychology behind folk-economic beliefs.

3. Our Model: Inference Systems, Beliefs, Cultural Transmission

In the model we propose here, the emergence and spread of folk-economic beliefs is influenced by specific intuitions about interpersonal exchange. These are not the outcome of explicit scholarly training. Nor are they the simple consequence of persuasion from political elites (politicians, journalists, pundits, etc.), or the straightforward absorption of particular cultural values. Rather, because of evolution in the context of small groups with intensive exchange, humans have developed an intuitive psychology of exchange, for which there is independent anthropological and psychological evidence (Cosmides & Tooby, 2015a). This psychology consists of a collection of highly specialized inference systems, each of which is designed to solve one kind of exchange problem recurrent in our ancestral environments.

3.1 Properties of Domain-Specific Inference Systems

We can describe the mind as consisting of many distinct, specialized systems, each of which corresponds to recurrent adaptive challenges in human evolution, attends to limited domains of available information, is organized along specific inferential principles, orchestrates neural structures in a specific functional manner, and is the outcome of a specific developmental pathway (Boyer & Barrett, 2015; Cosmides & Tooby, 2015b; Hirschfeld & Gelman, 1994).

A few examples may help illustrate the relevant functional properties of this broad class of cognitive systems. In the auditory stream, the sound events identified as instances of lexical items are handled by a parsing system that assigns various syntactic roles to the different words (Pickering & van Gompel). In the visual field, some configurations are identified as human faces by a face-recognition system that computes a holistic description of the face, which is then processed by other memory and affective systems (Kanwisher, 2000; Solomon-Harris et al., 2013; Tsao & Livingstone, 2008). Information from multiple modalities is integrated to compute the extent to which a particular person is attractive as a potential mate (Fink & Penton-Voak, 2002; Grammer & Thornhill, 1994).

However different the domains, there are some important functional properties common to these systems:

1. Specific input format. The face-identification systems respond to visual displays that include points or lines interpreted as eyes and mouth. Any such elements presented in the appropriate configuration trigger the system, which is why cartoons and other stylized renditions of human faces activate it, whereas displays with scrambled features, or features in the wrong alignment, do not. The parsing system responds only to words in the stream of speech. Other sounds are not processed. Sexual attractiveness computations only consider very narrow aspects of information about a person, for example, the pitch of the voice rather than prosody, skin-reflectance (an index of youth) rather than skin-tone, facial symmetry rather than facial length, and so on. In general, then, domain-specific inference systems may ignore information that might be relevant to an organism but fails to meet the input conditions.

2. Automatic activation. Specialized inference systems are neither initiated nor stopped by deliberate intentions. Once information with the appropriate input format is detected, the systems proceed to produce the relevant inferences, which are then passed on to other inference systems.

3. Specific inference rules. Each system operates on highly specific inferential rules. The computational principles that assign words to their syntactic roles are found only in that domain, and the same goes for the matching between faces and memories about persons, or the computation of sexual attractiveness.

4. Unconscious computation. The operation and inference rules of each system are generally outside conscious access. Only some outputs of these computational systems can be accessed, such as, for example, the meaning of a sentence or the general attractiveness of an individual.

5. Intuitive output. The output of specialized inference systems, when consciously accessible, consists of intuitions—that is, a description of a particular situation or a motivation to behave in a particular way—that do not include any indication of the computational steps that resulted in that particular description or motivation.

3.2 Intuitive Systems Output Can Lead to Reflective Beliefs

It is important here to keep in mind the difference between intuitive output on the one hand, and reflective representations on the other (Sperber, 1997). Reflective representations add information to intuitions, explicate them, extend or restrict their scope, offer a comment on the intuitions, or link them to specific sources, as in, for example, 'the reason this sentence is strange is that there is no verb,' or 'this person has the same round face as Humpty Dumpty,' or 'it is sad that this attractive person has a bad personality,' and so forth (Cosmides & Tooby, 2000; Sperber, 1997, 2000).

Most of our 'folk-theories' of particular domains consist of explicit, conscious reflective beliefs about our intuitions. That is why we can better understand the diffusion of beliefs in social groups, if we follow closely the interaction between intuitions delivered by specialized inference systems, on the one hand, and their reflective interpretation, on the other.

Here, again, examples may be of help. Human minds include an intuitive physics, a set of assumptions that helps us predict the trajectory of objects, expect solid objects to collide when their trajectories intersect, and so forth. These expectations appear early in infancy long before language acquisition (Baillargeon et al., 1995; Spelke et al.). But we can also entertain explicit thoughts that (to some extent) explicate and comment on these intuitions, for example, a belief that heavy objects have more momentum than lighter ones. Some of these reflective beliefs are wrong, others are too vague even to be wrong, and some are in agreement with physical science (Kaiser et al., 1986). In the same way, we have a set of intuitive biological expectations, for example, that all living things come in exclusive, taxonomically ordered categories (Atran, 1995), and that they are propelled by internal energy sources (R. Gelman et al., 1995; Tremoulet & Feldman, 2000). But we also have reflective and explicit beliefs, for example, that each species has unique essential properties that cannot change (S. A. Gelman & Wellman, 1991); that there must be some 'catness' about cats that makes them what they are. Here, the intuitive expectation (all cats share external features, their behavior is highly predictable, etc.) is explained by the reflective belief, which postulates a hidden, undefined essence inside organisms of the same species.

Folk-economic beliefs are widespread, culturally transmitted, explicitly held reflective beliefs about economic processes. These are to be distinguished from the intuitive thoughts that emerge as a result of the operation of specialized intuitive systems. We reserve the term 'folk' for beliefs held by layfolk as a result of the interaction between information about the economy, and the operation of some inference systems. (This is in contrast to some parts of the psychological literature, where the term folk has been sometimes, confusingly, used to characterize both the products of intuitive inference systems and the cultural beliefs that emerge as a result of their operation.)

3.3 Why We Should Not Expect Consistency or Coherence in FEBs

Explicit reflective beliefs may be extremely vague in their implications. One may hold that there must be a special essence present in all cats that makes them different from dogs, without specifying what that essence consists of—in fact, that is the most common form of essentialism (S. A. Gelman, 2004).

Also, reflective beliefs may be inconsistent or incoherent, mostly because they come in a meta-representational format. In contrast to the output of intuitive systems, for example, the intuitive belief that 'there is a cat here on the mat,' reflective beliefs consist in comments on intuitions, for example, 'it is true in some sense that "the market is bad."' A meta-representational format allows one to be committed to a belief, without the contents of the belief being processed in detail (Cosmides & Tooby, 2000; Mercier & Sperber, 2009; Sperber, 1997). That is the case for mystical or religious statements, for example, 'the true path is not a path' or 'three persons are one being,' which people can hold to be true, in the form 'the proper interpretation of 'p' is true,' without processing their contents (Mercier & Sperber, 2009; Sperber, 1997).

This applies to the domain of folk-economic beliefs as well. A belief that markets are socially negative can be held true, without triggering specific representations about, for example, how markets would decrease social welfare, in what domains of activity, to what extent, through what economic mechanisms, and so forth, as long as it is held in a meta-representational format, for example, 'It is true in some sense that "markets are bad for society."' For the same reason, one can hold that meta-representational belief, and also hold other beliefs that may seem to contradict it, for example, 'It is a good thing that we have many butchers here, so they have to keep prices low.' Finally, if folk-economic opinions consist of reflective, meta-representational beliefs, then different beliefs can be held in relative isolation from each other without ever being integrated in a general theory of the economy. So, we should not expect precision, consistency, or integration in the domain of reflective folk-economic beliefs.

3.4 Proposed Mechanism: Intuitions, Beliefs, Cultural Transmission

Folk-economic beliefs are cultural beliefs—which simply means that they are represented in roughly similar ways in the minds of different individuals in a group, as a result of communication between individuals. Folk-economic beliefs are communicated—between laypeople, but also between media and their customers, and between political entrepreneurs and the public. That is why it is important to consider the mechanisms that lead to their cultural spread, that is, the extent to which they are likely to be entertained, in roughly similar ways, by different minds.

An essential component of cognitive theories of cultural transmission is that prior psychological assumptions and expectations make certain representations easier to acquire, store, and communicate than others (Boyd & Richerson, 1985; Sperber, 1991). Cognitive dispositions make people transform input in such a way that it is more similar to the types that match these dispositions, an 'attraction' process that results in the spread of highly particular mental representations (Claidière et al., 2014).

In Section 4, we document the existence of various intuitive inference systems dedicated to representing social exchange. We then examine how these different systems make particular views of the economy, in general, particularly easy to acquire and represent, turning them into cultural beliefs.

4. Relevant Cognitive Systems

4.1 Relevant Systems Evolved before and outside Markets

Evolutionary theory predicts that cognitive systems are geared towards solving specific, recurrent problems in environments in which humans evolved. Specifically, what evolutionary theorists call the environment of evolutionary adaptedness (or EEA) for a trait is a statistical construct, an aggregate of the conditions under which there was selection for or against that trait, weighted for frequency and time. In that sense, the EEA is not a particular time or place, but a collection of features. As an illustration, we can consider that optimization problems such as hunting, foraging, choosing the best mate, selecting nutritious foods, and garnering social support were present, and relevant to fitness, throughout human evolution. By contrast, urban life, mass-communication, rapid long-distance travel, and mass-market economies only occurred for a small duration and only in some places at first. So it is more plausible that human minds were selected for systems geared to the first kind of adaptive problems, than to the second.

One feature that is universally prominent in both modern and ancestral human societies is the exchange of goods (e.g., tools, food) and services (everything from back-up in conflicts to help with hunting, foraging, parenting, or shelter-building) (Brown, 1991). Developmental psychology studies show that children readily engage in exchange in early years (Levitt et al., 1985). Exchange provides significant fitness benefits. It allowed our ancestors, as it allows us, to exploit cooperative positive-sum games, engage in collective action, and buffer against predicaments such as hunger and injury (Gurven, 2004; Sugiyama, 2004). For us and for our ancestors, engaging in exchange requires the existence of distinct, specialized cognitive mechanisms (Cosmides & Tooby, 1992), including mechanisms for estimating costs and benefits of goods and services for the self and other; for comparing them in an abstract format (equivalent to utility in the vocabulary of economics); and for motivating exchange when the benefits of exchange exceed the costs for oneself.

The human mind, in other words, contains a rudimentary exchange psychology, evolved by natural selection to help facilitate transactions. Although it evolved within ancestral small-scale hunter-gatherer groups, the cues inherent in modern markets economies (transactions, bargaining, prices, etc.) also bring it online. However, market economies are a novelty at the scale of biological evolution, so we should not expect specific adaptations to their features, as the differences between ancestral exchange and the market are vast (Rubin, 2003).

A crucial difference is that economic activity in nonmarket societies, and by extension during most of human evolution, does not and did not take place in isolation from other aspects of social interaction. Indeed, the clear separation between economic exchange and other forms of social interaction is a by-product of market conditions (Polanyi, 2001). Throughout human evolution, most transactions affected not only the agents' welfare, what they gained or lost on the spot, but also their reputation, their social standing, the nature of their relationship to exchange partners, the extent to which they could rely on others, the cohesiveness of the groups they belonged to, and so forth. That is why mechanisms for reasoning about exchange are designed to take in a whole range of social considerations that are not relevant in the impersonal modern market.

In the following pages, we examine some of the systems that evolved to facilitate exchange, the evidence for their operating principles, and their potential effects on the perception of modern market phenomena.

4.2 Detecting Free-Riders in Collective Action

In any exchange, it is crucial to monitor whether the implicit or explicit terms of the exchange are being followed. For example, if two individuals take turns helping each other forage, does one person provide less help than he receives? To solve this problem, human exchange psychology needs to contain specific mechanisms for detecting and responding to free-riders. There is considerable evidence that humans, in general, are attentive to potential cheating in social exchanges, so proximate psychological mechanisms are congruent with the ultimate fitness benefit of detecting and deterring free-riders. Indeed, a situation where some agent has taken a benefit without paying the cost for it is psychologically more salient than the opposite situation of an agent paying some cost but not getting the associated benefit (Cosmides, 1989; Cosmides & Tooby, 2005; Gigerenzer & Hug, 1992; Sugiyama et al., 2002). Also, information that some agent received benefits from cooperation without contributing triggers punitive motivations, as a way of depriving them of the benefits of free-riding (Price et al., 2002). The ultimate rationale for free-riding detection is to preserve cooperation, including in the future. This would suggest that we do not intuitively classify as free-riders those individuals who make honest mistakes or whom accidents bar from cooperating. Indeed, Delton et al. have shown that the intuitive freerider categorization is highly sensitive to intentions, rather than just tallying who contributed what to the collective action (Delton et al., 2012).

4.3 Partner-Choice for Exchange

To engage in exchange, one needs to choose among available social partners. Given the possibility of choice, human exchange and cooperation from ancestral times have taken place in the context of competition for cooperation (Noë & Hammerstein, 1994), as each agent could advertise a willingness to cooperate (and signal how advantageous cooperation would be), and could choose or reject partners depending on their past and potential future behavior (Barclay, 2016; Delton & Robertson, 2012; Panchanathan & Boyd, 2004). Cases of mutualism between species illustrate the efficiency of partner-choice for stabilizing mutually beneficial cooperation, for example, between cleaner fish and their clients (Bshary & Grutter, 2005). Human communicative abilities allow this kind of mutualism to occur between conspecifics, with reputation as an essential factor in the selection of partners. Agents have access to information about other agents' past interactions as an index of likely future behaviors. In such conditions, there is of course a cost in engaging with free-riders, but also a cost in not cooperating with an honest partner (in terms of potential cooperative positive-sum games) (Krasnow et al., 2012; Milinski et al., 2002). Competition for cooperation has specific consequences on fairness intuitions in the context of collective action. Given that two (or more) partners contribute equal effort to a joint endeavor, and receive benefits from it, an offer to split the benefits equally is likely to emerge as the most frequent strategy— anyone faced with a meaner division of spoils will be motivated to seek a more advantageous offer from other partners. So, to the extent that people have partner options, the constraints of partner-choice explain the spontaneous intuition that benefits from collective action must be proportional to each agent's contribution (André, 2010; André & Baumard, 2011; André & Day, 2007).

The existence of partner-choice based on shared information and reputation may explain why people select partners, in the context of laboratory economic games, on the basis of criteria that may seem economically irrational, but that happened to be ecologically predictive in our environments of evolution. For instance, people prefer partners who express moral judgments in deontic (i.e., 'moral' and emotional) rather than rational terms (Everett et al., 2016). They also prefer potential partners whose faces suggest productivity, prosocial attitudes, and relatively high social status (Eisenbruch et al., 2016).

4.4 Exchange and Assurance by Communal Sharing

One important form of social relations is founded on communal sharing, where resources are pooled (Alan P Fiske, 1992). This is found to some variable extent in all human groups, particularly in food provision, and seems crucial to social interaction in small-scale societies, especially in foraging economies similar to those in which humans evolved (Kelly, 1995). That is why this form of apparently unconditional altruism has been the focus of so much research in evolutionary anthropology and psychology (Kaplan et al., 2005). A major result of those observations and models is that communal allocations is not the outcome of an indiscriminate motivation to share with others, but rather follows implicit rules that make sense given the conditions of human evolution.

For example, band-wide sharing in hunter-gatherer economies is generally confined to game, especially large game, whereas gathered and extracted foods are mostly shared with close kin. An explanation for this spontaneous preference in allocations lies in the differences in variance in the supply of these goods (Cosmides & Tooby, 1992), as gathering typically produces low-variance resources, in contrast with hit-or-miss hunting expeditions. So communal sharing provides insurance against random bad luck such as the vicissitudes of hunting expeditions (Kaplan & Hill, 1985) or injury that prevents hunters from going on expeditions (Sugiyama, 2004). This is reinforced by the low marginal value of food units when they come in large packages, like big game. Communal sharing, although typically presented as including all group members, is often in fact modulated by past or expected reciprocation. Even where there is a norm of unconditional sharing, those who give more freely also receive more (Gurven, 2004; Gurven et al., 2000). Communal sharing is founded on specific assumptions and principles, distinct from those that govern, for example, direct exchange or authority-based social relations (Alan P Fiske, 1992). The norm of communal sharing is readily acquired by children, and intuitively deployed by adults in the appropriate contexts (Birch & Billman, 1986; Hamann et al., 2011; Rao & Stewart, 1999). In different places, different sets of resources and occasions are designated as proper goods to share. People notice (and are usually shocked by) the application of one type of inference system to the wrong domain according to the local norms, for example, offering to pay your friends for coming to dinner, or asking for a discount as a personal favor at a supermarket checkout.

The structure of the psychology for exchange resources through communal sharing implies that if people find that a need is caused by random circumstances beyond their own control, they intuitively represent that need as potentially alleviated through communal sharing. By consequence, they would think it as unfair if others try to profit from this type of need (i.e., turning the exchange into a direct form of exchange rather than communal sharing).

4.5 Coalitional Affiliation

Humans are special in that they build and maintain highly stable associations bounded by reciprocal and mutual duties and expectations. Such groups—called alliances or coalitions—may be found at many different levels of organization, such as political parties, street gangs, office cliques, academic cabals, and groups of close friends, and can include thousands or millions of individuals when ethnic or national categories are construed as coalitions (Tooby & Cosmides, 2010).

The psychology underlying coalitional strategies include the following assumptions: (a) relevant payoffs to other members of the coalition are considered as gains for self (and obviously, negative payoffs as losses to self); (b) payoffs for rival coalitions are assumed to be zero-sum—the rival coalition's success is our loss, and vice-versa; and (c) the other members' commitment to the common goal is crucial to one's own welfare (Pietraszewski, 2013, 2016). These assumptions reflect two crucial selection pressures operating on human groups: First, that alliances are competitive and exclusive, because social support is a rival good. Second, that resources, status, and many other goods are zero-sum and, hence, the object for rivalry between alliances. As consequence, allied agents spontaneously share the intuition that achieving their goal requires avoiding or overcoming opposition from other, similar alliances and coalitions in a zero-sum fashion (Tooby & Cosmides, 2010).

A vast literature in social psychology and behavioral economics documents the proximate psychological mechanisms involved in coalitional situations. For instance, people do indeed consider benefits for the coalition as (presumed) benefits for themselves (Baron, 2001). Second, social psychology studies of in-group favoritism show how very subtle cues of group membership and coalitional rivalry can activate coalitional assumptions. In so-called minimal group paradigms, people favor fellow members of an arbitrarily constructed category (Tajfel, 1970). This occurs when the categories in question are construed by participants as groups within which members can reciprocate favors (Karp et al., 1993; Kiyonari & Yamagishi, 2004).

In human coalitions, members monitor each other's level of commitment, are motivated to demonstrate their commitment to the other members, and are also motivated to make defection less likely, notably by making it costly. Monitoring of other people's behavior is frequent, all the more so if the collective action is risky and success is crucially dependent on numbers. Such surveillance is manifest in voluntary groups and associations, and the extent to which monitoring is possible is a predictor of group stability (M Hechter, 1987, pp. 146–156).

4.6 Ownership Psychology

For exchange to happen over human evolutionary history, our ancestors needed an elaborate psychology of ownership. Who is entitled to enjoy possession of a good, and to exchange it? Ownership is expressed in all human languages (Heine, 1997); in all human cultures, there is a principled distinction between mere possession and ownership; and ownership is associated everywhere with specific emotions and motivations (Brown, 1991). At the same time, explicit norms of ownership and property rights differ from one place or time to another in terms of both scope (who can own things and what things can be owned) and implications (what one may do with specific types of property) (Hann, 1998). Surprisingly, despite a long history of legal and economic reflection on property, there are only recent and relatively sparse experimental studies of our spontaneous intuitions about use, possession, and ownership (Boyer, 2015; DeScioli & Karpoff, 2015; O. Friedman, 2010).

We must distinguish between intuitions and reflective representations about ownership. Adults and even very young children have definite intuitions about who owns what particular good, in a specific situation. For instance, they generally assume that ownership applies to rival resources (that is, such that one person's enjoyment of the resource diminishes another person's); that prior possession implies ownership; that extracting a resource from the environment makes one the owner; that transforming an existing resource confers ownership rights; and that ownership can be transferred, but only through codified interactions (O. Friedman et al., 2011). By contrast, people's explicit beliefs about ownership are often vague and sometimes incoherent (Noles & Keil, 2011). Also, these explicit, reflective norms often do not even reflect actual legal practices. In fact, people who live in societies with legal systems generally (and often wrongly) assume that the law must somehow accord with their intuitions—see County and Ellickson (1991) for an illustration in the domain of externalities and tort.

In terms of proximate mechanisms, this suggests that the inference system takes as its input information about specific connections between a thing and an agent and outputs an 'owner' tag. In particular, this system is highly sensitive to such cues as first possession (O. Friedman & Neary, 2008), but also to information about an object's history (e.g., past possession, transactions between past and present possessor) (Blake & Harris, 2009; O. Friedman et al., 2011), as well as the work invested in the object by its current possessor; even young children consider that creative work that transforms an object creates, at least presumptively, a claim to ownership (Kanngiesser et al., 2010).

5. Effects of Intuitive Systems on Folk-Economic Beliefs

In our model, folk-economic beliefs are a result of the activation of the intuitive systems for exchange described above (and many others). The processes are illustrated in Figure 2 below. Information about economic processes, from news media, political discourse, from occasional pronouncements by economists, from other individuals, or any other sources, sometimes happens to match the input conditions of some intuitive inference system. As a consequence, the system is activated and produces specific inferences in the form of intuitive representations. These intuitive representations, in some cases, become the object of explicit, deliberate reflections, which may attribute an intuition to a source, put together several intuitive inferences, or compare them, or provide an explanatory context for intuitions, giving rise to folk-economic beliefs.

In this context, it is also worth emphasizing again that a single belief need not be the product of a single, intuitive inference system. The more inference systems that are underlying a particular belief, the more cognitive scaffolding it receives (see Fig. 2).

In the following sections (5.1. to 5.6), we discuss the possible connections between specific evolved inference systems and specific folk-economic beliefs—that is, how activation of the systems may make a particular belief received from external sources more natural and compelling. The examples that we draw on are meant as mere

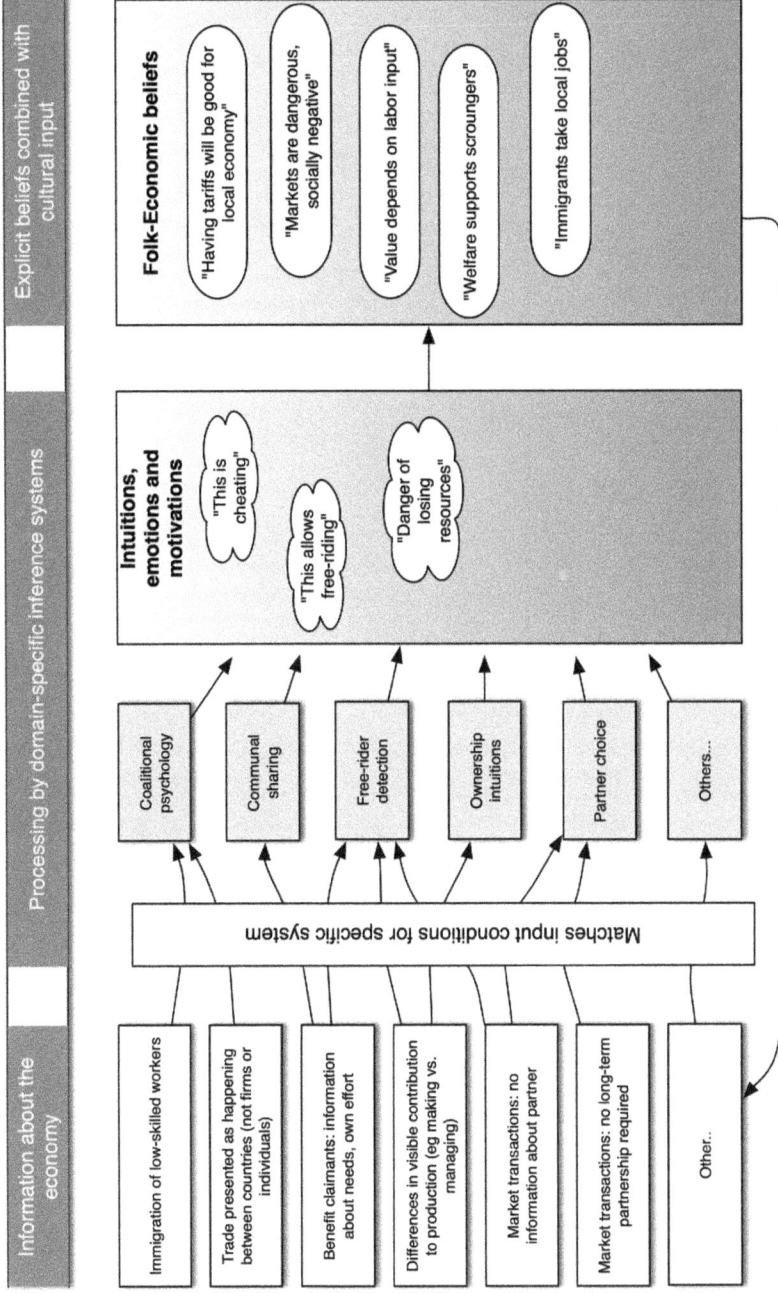

Fig. 2. Illustration of the sequence of cognitive processes involved in acquisition of economy-related information and generation of folk-economic beliefs. (Figure by P Boyer. 2017)

illustrations of many potential connections, providing the first small steps towards an empirical research program.

5.1 Explaining FEB 1: International Trade as Coalitional Rivalry

We begin with what we referred to above as FEB 1, the statement that international trade has negative consequences. This contains several pieces of information likely to activate specific inference systems. Let us consider a news headline like 'China sells more to the U.S. than to Russia.' Selling involves receiving resources and, importantly, resources in this case transfer from one nation to another. In psychological terms, nations are 'imagined communities' (Anderson, 1983) or, with the vocabulary presented above, nations are coalitions to the mind and, hence, mention of nations activates the coalitional psychological machinery (Gat, 2006; Michael Hechter, 1987). Nations are exclusive groups, citizens of a nation are assumed to have common interests, and nations are equipped with armies to fight each other. The activation of this machinery has the downstream consequence, we argue, that Americans will evaluate the transfer of resources to China—and, hence, the headline—negatively. As argued above, one key assumption of the coalitional system, once activated about two categories or groups, is that there is a zero-sum interaction between the mutually exclusive groups. As a consequence, there is a strong prior belief that any advantage to another group is detrimental to one's own (Hiscox, 2006). Any information to the effect that other groups are prosperous, or getting better, is equivalent to a threat-cue, indicating that our group stands to lose out.

It is relevant to note how this interpretation of FEB 1 (i.e., the disadvantage of trade) is different from the standard 'fallacy'-oriented interpretation. According to our view, FEB 1 does not occur as a result of any cognitive or intellectual dysfunction. Instead, we argue that the zero-sum assumption is part of the design of coalitional reasoning. The resulting motivations are part of the architecture of this system. To maintain stable and efficient coalitions, humans in many different contexts must have assumed that other groups' advantage was a potential loss.

Viewing the 'international trade is bad' belief as supported by coalitional psychology does not just explain the belief but also suggests novel testable predictions. In particular, we should expect the view that trade is bad to be particularly attractive when the trading crosses perceived coalitional boundaries. It is predicted to invariably occur in the context of, precisely, debates about trade between countries. American consumers may find it intuitive that the United States might suffer from Chinese prosperity, but, on this theory, they would find it less compelling that development in Vermont damages the economy of Texas. Similarly, the survival value of the belief might depend on the relationship between the countries. Trading between long-term allies (e.g., trading between Great Britain and the United States) should be viewed as less problematic than trading between rivals (e.g., trading between China and the United States), even if all else were equal.

5.2 Explaining FEB 2 and FEB 3: Immigration and the Dual Activation of the Psychologies of Coalitions and Cheater-Detection

In Section 2, we outlined two FEBs about immigration. FEB 2 is the belief that immigrants 'steal' jobs and FEB 3 the somewhat contrary belief that 'immigrants abuse welfare systems.' Although these two beliefs seem inconsistent (how can immigrants take both jobs and unemployment benefits?), they do share a key common assumption, a stipulation that immigrants use up valuable resources to which they are not entitled. This assumption, we argue, is what makes either of these ideas resonate with the evolved psychology of social exchange.

Specifically, the representation of recipients as not entitled to resources receives support from the interaction of two crucial inference systems: (a) coalitional psychology, and (b) cheater-detection. Immigrants are by definition newcomers to the community. Psychological research has shown that newcomers to groups activate this connection between coalitional cognition and cheater-detection, in particular, in situations where group membership is construed as conferring particular benefits. In such situations, newcomers are typically regarded with great suspicion.

Cimino and colleagues interpret this in terms of cheater-detection. When new members join a group, they are in a position to receive some of the benefits of membership (e.g., becoming a Marine makes one a respected member of a prestigious military corps), without having (yet) paid any costs (e.g., risked one's life in action). This combination of features may activate cheater-detection mechanisms, as persons in this situation effectively meet the input criterion of Benefit Received without Cost Paid, which would explain the considerable hostility towards newcomers in many voluntary groups that is sometimes expressed in the form of painful hazing and initiation rituals (Cimino, 2011). Experiments show that there is indeed an implicit concept of NEWCOMER that motivates such aggressive attitude, even when people consider membership in imaginary groups (Cimino & Delton, 2010; Delton & Cimino, 2010).

The tight relationship between the concepts of nation and coalition may explain the attractiveness of the statement that immigrants must be free-riders, scrounging on the past efforts of the host community. But, at the same time, the involved psychological systems leave open whether it is on job creation or on the welfare system that immigrants free-ride.

This interpretation suggests new research avenues. The argument is that the public's intuitions about the economic effects of immigration does not just reflect diffuse prejudice (Stephan et al., 1999) but is the outcome of very precise psychological mechanisms that work in tandem with beliefs about jobs, the welfare state, and so on, as collectively produced resources. As a consequence, it will be difficult for immigrant populations to behave in ways that increase acceptance by the native population. Any involvement with what is construed as a 'resource' is likely to trigger intuitions of free-riding—see, for example, Guimond et al. (2010). Furthermore, our interpretation suggests that there is an intimate connection between the perceived motivations of immigrants and the presumed economic consequences of immigration. Only in instances where specific immigrant groups are seen as willing to sacrifice self-interest for collective goods—that is, the exact opposite of free-riding motivations—should the public view the economic effects as positive.

Finally, this shows that there is no one-to-one mapping from specific systems for social exchange and specific FEBs. When FEBs—sometimes contradictory ones like FEB 2 and FEB 3—become culturally available, their acceptance depends on the degree to which they resonate with human exchange psychology. In this particular case, it is the dual appeal of the FEBs to both coalitional psychology and cheater-detection psychology that ensures their cultural survival in the minds of the public.

5.3 Explaining FEB 4: Social Welfare and Intuitions about Free Riding and Communal Sharing

FEB 4 refers to beliefs about the effects of economic investments in welfare programs. In fact, as laid out in Section 2, folk-economic beliefs about these effects consist of two separate and diametrically opposed beliefs. One belief is that unemployment benefit programs, for instance, lead to decreased economic activity because welfare programs benefit unproductive individuals. Another belief is that, in the long run, these benefits increase economic activity because they sustain productive individuals during periods of bad luck and, hence, facilitate the transition to new jobs. These opposite beliefs are not randomly distributed. In fact, their distribution demonstrates our key point about the relevance of FEBs: that they are associated with particular political positions. Support for welfare programs is strongly related to the belief that they sustain unfortunate individuals. Opposition to welfare programs is strongly related to the belief that they sustain unproductive—that is, lazy—individuals.

In our perspective, beliefs surrounding welfare programs—and, in particular, the link between beliefs about welfare recipients' productivity and support for welfare programs—are a key example of how psychological adaptations designed for social exchange shape economic policy views. What is surprising is not just the existence but also the strength of this link between perceived character of recipients and presumed economic benefits of welfare programs. In one of the most extensive studies of Americans' views on welfare, Gilens (1999) concluded that the perception of welfare recipients as 'undeserving' is the strongest predictor of individual-level opposition to welfare programs. This, we argue, is a consequence of the way in which the cues surrounding welfare programs activates mechanisms designed for cheater-detection.

Debates about welfare programs contain a number of cues that should elicit cheater-detection psychology. Welfare recipients are in need, and welfare programs provide benefits to the recipients and does so at a cost for the collective. For a mind designed to scan the social environment for cheaters, this particular set of cues automatically raises the question: Have the recipients paid sufficient costs in order to be entitled to these benefits? (Petersen et al., 2012). Or, more specifically: Are the recipients valuable enough as cooperation partners to be included within the exchange system? This, then, motivates scanning for additional information about the cooperative motivations of welfare recipients, activating either cheater-avoidance motivations (if low) or communal sharing motivations (if high), and, in the end, providing an exceptionally fertile soil for infusing economic opinions with beliefs about whether or not welfare recipients are lazy.

This psychological process is one of the more well studied aspects of folk-economics. The most direct test comes from a series of studies utilizing the memory confusion paradigm. They suggest that welfare recipients are mentally represented by activating the exact same psychological categories that people use to represent cheaters and reciprocators in everyday social interaction (Petersen, 2012). The results show that memory processes confuse lazy welfare recipients with everyday cheaters and unfortunate recipients with everyday reciprocators (but not lazy recipients and everyday reciprocators or unfortunate recipients with cheaters). Participants in these studies even forget whether those specific individuals were presented in the context of economically relevant welfare debates or everyday face-to-face interaction. This process operates in a similar fashion, regardless of people's political ideology, their level of political engagement, and whether they live in a society with an expansive welfare state (Denmark) or a reduced one (United States).

This particular explanation for FEB 4 makes sense of empirical findings concerning the relationship between cultural factors and beliefs about welfare. Individuals with liberal or left-leaning views tend to view social welfare recipients as productive individuals. Individuals with conservative or right-leaning views tend to view welfare recipients as unproductive individuals. Similarly, in social democratic societies, the former belief tends to dominate, whereas the latter belief dominates in societies with minimal welfare states. As consequence, cultural explanations have largely dominated the literature. For example, Americans' perception that many welfare recipients are lazy, and the association with anti-welfare sentiments, has been argued to reflect an 'individualistic' American culture (Gilens, 1999). Similar arguments have been made with regard to right-wing ideology: that it contains an 'ideological script' that binds together perceptions of laziness and welfare opposition in the mind of right-wing individuals (Skitka & Tetlock, 1993). From the evolutionary cognitive perspective, however, this structure is imposed by evolved mechanisms for exchange that are operating flexibly on the available cues. As a consequence, it should be easy to reverse apparently stable cultural patterns in welfare beliefs, if the right cues are provided. Research shows that this is indeed the case. Among a sample of Danish political science majors (who should be able to reason ideologically), ideological differences in opinions completely disappear when the participants form views about the deservingness of recipients cast as either lazy or unfortunate (Petersen et al., 2012). Even more dramatically, cultural differences between Scandinavians and Americans in support for the welfare state completely disappear when participants from these populations have to form views about specific recipients. Two sentences of text that contain evolutionarily relevant cues for cheater-detection are enough to displace 150 years of historical experience with two very different welfare systems (Aarøe & Petersen, 2014).

Another insight from the evolutionary cognitive perspective is that people's priority with regard to welfare economy is not so much to ensure a particular overall distribution of resources but more to ensure that resources go to the right individuals. Although the notion that people generally prefer equal to unequal distributions of resources (Fehr & Schmidt, 2006) has been popular, recent research suggests that people are much more concerned with a fair distribution. Unequal distributions are perfectly acceptable, if those who are bypassed are viewed as cheaters (Starmans et al., 2017).

5.4 Explaining FEBs 5 and 6: Impersonal Markets and Mechanisms for Partner-Choice

A common feature across numerous FEBs is the notion that markets are, in different ways, 'bad' for general welfare. FEB 5 is an expression of what Rubin (2014) called emporiophobia. FEB 6 refers to the more specific notion that transactions on the market are somehow 'unfair.' There is a common thread in these beliefs, the role of perceived social motivations. In most cases, the perceived negative effects of the market are seen as originating from particular sets of social motivations, believed to be pervasive in market transactions. From a cognitive evolutionary perspective, we argue, these beliefs emerge naturally due to the way market interactions differ from the types of social exchanges we evolved to value.

Specifically, to explain these FEBs, we need to describe in cognitive terms, in what way market transactions are, as is often claimed, 'impersonal.' This description combines several features of potential relevance to our intuitive systems. First, people in modern conditions do not in principle need information about their exchange partners, beyond knowledge of their positions (seller, buyer), the particular goods they sell or buy, and their price. Second, there is no expectation that considerations other than price and utility should govern people's behaviors in such exchanges. That is, you may be interested in patronizing local stores because that helps keep the town pleasant, but that motivation is clearly extrinsic to the terms of exchange. Third, there is no expectation of reiterated transactions. One can in principle behave in opportunistic ways, patronizing Baker A when his prices are lower and defecting to Baker B when that is more advantageous.

These features all constitute advantages of market transactions from an economic standpoint. Yet, for intuitive inference systems designed for established, long-term, cooperative exchange, these same features will be interpreted in a different manner—as threat-cues. First, our partner-choice system requires that the parties in a transaction be identifiable as specific individuals. In small-scale interactions, the balancing of costs and benefits occurs over reiterated exchanges, and, in order to predict these long-term outcomes, information about the partner's reputation and past exchanges are key. Impersonal transactions, in contrast, are often anonymous, and therefore make it more difficult to track the reputation of one's partners. To a psychology designed for partner-choice, this is likely to trigger an alarm signal, indicating that such a situation should be avoided. Second, strictly impersonal exchange goes against motivations to generate bonds of cooperation with particular individuals, as a form of social insurance. This may reinforce the intuition that impersonal transactions involve, if not danger, at least a missed opportunity. Finally, systems for partner-choice are set up to avoid engaging in exchange relationships with individuals who are much more powerful, in order to avoid exploitation (Petersen, 2013; Trivers, 1971). In modern markets, however, many exchanges take place with corporations or business that seem exceptionally powerful from the perspective of the individual. While these corporations are actually affected by consumer choice, this only occurs at the aggregate level. As a result, each individual can form the perception that powerful corporations set the terms of exchange in potentially exploitative ways.

Such intuitive computations would provide the cognitive context in which the mind processes socially transmitted information, for example, to the effect that it seems true that 'markets are cruel and selfish,' or that 'a free market makes wolves free to attack sheep.' In such circumstances, external information provides a context in which some of the intuitions described here receive an explanation or a justification. Conversely, such explicit discourse about the economy is attention-grabbing for people to the extent that it matches some of these intuitions.

This perspective on the emergence of emporiophobia is a recent theoretical proposal (Rubin, 2014). There is no specific test of the hypothesis as yet. However, a range of evidence on related phenomena is congruent with this psychological description. Behavioral economics studies show how trust and cooperation are inhibited when social situations are made anonymous (Bohnet, 1999; Hoffman et al., 1996); neuro-economic studies show how monetary rewards elicit greater emotional responses if we experience the source as a human rather than, for example, an impersonal computer—for a review, see Petersen et al. (2009); and management studies show that more impersonal forms of interaction (e.g., e-mail rather than face-to-face interaction) reduce satisfaction with the interaction, in part because of a lack of emotional coordination (Baltes et al., 2002; Hibbing et al., 2013).

Future research could test the proposed explanation directly by utilizing an individual differences approach: Do individual differences in attention to cooperative positive-sum games in everyday life predict endorsement of emporiophobia-related beliefs? This would not only provide a test of the link between perceptions of the market and social motivations, but also could illuminate some of the political implications of FEBs. Emporiophobia is more outspoken among liberals than conservatives and, consistent with the proposed explanation, there is evidence that liberals in general are more oriented towards cooperative, positive-sum games, in particular with strangers (Hibbing et al., 2013). In this regard, it is important to note, again, that emporiophobia is a matter of stated, explicit beliefs, which may or may not reflect the intuitive principles that actually guide people's economic behavior. People who say that markets are 'bad' may still behave as roughly rational agents in markets, and they may even detect the advantages of competition in their everyday economic behavior. But, if asked whether a given domain of activity should be left to a market of competitors, or when asked the extent to which markets should be regulated, they readily express the view that market outcomes are socially detrimental.

5.5 Explaining FEB 7: Wages, Labor, and the Effects of Ownership Intuitions

FEB 7 is the belief that labor is the source of 'value.' Experimental studies have carefully documented this effect. For instance, adults and even young children assume that working to transform an object carries a potential claim to ownership such that, for example, the artist, not the owner of the quarry, is the owner of a sculpture. This ownership claim is made stronger by the extent of the transformation (O. Friedman, 2010; O. Friedman & Neary, 2008; O. Friedman et al., 2011).

From a cognitive evolutionary perspective, human ownership psychology reflects the features of evolutionarily recurrent environments. Ancestrally, most valued and owned goods were previously unclaimed natural resources that time and effort turned into something useable (whether food, tools, or shelter). In such situations, labor is indeed the exclusive generator of both 'value' and ownership. Features of modern economies that influences ownership and price, such as ownership of capital and consumer demand, were not crucial features of ancestral environments in the context of production. For example, claiming ownership over something processed by an unrelated person ancestrally would instead signal the existence of a clear dominance relationship.

Although good evidence exists for the importance of labor for intuitions of ownership and value, future studies should seek to directly test people's intuitions about the relative contributions of labor, as well as capital provision and consumer demands, in determining ownership. The prediction that emerges from the cognitive evolutionary perspective is that labor should be intuitively associated with ownership, while other factors are represented in explicit afterthoughts rather than through automatic intuitions. Studies utilizing measures of explicit and implicit processing could tease such effects apart.

This set of folk-economic beliefs (and, in particular, intuitions about value) illustrates an important point: that information that does not meet the input conditions of a system is simply not handled by that system. Here, our ownership inference system takes as its input the fact of original possession, the original state, and the amount of work that transformed a thing. These are the conceptual slots, the place-holders, to be filled by appropriate information. By contrast, the fact that there is, or is not, some demand for the work in question, does not fit any specific conceptual slot in our intuitive ownership system. So, it is simply not processed at all by the relevant intuitive system.

These beliefs also illustrate the political importance of FEBs. Intuitions about ownership and value resonate with arguments about large wage differentials between, for example, managers and frontline workers being unfair, and that the latter contribute more 'value' than the former. Such arguments have particular appeal if used to argue in favor of higher taxation or the regulation of business. Historically, Marxian ideologies have also continuously framed owners of capital as exploitive. In this regard, the evolutionary cognitive model entails novel testable predictions: The underlying intuition that owners of companies or factories are exploiting workers may not ultimately stem from observed differences in wealth, or poor conditions for the workers. Instead, an important contribution may lie in the fact that workers are perceived as investing more effort, often in the form of more physically demanding labor. To the evolved mind, this may trigger the intuition that workers are natural owners of products. Future studies could directly test this by examining how different factors such as wealth differences between management and workers, differences in working conditions, and differences in effort, shape the view that particular corporations are exploiting their employees.

5.6 Explaining FEB 8: Large-Scale Regulation and Small-Scale Minds

FEB 8 is the belief that regulation has the intended economic effects. Specific examples include the belief that rent controls drive down the average rent, that minimum wages increase average income, or that there is a fixed amount of work to be done, so that limiting the working hours will palliate unemployment by distributing that amount (Worstall, p. 75). Economists generally point out that, even in the best scenario, unintended effects occur and, in some cases, reverse the desired outcome. Trust in regulation seems to be based on specific non-economic assumptions (Hirshleifer, 2008) and, in particular, an assumption of stable supply. For example, people expect price-controls to affect market prices but have no effect on quantities supplied.

To explain this FEB, we need to take into account the fact that unintended consequences of this kind are second-order effects that occur in large-scale social systems. They reflect aggregate market responses to changes in costs and benefits (e.g., if the price of the good is regulated downwards, the market responds by decreasing quantities supplied). But our psychology of social exchange is designed for small-scale social systems, for personal exchanges between oneself and one or more identified others. The intuitive inference systems that evolved to deal with such situations do not, because of the small-scale nature of the situations, include any conceptual slots for aggregate dynamics such as origins of supply. In this way, FEBs about regulation do not emerge from a single set of intuitive inference systems. Rather, they emerge from the failure of particular pieces of information to be processed by any intuitive inference system.

Let us consider the specific example of rent control to illustrate this interpretation in more detail. To the evolved mind, rent control can be intuitively construed as a form of assistance that makes sense from a small-scale perspective, as it seems that resources are transferred from richer landlords to poorer tenants. It is likely that systems designed for cheater-detection provides the motivational impetus to support such policies. The situation can be mentally represented as including a generic landlord who intentionally takes an extra benefit (increasing rent) without incurring an extra cost (providing better housing), thereby meeting the input conditions for the 'cheater' concept. In this context, the regulatory state appears to redress the situation; the rent ideally decreases, so that the situation no longer activates free-riding detection. Economists have pointed out that the adverse consequences of rent controls (i.e., a lower supply of rental units) may offset any positive effects, although there is disagreement over the size of these negative dynamics (Jenkins, 2009). From an evolutionary cognitive perspective, people will fail to consider such aggregate effects, as the activation of evolved categories entails a perception of the situation as small-scale interaction. The cheater-detection system has no slot for information about the origin of supply and takes quantity supplied as a given. Indeed, in the exchange situations typical of our ancestral past, distribution typically had little effect on production. As described above, opportunity costs, insurance expectations, and reputation management made it possible for people to both distribute most of the game they caught and be motivated to hunt again. Since there is no conceptual slot for information about the origin of supply—for example, the incentives that make people offer housing for rent—this information does not enter into computations about regulations, thereby allowing a belief that regulation will have only the intended effects.

No existing studies have directly tested this argument, and there is only scant evidence at present concerning the psychological representation of regulation (Hirshleifer, 2008). An initial set of evolutionary cognitive studies on regulation should test (1) whether the presence of evolutionarily recurrent cues (e.g., cues of cheaters) automatically induces the intuition that regulation in the relevant domain (e.g., rent) works, and (2) whether explicit information about second-order dynamics (e.g., decreased supply) are discounted in the face of such cues.

6. Transmission and Effects of Folk-Economic Beliefs

6.1 Intuitive Systems Create Cultural Attractors

So far, we have analyzed the ways in which various cognitive systems could affect the relevance of particular pieces of information about the economy, making some views about, for example, unemployment or trade, particularly salient because of their fit with the contents of intuitive assumptions. We can now examine how the agreement or discrepancy between intuitions and some explicit notions of the economy impacts the transmission of information between individuals, thereby creating culturally successful representations. Here we are extending the work of economists who emphasized some particular ways in which individual psychology may influence economic beliefs (Caplan, 2008; D. D. Friedman, 2004; Rubin, 2002). Closest to the kind of model presented here, David Hirshleifer proposed a 'psychological attraction' account of popular opinion on regulation, following which 'certain beliefs [...] are especially good at exploiting psychological biases to attract attention and support' (Hirshleifer, 2008, p. 857).

Our model extends this form of explanation to most domains of folk-economic opinion. We predict that information about economic matters will be all the more widespread, easy to acquire, natural, compelling, and so forth, when it matches the input conditions of the inference systems described above, thereby creating widespread folk-economic beliefs.

Human communication does not consist in 'downloading' representations from one mind to another. Rather, it consists of inferential processes, whereby a listener makes use of observable cues provided by a speaker to reconstruct that individual's possible communicative intentions (T. Scott-Phillips, 2014; Sperber & Wilson, 1995). Because of this interpretive quality of communication, cultural transmission will often follow unpredictable paths. We should not expect the contents of two minds from the same social group to be similar. And to a large degree, of course, they are not. Among the myriad mental representations created and sustained in individual human minds, only a minuscule fraction are shared with other individuals. Precisely for that reason, these common beliefs require special explanation. Why do people in a social group sometimes hold roughly similar representations? This question stands in contrast to the questions of classical social science, for which social change was the problem, while the continuity of traditions was taken for granted (Morin, 2016).

A crucial insight of evolutionary anthropology is that cultural transmission processes are strongly constrained by the structure of human psychology (Sperber, 1985, 1996). The mind is prepared to acquire certain representations more easily than others. As a consequence, these representations are found, in roughly similar forms, in many different minds, becoming what we call cultural beliefs. The combination of expectations from our domain-specific intuitive systems, with communicative input from other members of our group, form what anthropologists call cultural attractors, positions in the space of possible representations where many minds seem to converge (Claidière et al., 2014; Claidière & Sperber, 2007). Cultural transmission creates stable representations, not just because people discard or forget material that is far from the attractors, but also because human minds actively distort fragmentary or deviant material. In other words, transmission is reconstructive rather than just selective (Claidière & Sperber, 2007; Morin, 2013).

This perspective on cultural transmission helps make sense of the cultural recurrence of some folk-economic beliefs, explaining for instance why the belief that imports from other countries are a bad thing, or the notion that immigrants are welfare-scroungers, are made more salient by their interaction with intuitions about coalitions and communal sharing. It is important to notice that the effect of intuitive systems on the spread of cultural beliefs are probabilistic. For example, our intuitive free rider detection system, or our evolved set of preferences for partner-choice, do not by themselves directly generate particular views of the economy. The intuitive systems only provide a context against which external information, provided by mass media, economists, political entrepreneurs, or simply other individuals, is likely to become relevant, attention-grabbing, and therefore susceptible of cultural transmission.

Conversely, we are obviously not suggesting that the human mind is condemned to process only mental representations that are relevant to our intuitive systems. There are many circumstances in which humans have acquired and communicated thoughts that are entirely non-intuitive, in the sense that they do not match our evolved inference systems. People can, for instance, learn to think in terms of scientific physics, which often go against our intuitive physics. In the case at hand, people can learn economics and produce reasoning that diverges from the beliefs described here. However, acquisition of such non-intuitive thoughts requires effort, and in most cases institutional support for sustained learning (Boyer, 1998).

6.2 Folk-Beliefs Do Not Reveal an Implicit Theory of the Economy

Is there an economic system in the mind, a set of processes specially dedicated to economic transactions? It would be tempting, though in our view seriously misleading, to consider the set of folk-economic beliefs as a (spontaneous, popular, perhaps misguided) alternative to economic theory. In this view, FEBs would be the outcome of a particular vision of society and the economy.

We resist this interpretation, as there is little evidence for such an integrated, quasi-theoretical picture of the economy among layfolk. In fact, the few studies of lay models clearly suggest the opposite. For instance, Williamson and Wearing interviewed 95 individuals and extracted from this material their implicit views about economic processes. They conclude that 'the outcome was 95 unique cognitive models' (Williamson & Wearing, 1996, p. 3).

Indeed, folk-economic beliefs may vary not just between individuals, but also within the same person, at different times or in different contexts. That is, people do not seem to have stable economic beliefs, in long-term memory, that they could pull out on demand. In the field of public opinion, researchers have made a strong case that we should dispense with such 'file-drawer' models of opinion formation (Wilson & Hodges, 1992; Zaller, 1992). People do not build and store stable, organized beliefs about the economy, ready to be made available when surveyed by a pollster. Instead, they make up their attitudes and beliefs 'on the spot,' by retrieving relevant cultural representations, and (in our view) activating the relevant intuitive inference systems. For most individuals in modern mass-societies, there is little monetary incentive to evaluate one's own beliefs about the economy or the political process (in contrast to many other domains in their everyday lives), and there is almost no price to pay for being factually wrong, which would explain why there is relatively little cognitive investment in evaluating their validity (Caplan, 2008).

The exceptional range of different understandings of the model identified by Williamson and Wearing (1996) also suggests that, for each individual, the model might be different if surveyed in another context. Indeed, there is evidence for such systematic changes. In an analysis of

British voters during the recent economic crisis, Martin Bisgaard (2015) found that people rapidly shift their understanding of how much control the government has over the economy, depending on how the economy is doing and whether or not their favored party is in government. If the economy gets worse and people support the governing party, the government is suddenly no longer viewed as in control. From an evolutionary cognitive perspective, such partisan motivations most likely stem from the operations of coalitional psychology (Haidt, 2012; Petersen, 2015). People signal support to their coalition by construing beliefs that protect it against criticism. Experimental results show that, like national or ethnic identities, partisanship is processed as a coalitional affiliation to the evolved mind (Pietraszewski et al., 2015). Hence, it might matter for people whether they have the 'right' FEBs from a coalitional perspective but not whether they have the 'true' FEBs from an epistemic perspective.

The fact that folk-economic beliefs can change rapidly should not be surprising, as most of them are reflective, not intuitive beliefs. To illustrate this reflective nature of FEBs, consider 'emporiophobia.' Information about the fact that market transactions are one-shot interactions can lead to the intuition 'there is danger here,' because our evolved social exchange preferences include reiterated transactions with known individuals. This intuition of danger can then lead to forming, acquiring, or accepting explicit reflective beliefs of the form 'the market is bad.'

From an evolutionary standpoint, it should come as no surprise that human minds do not comprise a specific 'economics' module. Decision-making under scarcity, traditionally described as the domain of economic models, is not a unified domain of social interaction, for which evolution would have given us specific inference systems. Instead, the evidence from experimental psychology studies suggests that human evolution resulted in specialized systems for scarcity in food provision (foraging), in mates (sexual preferences), in social support (coalitional psychology), and so on Buss (2015). Even in the domain of social exchange, as described above, we spontaneously activate diverse systems with different principles and potentially inconsistent responses.

6.3 Relationship Between FEBs and Economic Behavior

The model presented here leaves a gap in our understanding, as concerns the connections (or lack thereof) between folk-economic views on the one hand, and economic behavior on the other. Many people in modern societies have explicit folk-economic views that do not just fly in the face of economic theory, but are also incompatible with their own behavior in markets. For example, people may both have the explicit belief that 'markets produce negative outcomes' and an implicit trust in competition in their search for the best prices.

We propose here that economic beliefs are largely constrained by evolved, domain-specific systems concerned with social exchange. So, there might be connections between FEBs and economic behavior, to the extent that these same domain-specific intuitive systems are activated when people engage in actual economic transactions.

Unfortunately, this aspect of economic cognition is still very much a terra incognita. We can assume that economic decision-making is governed by a variety of intuitive systems, the aggregate output of which is an intuition that the transactions is desirable or best avoided, and that intuition motivates the eventual decision. Over the last decades, studies within behavioral economics have demonstrated how this intuitive output diverges, in relatively systematic ways, from the subjective utility maximization predictions of standard microeconomics (Plott, 2001; Smith, 2003).

However, we still lack a computationally precise and reasonably predictive description of the cognitive processes engaged (Ross, 2005). Indeed, a large part of the behavioral economic literature assumes what could be called a person-level description of economic decision-making, in which information about possible strategies is combined and evaluated by a general-purpose, centralized utility-evaluating system—the difference from neoclassical models being that considerations of fairness, reputation, and other nonstandard forms of utility are added to the classical homo economicus agent. This notion of utility as considered by a centralized agent corresponds to what Dennett calls the 'intentional stance,' in which we explain behavior in terms of reasons, knowledge, and intentions (Dennett, 1989). This way of explaining behaviors is produced by our intuitive psychology, or 'theory of mind.' It is very successful in explaining and predicting other human beings' behavior. The operation of this intuitive psychology is so natural and invisible that it often seems difficult even to imagine another way of explaining behavior.

But there is an alternative, what Dennett called a 'design stance,' in which we consider behavior in terms of the various computational systems involved in acquiring information about the environment and motivating specific behaviors (Dennett, 1989). Approaching economic decision-making in this perspective could make economic theory more congruent with findings and models from the cognitive sciences (Ross, 2005). In that perspective, decision-making in any domain is the outcome of a competition between distinct computational processes— and this of course applies to economic decisions as well (Kenrick et al., 2012), a view that is supported by behavioral evidence (Ainslie & Monterosso, 2004) and neurocognitive findings (Glimcher, 2009; Loewenstein et al., 2008). However, it is still difficult to describe how these models and findings could be integrated with classical, and often empirically successful, descriptions of economic behavior in terms of rationality (Ross, 2005) and utility (Burnham, 2013). As a consequence, the actual connections between micro-processes of economic decision-making on the one hand, and folk-economic beliefs on the other, remain unexplored.

6.4 Political Relevance of Folk-Economic Beliefs

In this model, because of the activation of intuitive inference systems, some ways of presenting economic processes are more compelling than others. This would constrain political communication, not just from elites to the rest of the population, but also among layfolk, with important consequences for political debate. Importantly, this would imply that a particular economic issue is often not discussed in the format that provides most information about the causes and consequences of policy, but in the format that is intuitively compelling, even if that obscures a great deal of the relevant information.

FEBs are politically important because they act as a set of background assumptions that forms the basis of the formation of political opinions. One important area of opinions relates to political candidates. A wealth of research within political science has shown that incumbent parties or candidates are punished and rewarded for bad and good economic developments, respectively. When unemployment soars, incumbents are more likely to lose. Importantly, however, research also shows that the link between economic circumstances and voting behavior is mediated by the perceived responsibility of the incumbents (Rudolph, 2003a, 2003b). Assignment of responsibility for macro-economic events necessarily relies on FEBs and an interpretation of the relationship between the actions of the candidate and the economic developments. Beliefs about the relationship between economic hardship, on the one hand, and international trade and immigration, on the other hand, could be influential. If the economy is doing badly and the incumbent government has increased immigration and trade, then our analyses suggest that it is more likely that the government will be held accountable on Election Day.

Such effects of intuitive systems are also relevant to policy choices. FEBs, and the intuitive systems underlying them, shape political behavior because they make certain ways of organizing the economy more compelling. Importantly, these compelling policies will in some cases be misguided, as the psychological systems were designed for small-scale exchange rather mass markets. For example, in the small-scale environments of our ancestors, helping was a matter of transferring resources to a needy individual. Arguments for welfare policy that are framed that way should be persuasive. In modern markets, however, the effectiveness of any social solutions is also affected by equilibrium considerations. Consider the difference between targeted versus universal welfare programs. From a small-scale perspective, targeted programs should be most effective in helping the needy, because they bring resources specifically to those in need. Yet, in market economies, comparative studies provide compelling evidence that welfare programs are more redistributive, and help the neediest people more, when they are universal rather than targeted. That is due, again, to macro-level dynamics ignored by our intuitive systems. Research shows that it is possible to sustain high levels of benefits from a welfare program, but only when the politically influential middle-class are among those benefiting from that program (Korpi & Palme, 1998; Rothstein, 1998). When they do not benefit, most voters are persuaded that the benefits should be scaled down. Because of this electoral dynamic, universal programs are on balance more redistributive than targeted programs. This net result arises from both their high benefit rates and the fact that higher-income groups contribute more to the program by means of taxation than low-income groups. But, again, evolved exchange intuitions would make people less likely to be persuaded by arguments that touch on such dynamics, compared to arguments that fit our intuitive systems for allocating benefits between individuals.

Folk-economic beliefs are politically important because they constrain how politicians can talk about policies to the public. Political scientists have documented the effects of 'framing' on policy views (Chong & Druckman, 2007). The model presented provides a more specific understanding of these processes. In our view, certain policy-related messages are more compelling or persuasive, not just because they are framed in more 'concrete' or 'simple' or 'vivid' terms, as is often suggested, but also because they meet specific expectations from our intuitive systems. For instance, policies that increase international trade with rival countries or that allow more immigrants to enter the country can be more easily framed as economically problematic than as beneficial, not because the former description is 'simpler' but because of the match it offers between intuitive inference systems and a particular constellation of arguments (Arceneaux, 2012).

7. Conclusion

In 1922, the American journalist Walter Lippmann grasped the characteristic of modern mass societies when he wrote: 'Our opinions cover a bigger space, a longer reach of time, a greater number of things, than we can directly observe' (Lippmann, 1922, p. 42). If this was true in 1922, it is even more true in the twenty-first century. And if it is true about mass societies, in general, it is nowhere else as true as with the market. No citizen can ever observe each of the distant transactions that comprise the market economy. It is not just a matter of practicality. The market mechanism is in principle unobservable. Even if all transactions could be observed, one would still not observe the economy as such— such a claim would be a category-mistake in the sense of Ryle (1949). The 'hand' that governs the causal processes of the market is, as already pointed out by Adam Smith, invisible—that is, not just hidden but in principle difficult to detect (Nozick, 1994). As consequence, laypeople, when forming their internal representations of the economy, cannot rely on much, if any, feedback from direct experience. And without external experiences as a reality-check on their beliefs, they are left with what others report and what they themselves can imagine.

We proposed a new explanation for the differences between laypeople and economists' views on a number of economic issues. Instead of considering folk-economic views as irrational deviations from normative understandings of economic processes, we explain them as the outcome of principled cognitive systems. These appeared in human evolution as adaptive response to specific challenges, and they are automatically activated whenever a situation meets their input criteria. The intuitions provide support for deliberate, explicit, reflective thoughts, among which are the culturally transmitted folk-economic beliefs considered here.

How and why people acquire and stabilize beliefs about the economy is, obviously, crucial to understanding political dynamics. Economic policies are central to the overt choices offered in most liberal democracies, but we are only starting to figure out the effects of intuitive systems, typical of all normal human minds, on the acquisition and transmission of people's explicit beliefs about the economy.

References

Aarøe, L., & Petersen, M. B. (2014). Crowding out culture: Scandinavians and Americans agree on social welfare in the face of deservingness cues. *The Journal of Politics, 76*, 684–697. https://doi.org/10.1017/S002238161400019X

Ainslie, G., & Monterosso, J. (2004). A Marketplace in the Brain? *Science, 306*, 421–423.

Alesina, A., & Glaeser, E. L. (2004). *Fighting Poverty in the US and Europe: A World of Difference.* New York: Oxford University Press.

Anderson, B. R. (1983). *Imagined Communities: Reflections on the Origin and Spread of Nationalism.* London: Verso.

André, J.-B. (2010). The Evolution of Reciprocity: Social Types or Social Incentives? *American Naturalist, 175*, 197–210. https://doi.org/10.1086/649597

André, J.-B., & Baumard, N. (2011). The evolution of fairness in a biological market. *Evolution*, 650, 1447–1456.

André, J.-B., & Day, T. (2007). Perfect reciprocity is the only evolutionarily stable strategy in the continuous iterated prisoner's dilemma. *Journal of Theoretical Biology*, 247, 11–22. https://doi.org/ 10.1016/j.jtbi.2007.02.007

Arceneaux, K. (2012). Cognitive biases and the strength of political arguments. *American Journal of Political Science*, 56, 271–285.

Atran, S. A. (1995). Causal constraints on categories and categorical constraints on biological reasoning across cultures. In D. Sperber, D. Premack, et al. (Eds.), *Causal Cognition: A Multidisciplinary Debate.* (pp. 205–233). New York: Clarendon Press/Oxford University Press.

Baillargeon, R., Kotovsky, L., & Needham, A. (1995). The acquisition of physical knowledge in infancy. In D. Sperber, D. Premack, & A. James-Premack (Eds.), *Causal Cognition: A Multidisciplinary Debate* (pp. 79–115). Oxford: Clarendon Press.

Baltes, B. B., Dickson, M. W., Sherman, M. P., Bauer, C. C., & LaGanke, J. S. (2002). Computer-mediated communication and group decision making: A meta-analysis. *Organizational Behavior and Human Decision Processes*, 87, 156–179.

Barclay, P. (2016). Biological markets and the effects of partner choice on cooperation and friendship. *Current Opinion in Psychology*, 7, 33–38. doi:http://dx.doi.org/10.1016/j.copsyc.2015.07.012

Baron, J. (2001). Confusion of group interest and self-interest in parochial cooperation on behalf of a group. *Journal of Conflict Resolution*, 45(3), 283–296. https://doi.org/10.1177/0022002701045003002

Baron, J., & Kemp, S. (2004). Support for trade restrictions, attitudes, and understanding of comparative advantage. *Journal of Economic Psychology*, 25(5), 565–580. https://doi.org/10.1016/S0167-4870(03)00064-3

Bhattacharjee, A., Dana, J., & Baron, J. (2017). Anti-profit beliefs: How people neglect the societal benefits of profit. *Journal of Personality and Social Psychology*, 113(5), 671–696. https://doi.org/10.1037/pspa0000093

Birch, L. L., & Billman, J. (1986). Preschool children's food sharing with friends and acquaintances. *Child Development*, 387–395.

Bisgaard, M. (2015). Bias will find a way: Economic perceptions, attributions of blame, and partisan-motivated reasoning during crisis. *The Journal of Politics*, 77(3), 849–860.

Bisgaard, M., & Slothuus, R. (2018). *How Powerful Are Political Parties in Shaping Public Opinion? Evidence from Two Quasi-Experiments*. Paper presented at the Annual Meeting of the Midwest Political Science Association, Chicago.

Blake, P. R., & Harris, P. L. (2009). Children's understanding of ownership transfers. *Cognitive Development, 24*(2), 133–145. https://doi.org/10.1016/j.cogdev.2009.01.002

Blinder, A. S., & Krueger, A. B. (2004). *What Does the Public Know about Economic Policy, and How Does It Know It?* National Bureau of Economic Research, Working paper 10787. https://doi.org/10.3386/w10787

Bohnet, I. (1999). The sound of silence in prisoner's dilemma and dictator games. *Journal of Economic Behavior and Organization* 38(1): 43–57. https://doi.org/10.1016/S0167-2681(98)00121-8

Boyd, R., & Richerson, P. J. (1985). *Culture and the Evolutionary Process.* Chicago, IL: University of Chicago Press.

Boyer, P. (1998). Cognitive Tracks of Cultural Inheritance: How Evolved Intuitive Ontology Governs Cultural Transmission. *American Anthropologist,* 100, 876–889.

——. (2015). How Natural Selection Shapes Conceptual Structure: Human Intuitions And Concepts Of Ownership. In E. Margolis & S. Laurence (Eds.), *The Conceptual Mind. New Directions in the Study of Concepts* (pp. 185–200). Cambridge, MA: MIT Press.

Boyer, P., & Barrett, H. C. (2015). Domain Specificity and Intuitive Ontologies. In D. M. Buss (Ed.), *The Handbook of Evolutionary Psychology.* (pp. xx–xx). Hoboken, NJ: John Wiley & Sons Inc.

Brown, D. E. (1991). *Human Universals.* New York: McGraw Hill.

Bshary, R., & Grutter, A. S. (2005). Punishment and partner switching cause cooperative behaviour in a cleaning mutualism. *Biology Letters,* 1, 396–399. https://doi.org/10.1098/rsbl.2005.0344

Burnham, T. C. (2013). Toward a neo-Darwinian synthesis of neoclassical and behavioral economics. *Journal of Economic Behavior & Organization,* 90, 113–127.

Buss, D. M. (2015). *The Handbook of Evolutionary Psychology, Volume 1: Foundation.* Hoboken, NJ: John Wiley & Sons.

Buss, D. M., Haselton, M. G., Shackelford, T. K., Bleske, A. L., & Wakefield, J. C. (1998). Adaptations, exaptations, and spandrels. *American Psychologist,* 53(5), 533.

Camerer, C. F., Bhatt, M., & Hsu, M. (2007). *Neuroeconomics: Illustrated by the Study of Ambiguity aversion.* In B. S. Frey & A. Stutzer (Eds.), *CESifo seminar series. Economics and psychology: A promising new cross-disciplinary field* (pp. 113–151). Cambridge, MA: MIT Press.

Caplan, B. (2006). How do voters form positive economic beliefs? Evidence from the Survey of Americans and Economists on the Economy. *Public Choice,* 128(3–4), 367–381. https://doi.org/10.1007/s11127-006-9026-z

Caplan, B. (2008). *The Myth of the Rational Voter: Why Democracies Choose Bad Policies* (. Princeton, NJ; Woodstock: Princeton University Press.

Chong, D., & Druckman, J. N. (2007). Framing theory. *Annual Review of Political Science*, 10, 103–126. https://doi.org/10.1146/annurev.polisci.10.072805.103054

Cimino, A. (2011). The evolution of hazing: Motivational mechanisms and the abuse of newcomers. *Journal of Cognition and Culture*, 11(3–4), 241–267. https://doi.org/10.1163/156853711X591242

Cimino, A., & Delton, A. W. (2010). On the perception of newcomers. *Human Nature*, 21(2), 186–202. https://doi.org/10.1007/s12110-010-9088-y

Claidière, N., Scott-Phillips, T. C., & Sperber, D. (2014). How Darwinian is cultural evolution? *Philosophical Transactions of the Royal Society B: Biological Sciences*, 369(1642), 20130368. https://doi.org/10.1098/rstb.2013.0368

Claidière, N., & Sperber, D. (2007). The role of attraction in cultural evolution. *Journal of Cognition and Culture*, 7(1–2), 89–111. https://doi.org/10.1163/156853707X171829

Converse, P. E. (1964). The nature of belief systems in mass publics. Ideology and discontent. *Ideology and Discontent*, 206–261.

Cosmides, L. (1989). The logic of social exchange: Has natural selection shaped how humans reason? Studies with the Wason selection task. *Cognition*, 31(3), 187–276.

Cosmides, L., & Tooby, J. (1992). Cognitive adaptations for social exchange. In J. H. Barkow, L. Cosmides, & J. Tooby (Eds.), *The Adapted Mind: Evolutionary Psychology and the Generation of Culture*. (pp. 163–228). New York: Oxford University Press.

———. (2000). Consider the source: The evolution of adaptations for decoupling and metarepresentation. In D. Sperber (Ed.), *Metarepresentations: A Multidisciplinary Perspective* (pp. 53–115). New York: Oxford University Press.

———. (2015a). Adaptations for reasoning about social exchange. In D. Buss (Ed.), *The Handbook of Evolutionary Psychology, Second edition.* (II, pp. 625–668). Hoboken, NJ: John Wiley & Sons.

———. (2015b). The theoretical foundations of evolutionary psychology. In D. Buss (Ed.), *The Handbook of Evolutionary Psychology, Second edition.* (II, pp. 3–87). Hoboken, NJ: John Wiley & Sons.

———. (Eds.). (2005). *Neurocognitive Adaptations Designed for Social Exchange.* Hoboken, NJ: John Wiley & Sons Inc.

Ellickson, R. C. (1991). *Order without law: How neighbors settle disputes.* Cambridge, Mass.: Harvard University Press.

Dahl, G. B., & Ransom, M. R. (1999). Does Where You Stand Depend on Where You Sit? Tithing Donations and Self-Serving Beliefs. *The American Economic Review*, 89, 703–727. https://doi.org/10.1257/aer.89.4.703

Delton, A. W., & Cimino, A. (2010). Exploring the evolved concept of NEWCOMER: Experimental tests of a cognitive model. *Evolutionary Psychology*, 8(2), 147470491000800214. https://doi.org/10.1177/147470491000800214

Delton, A. W., Cosmides, L., Guemo, M., Robertson, T. E., & Tooby, J. (2012). The psychosemantics of free riding: dissecting the architecture of a moral concept. *Journal of Personality and Social Psychology*, 102(6), 1252. https://doi.org/10.1037/a0027026

Delton, A. W., & Robertson, T. E. (2012). The social cognition of social foraging: Partner selection by underlying valuation. *Evolution and Human Behavior*, 33(6), 715–725. https://doi.org/10.1016/j.evolhumbehav.2012.05.007

Dennett, D. C. (1989). *The Intentional Stance*. Cambridge, MA: MIT press.

DeScioli, P., & Karpoff, R. (2015). People's judgments about classic property law cases. *Human Nature*, 26(2), 184–209. https://doi.org/10.1007/s12110-015-9230-y

Dreier, P. (1999). The politics of rent control in California and Massachusetts. *Research in Politics and Society*, 7, 207–250.

Eisenbruch, A. B., Grillot, R. L., Maestripieri, D., & Roney, J. R. (2016). Evidence of partner choice heuristics in a one-shot bargaining game. *Evolution and Human Behavior*, 37(6), 429–439. https://doi.org/10.1016/j.evolhumbehav.2016.04.002

Everett, J. A., Pizarro, D. A., & Crockett, M. J. (2016). Inference of trustworthiness from intuitive moral judgments. *Journal of Experimental Psychology: General*, 145(6), 772–787. http://dx.doi.org/10.1037/xge0000165.supp

Fehr, E., & Schmidt, K. M. (2006). The economics of fairness, reciprocity and altruism—experimental evidence and new theories. *Handbook of the Economics of Giving, Altruism and Reciprocity*, 1, 615–691.

Fink, B., & Penton-Voak, I. (2002). Evolutionary psychology of facial attractiveness. *Current Directions in Psychological Science*, 11(5), 154–158. https://doi.org/10.1111/1467-8721.00190

Fiske, A. P. (1992). The four elementary forms of sociality: framework for a unified theory of social relations. *Psychological Review*, 99(4), 689.

Fiske, A. P., & Tetlock, P. E. (1997). Taboo trade-offs: Reactions to transactions that transgress the spheres of justice. *Political Psychology*, 18(2), 255–297. https://doi.org/10.1111/0162-895X.00058

Friedman, D. D. (2004). Evolutionary Psychology and Economic Theory. *Advances in Austrian Economics*, 7, 17–33.

Friedman, O. (2010). Necessary for possession: How people reason about the acquisition of ownership. *Personality and Social Psychology Bulletin*, 36(9), 1161–1169. https://doi.org/10.1177/0146167210378513

Friedman, O., & Neary, K. R. (2008). Determining who owns what: Do children infer ownership from first possession? *Cognition*, 107(3), 829–849. https://doi.org/10.1016/j.cognition.2007.12.002

Friedman, O., Neary, K. R., Defeyter, M. A., & Malcolm, S. L. (2011). Ownership and object history. *New directions for child and adolescent development*, 2011(132), 79–89. https://doi.org/10.1002/cd.298

Gat, A. (2006). *War in Human Civilization*. New York: Oxford University Press.

Gelman, R., Durgin, F., & Kaufman, L. (1995). Distinguishing between animates and inanimates: Not by motion alone. *Causal Cognition: A Multidisciplinary Debate*, 150–184.

Gelman, S. A. (2004). Psychological essentialism in children. *Trends in Cognitive Sciences*, 8(9), 404–409.

Gelman, S. A., & Wellman, H. M. (1991). Insides and essences: Early understandings of the non-obvious. *Cognition*, 38(3), 213–244. https://doi.org/10.1016/0010-0277(91)90007-Q

General Social Survey. (2011). General Social Survey (GSS) Cumulative Datafile 1972–2010. https://sda.berkeley.edu/archive.htm

Gigerenzer, G. (1991). How to Make Cognitive Illusions Disappear: Beyond 'Heuristics and Biases'. *European Review of Social Psychology*, 2, 83–115.

Gigerenzer, G., & Hug, K. (1992). Domain-specific reasoning: Social contracts, cheating, and perspective change. *Cognition*, 43, 127–171.

Gigerenzer, G., Todd, P. M., & Group, A. B. C. R. (1999). *Simple Heuristics that Make us Smart*. New York: Oxford University Press.

Gilens, M. (1999). *Why Americans Hate Welfare: Race, Media, and the Politics of Antipoverty Policy*. Chicago, IL: University of Chicago Press.

Gilovich, T., Griffin, D., & Kahneman, D. (2002). *Heuristics and Biases: The Psychology of Intuitive Judgment*. Cambridge: Cambridge University Press.

Glimcher, P. (2009). Neuroeconomics and the study of valuation. In D. Poeppel, G. R. Mangun, & M. S. Gazzangia (Eds.), *The Cognitive Neurosciences* (pp. 1085–1092). Cambridge, MA: MIT Press.

Grammer, K., & Thornhill, R. (1994). Human (Homo sapiens) facial attractiveness and sexual selection: the role of symmetry and averageness. *Journal of Comparative Psychology*, 108(3), 233.

Green, D. P., & Shapiro, I. (1994). *Pathologies of Rational Choice Theory: A Critique of Applications in Political Science*. New Haven, CT: Yale University Press.

Guimond, S., De Oliveira, P., Kamiesjki, R., & Sidanius, J. (2010). The trouble with assimilation: Social dominance and the emergence of hostility against immigrants. *International Journal of Intercultural Relations*, 34(6), 642–650. https://doi.org/10.1016/j.ijintrel.2010.01.002

Gurven, M. (2004). To give and to give not: the behavioral ecology of human food transfers. *Behavioral and Brain Sciences*, 27(4), 543–559. https://doi.org/10.1017/S0140525X04000123

Gurven, M., Hill, K., Kaplan, H., Hurtado, A., & Lyles, R. (2000). Food transfers among Hiwi foragers of Venezuela: tests of reciprocity. *Human Ecology*, 28(2), 171–218. https://doi.org/10.1023/A:1007067919982

Haferkamp, A., Fetchenhauer, D., Belschak, F., & Enste, D. (2009). Efficiency versus fairness: The evaluation of labor market policies by economists and laypeople. *Journal of Economic Psychology*, 30(4), 527–539. https://doi.org/10.1016/j.joep.2009.03.010

Haidt, J. (2012). *The Righteous Mind: Why Good People Are Divided by Politics and Religion*. New York: Vintage.

Hainmueller, J., & Hiscox, M. J. (2007). Educated preferences: Explaining attitudes toward immigration in Europe. *International Organization*, 61(2), 399–442. https://doi.org/10.1017/S0020818307070142

——. (2010). Attitudes toward highly skilled and low-skilled immigration: Evidence from a survey experiment. *American Political Science Review*, 104(1), 61–84. https://doi.org/10.1017/S0003055409990372

Hamann, K., Warneken, F., Greenberg, J. R., & Tomasello, M. (2011). Collaboration encourages equal sharing in children but not in chimpanzees. *Nature*, 476(7360), 328–331. https://doi.org/10.1038/nature10278

Hann, C. M. (1998). *Property Relations: Renewing the Anthropological Tradition*. Cambridge: Cambridge University Press.

Hazlitt, H. (2010). *Economics in One Lesson: The Shortest and Surest Way to Understand Basic Economics*. New York: Random House.

Hechter, M. (1987). Nationalism as group solidarity. *Ethnic and Racial Studies*, 10(4), 415–426. https://doi.org/10.1080/01419870.1987.9993580

——. (1987). *Principles of Group Solidarity*. Berkeley, CA: University of California Press.

Heine, B. (1997). *Possession: Cognitive sources, forces, and grammaticalization. Cambridge Studies in Linguistics* (83). Cambridge: Cambridge University Press.

Hibbing, J. R., Smith, K. B., & Alford, J. R. (2013). *Predisposed: Liberals, Conservatives, and the Biology of Political Differences*. London: Routledge.

Hirschfeld, L., & Gelman, S. A. (1994). *Mapping the Mind: Domain Specificity in Cognition and Culture*. Cambridge; New York: Cambridge University Press.

Hirshleifer, D. (2008). Psychological Bias as a Driver of Financial Regulation. *European Financial Management,* 14, 856–874. https://doi.org/10.1111/j.1468-036X.2007.00437.x

Hiscox, M. J. (2006). Through a Glass and Darkly: Attitudes Toward International Trade and the Curious Effects of Issue Framing. *International Organization,* 60, 755–780. https://doi.org/10.1017/S0020818306060255

Hoffman, E., McCabe, K., & Smith, V. L. (1996). Social distance and other-regarding behavior in dictator games. *The American Economic Review,* 86, 653–660.

Jenkins, B. (2009). Rent control: Do economists agree? *Econ Journal Watch,* 6(1): 73–112.

Kaiser Foundation. (1996). *Survey of Americans and Economists on the Economy.* https://www.kff.org/other/poll-finding/survey-of-americans-and-economists-on-the/

Kaiser, M. K., Jonides, J., & Alexander, J. (1986). Intuitive reasoning about abstract and familiar physics problems. *Memory & Cognition,* 14(4), 308–312.

Kameda, T., Takezawa, M., Tindale, R. S., & Smith, C. M. (2002). Social sharing and risk reduction: Exploring a computational algorithm for the psychology of windfall gains. *Evolution and Human Behavior,* 23(1), 11–33. https://doi.org/10.1016/S1090-5138(01)00086-1

Kanngiesser, P., Gjersoe, N., & Hood, B. M. (2010). The effect of creative labor on property-ownership transfer by preschool children and adults. *Psychological Science,* 21(9), 1236–1241. https://doi.org/10.1177/0956797610380701

Kanwisher, N. (2000). Domain specificity in face perception. *Nature Neuroscience,* 3(8), 759–763. https://doi.org/10.1038/77664

Kaplan, H., Gurven, M., Hill, K., & Hurtado, A. M. (2005). The natural history of human food sharing and cooperation: a review and a new multi-individual approach to the negotiation of norms. *Moral sentiments and material interests* 6, 75–113.

Kaplan, H., & Hill, K. (1985). Hunting ability and reproductive success among male Ache foragers: Preliminary results. *Current Anthropology,* 26(1), 131–133.

Karp, D., Jin, N., Yamagishi, T., & Shinotsuka, H. (1993). Raising the minimum in the minimal group paradigm. *The Japanese Journal of Experimental Social Psychology,* 32(3), 231–240.

Kelly, R. L. (1995). *The Foraging Spectrum: Diversity in Hunter-Gatherer Lifeways.* Washington, DC: Smithsonian Institution Press.

Kenrick, D. T., Li, Y. J., White, A. E., & Neuberg, S. L. (2012). Economic subselves: Fundamental motives and deep rationality. *Social Thinking and Interpersonal Behavior,* 14, 23–43.

Kiyonari, T., & Yamagishi, T. (2004). Ingroup Cooperation and the Social Exchange Heuristic. In R. Suleiman, D. V. Budescu, I. Fischer, & D. M. Messick (Eds.), *Contemporary Psychological Research on Social Dilemmas* (p. 269–286). Cambridge: Cambridge University Press.

Korpi, W., & Palme, J. (1998). The paradox of redistribution and strategies of equality: Welfare state institutions, inequality, and poverty in the Western countries. *American Sociological Review*, 63(5), 661–687. https://doi.org/10.2307/2657333

Krasnow, M. M., Cosmides, L., Pedersen, E. J., & Tooby, J. (2012). What are punishment and reputation for? *PloS one*, 7(9). https://doi.org/10.1371/journal.pone.0045662

Levitt, M. J., Weber, R. A., Clark, M. C., & McDonnell, P. (1985). Reciprocity of exchange in toddler sharing behavior. *Developmental Psychology*, 21(1), 122.

Lippmann, W. (1922). *Public Opinion*. NY: The Free Press.

Loewenstein, G., Rick, S., & Cohen, J. D. (2008). Neuroeconomics. *Annual Review of Psychology*, 59, 647–672. https://doi.org/10.1146/annurev.psych.59.103006.093710

Magalhães, P., & Geoffrey White, K. (2016). The sunk cost effect across species: A review of persistence in a course of action due to prior investment. *Journal of the Experimental Analysis of Behavior*, 105(3), 339–361. https://doi.org/10.1002/jeab.202

Mansfield, E. D., Mutz, D. C., & Brackbill, D. (2019). Effects of the Great Recession on American attitudes toward trade. *British Journal of Political Science*, 49(1), 37–58. https://doi.org/10.1017/S0007123416000405

Mercier, H., & Sperber, D. (2009). Intuitive and reflective inferences. In J. Evans & K. Frankish (Eds.), *In Two Minds: Dual Processes and Beyond* (pp. 149–170). Oxford: Oxford University Press. https://doi.org/10.1093/acprof:oso/9780199230167.001.0001

Milinski, M., Semmann, D., & Krambeck, H.-J. (2002). Reputation helps solve the 'tragedy of the commons'. *Nature*, 415(6870), 424–426. https://doi.org/10.1038/415424a

Morin, O. (2013). What does communication contribute to cultural transmission? *Social Anthropology*, 21(2), 230–235. https://doi.org/10.1111/1469-8676.12014

——. (2016). *How Traditions Live and Die*. Oxford; New York: Oxford University Press.

Nannestad, P., & Paldam, M. (1994). The VP-function: A survey of the literature on vote and popularity functions after 25 years. *Public Choice*, 79(3–4), 213–245.

Noë, R., & Hammerstein, P. (1994). Biological markets: supply and demand determine the effect of partner choice in cooperation, mutualism and mating. *Behavioral Ecology and Sociobiology*, 35(1), 1–11.

Noles, N. S., & Keil, F. C. (2011). Exploring ownership in a developmental context. *New directions for child and adolescent development*, 2011(132), 91–103. https://doi.org/10.1002/cd.299

Nozick, R. (1994). Invisible-hand explanations. *The American Economic Review*, 84(2), 314–318.

Panchanathan, K., & Boyd, R. (2004). Indirect reciprocity can stabilize cooperation without the second-order free rider problem. *Nature*, 432(7016), 499–502. https://doi.org/10.1038/nature02978

Peffley, M. (1984). The voter as juror: Attributing responsibility for economic conditions. *Political Behavior*, 6(3), 275–294.

Petersen, M. B. (2012). Social welfare as small-scale help: evolutionary psychology and the deservingness heuristic. *American Journal of Political Science*, 56(1), 1–16. https://doi.org/10.1111/j.1540-5907.2011.00545.x

——. (2013). Moralization as protection against exploitation: do individuals without allies moralize more? *Evolution and Human Behavior*, 34(2), 78–85. https://doi.org/10.1016/j.evolhumbehav.2012.09.006

——. (2015). Evolutionary political psychology. In D. M. Buss (Ed.), *The Handbook of Evolutionary Psychology* (pp. 1–19). Hoboken, NJ: John Wiley & Sons, Inc.

Petersen, M. B., Roepstorff, A., & Serritzlew, S. (2009). Social capital in the brain? In G. T. Svendsen & G. L. H. Svendsen (Eds.), *Handbook of Social Capital* (pp. 75–92). Cheltenham; Northampton, MA: Edward Elgar.

Petersen, M. B., Sznycer, D., Cosmides, L., & Tooby, J. (2012). Who deserves help? Evolutionary psychology, social emotions, and public opinion about welfare. *Political Psychology*, 33(3), 395–418. https://doi.org/10.1111/j.1467-9221.2012.00883.x

Pickering, M., & van Gompel, R. G (2006). Syntactic parsing. In E. M. Fernández & H. S. Carins (Eds.), *The Handbook of Psycholinguistics* (pp. 455–503). Hoboken, NJ: John Wiley & Sons.

Pietraszewski, D. (2013). What is group psychology? Adaptations for mapping shared intentional stances. In M. R. Banaji & S. A. Gelman (Eds.), *Navigating the Social World: What Infants, Children, and Other Species Can Teach Us* (pp. 253–257). Oxford: Oxford University Press

——. (2016). How the mind sees coalitional and group conflict: the evolutionary invariances of n-person conflict dynamics. *Evolution and Human Behavior*, 37(6), 470–480. https://doi.org/10.1016/j.evolhumbehav.2016.04.006

Pietraszewski, D., Curry, O. S., Petersen, M. B., Cosmides, L., & Tooby, J. (2015). Constituents of political cognition: Race, party politics, and the alliance detection system. *Cognition*, 140, 24–39. https://doi.org/10.1016/j.cognition.2015.03.007

Plott, C. R. (1974). On game solutions and revealed preference theory. *none*(35).

——. (2001). *Public Economics, Political Processes and Policy Applications. Collected Papers on the Experimental Foundations of Economics and Political Science, Volume 1.* Cheltenham; Northampton, MA: Edward Elgar Publishing.

Polanyi, K. (2001). The Economy as Instituted Process, 1957. In M. Granovetter & R. Swedberg (Eds.), *The Sociology of Economic Life* (pp. 29–51). Boulder, CO: *Westview Press.*

Price, M. E., Cosmides, L., & Tooby, J. (2002). Punitive sentiment as an anti-free rider psychological device. *Evolution and Human Behavior,* 23(3), 203–231. https://doi.org/10.1016/S1090-5138(01)00093-9

Rao, N., & Stewart, S. M. (1999). Cultural influences on sharer and recipient behavior: Sharing in Chinese and Indian preschool children. *Journal of Cross-Cultural Psychology,* 30(2), 219–241.

Ross, D. (2005). *Economic Theory and Cognitive Science: Microexplanation.* Cambridge, MA: MIT Press.

Rothstein, B. (1998). *Just Institutions Matter: The Moral and Political Logic of the Universal Welfare State.* Cambridge: Cambridge University Press.

Rubin, P. H. (2002). *Darwinian Politics: The Evolutionary Origin of Freedom.* New Brunswick, NJ: Rutgers University Press.

——. (2003). Folk economics. *Southern Economic Journal,* 70(1), 157–171.

——. (2014). Emporiophobia (fear of markets): Cooperation or competition? *Southern Economic Journal,* 80(4), 875–889. https://doi.org/10.4284/0038-4038-2013.287

Rudolph, T. J. (2003a). Institutional context and the assignment of political responsibility. *The Journal of Politics,* 65(1), 190–215. https://doi.org/10.1111/1468-2508.00009

——. (2003b). Who's responsible for the economy? The formation and consequences of responsibility attributions. *American Journal of Political Science,* 47(4), 698–713. https://doi.org/10.1111/1540-5907.00049

Ryle, G. (1949). 2009, The Concept of Mind. Harmondsworth: Penguin Books.

Schipper, S. (2015). Towards a 'Post-Neoliberal' mode of housing regulation? The Israeli Social Protest of Summer 2011. *International Journal of Urban and Regional Research,* 39(6), 1137–1154. https://doi.org/10.1111/1468-2427.12318

Scott-Phillips, T. (2014). *Speaking Our Minds: Why Human Communication is Different, and How Language Evolved to Make it Special.* London: Red Globe Press.

Scott-Phillips, T. C., Dickins, T. E., & West, S. A. (2011). Evolutionary theory and the ultimate-proximate distinction in the human behavioral sciences. *Perspectives on Psychological Science,* 6(1), 38–47. https://doi.org/10.1177/1745691610393528

Simon, R. J., & Lynch, J. P. (1999). A comparative assessment of public opinion toward immigrants and immigration policies. *International Migration Review*, 33(2), 455–467. https://doi.org/10.1177/019791839903300207

Skitka, L. J., & Tetlock, P. E. (1993). Providing public assistance: Cognitive and motivational processes underlying liberal and conservative policy preferences. *Journal of Personality and Social Psychology*, 65(6), 1205.

Smith, V. L. (2003). Constructivist and ecological rationality in economics. *American Economic Review*, 93(3), 465–508. https://doi.org/10.1257/000282803322156954

——. (2007). *Rationality in Economics: Constructivist and Ecological Forms*. Cambridge: Cambridge University Press.

Sniderman, P. M., Petersen, M. B., Slothuus, R., & Stubager, R. (2014). *Paradoxes of Liberal Democracy: Islam, Western Europe, and the Danish Cartoon Crisis*. Princeton, NJ: Princeton University Press.

Solomon-Harris, L. M., Mullin, C. R., & Steeves, J. K. (2013). TMS to the 'occipital face area' affects recognition but not categorization of faces. *Brain and Cognition*, 83(3), 245–251.

Sowell, T. (2011). *Economic Facts and Fallacies*. New York: Basic Books.

Spelke, E., Phillips, A., & Woodward, A. L. 1995 Infants' knowledge of object motion and human action. In D. Sperber, D. Premack, & A. J. Premack (Eds.), *Causal Cognition: A Multidisciplinary Debate* (pp. 44–78). New York: Oxford University Press.

Sperber, D. (1985). Anthropology and psychology: Towards an epidemiology of representations. *Man*, 20(1), 73–89. https://doi.org/10.2307/2802222

——. (1991). The epidemiology of beliefs. In C. Fraser (Ed.), *Psychological Studies of Widespread Beliefs*. Oxford: Oxford University Press.

——. (1996). *Explaining culture: A naturalistic approach*. Malden, MA: Blackwell.

——. (1997). Intuitive and Reflective Beliefs. *Mind and Language*, 12 (1), 67–83.

——. (2000). Metarepresentations in an evolutionary perspective. In D. Sperber (Ed.), *Metarepresentations: A Multidisciplinary Perspective* (pp. 117–137). New York: Oxford University Press.

Sperber, D., & Wilson, D. (1995). *Relevance. Communication and Cognition*. Oxford: Blackwell.

Starmans, C., Sheskin, M., & Bloom, P. (2017). Why people prefer unequal societies. *Nature Human Behaviour*, 1(4), 0082. https://doi.org/10.1038/s41562-017-0082

Stephan, W. G., Ybarra, O., & Bachman, G. (1999). Prejudice toward immigrants 1. *Journal of Applied Social Psychology*, 29(11), 2221–2237.

Sugiyama, L. S. (2004). Illness, injury, and disability among Shiwiar forager-horticulturalists: Implications of health-risk buffering for the evolution of human life history. *American Journal of Physical Anthropology: The Official Publication of the American Association of Physical Anthropologists*, 123(4), 371–389. https://doi.org/10.1002/ajpa.10325

Sugiyama, L. S., Tooby, J., & Cosmides, L. (2002). Cross-cultural evidence of cognitive adaptations for social exchange among the Shiwiar of Ecuadorian Amazonia. *Proceedings of the National Academy of Sciences*, 99(17), 11537–11542. https://doi.org/10.1073/pnas.122352999

Tajfel, H. (1970). Experiments in intergroup discrimination. *Scientific American*, 223(5), 96–103.

Tetlock, P. E., Kristel, O. V., Elson, S. B., Green, M. C., & Lerner, J. S. (2000). The psychology of the unthinkable: taboo trade-offs, forbidden base rates, and heretical counterfactuals. *Journal of Personality and Social Psychology*, 78(5), 853. https://doi.org/10.1037//0022-3514.78.5.853

Tooby, J., & Cosmides, L. (2010). Groups in mind: The coalitional roots of war and morality. In H. Høgh-Olesen (Ed.), *Human Morality and Sociality: Evolutionary and Comparative Perspectives* (pp. 191–234). Basingstoke: Palgrave Macmillan.

Tremoulet, P. D., & Feldman, J. (2000). Perception of animacy from the motion of a single object. *Perception*, 29(8), 943–951. https://doi.org/10.1068/p3101

Trivers, R. L. (1971). The evolution of reciprocal altruism. *The Quarterly Review of Biology*, 46(1), 35–57.

Tsao, D. Y., & Livingstone, M. S. (2008). Mechanisms of face perception. *Annual Review of Neuroscience*, 31, 411–437. https://doi.org/10.1146/annurev.neuro.30.051606.094238

Williamson, M. R., & Wearing, A. J. (1996). Lay people's cognitive models of the economy. *Journal of Economic Psychology*, 17(1), 3–38.

Wilson, T. D., & Hodges, S. D. (1992). Attitudes as temporary constructions. In L. L. Martin & A. Tesser (Eds.), *The Construction of Social Judgments* (pp. 37–65). Hillsdale, NJ: Erlbaum.

Wood, G. (2002). Fifty economic fallacies exposed. *Institute of Economic Affairs Occasional Paper* (129). London: Institute of Economic Affairs.

Worstall, T. (2014). *20 Economics Fallacies*. Cambridge: Searching Finance Ltd.

Yuen, T. W., & Greene, M. (2011). Impact of the Recent Financial Crisis on Subjective Perceptions of the Economy: Findings from Hong Kong, Guangdong, and Beijing. *Chinese Economy*, 44(3), 45–58. https://doi.org/10.2753/CES1097-1475440303

Zaller, J. R. (1992). *The Nature and Origins of Mass Opinion*. Cambridge: Cambridge University Press.

6. Detecting Mental Disorder

Introductory Note

Who do we see as mad, and why? How do people decide that some person (possibly themselves) suffers from a mental disorder? History and anthropology tell us that in all human societies, people readily identify some forms of behavior as evidence for some dysfunction. In modern societies, we delegate final decisions about such matters to medical specialists. But that is of course a recent phenomenon (Porter, 2004). And, even in places with psychiatric experts, an individual must be identified as suffering from some disorder before medicine is involved. All this raises the question, how do people detect mental disorder?

I was surprised to find that there was very little description of these criteria in the literature. Anthropologists did describe various local interpretations and explanations of madness, e.g., as the work of spirits, a consequence of witchcraft, an imbalance in humors or elemental components of the person... but what behavior had prompted the initial perception of disorder? In brutal terms, what do you have to do to seem mad?

One might imagine that the criteria could be entirely specific to each culture, but that is certainly false. Manifestations of mental disorder are identified in strikingly similar ways in very different places. We can recognize what Horatio describes as Hamlet's 'wild and whirling words' (*Hamlet*, I–v), as well as the hallucinations, incoherent speech, inappropriate emotional reactions, conversations with non-existent interlocutors, etc. Anthropologists who do fieldwork have little difficulty in perceiving mental disorder in the most exotic (to them) cultural environments.

      https://doi.org/10.11647/OBP.0257.10

In this article, I proposed that people in different cultures use the same implicit criteria for mental disorder, which derive from our intuitive psychology, sometimes called 'theory of mind' (Leslie et al., 2004). It provides us with interpretations of people's observable behaviors, utterances, and gestures, in terms of things that we could not observe, such as other people's beliefs and intentions. Our intuitive psychology works on particular assumptions about the way minds work, how perception causes beliefs, how beliefs interact with intentions, how intentions explain behavior, etc. Naturally, all these assumptions are implicit. In our everyday interactions we need not be aware of their content or their operation.

Intuitive psychology is present in all normally functioning human minds, mostly as a result of natural selection pressures for cooperation (Tomasello, 2009). Humans cannot coordinate their behavior on joint goals unless they mentally represent other agents' intentions and beliefs. This evolutionary context explains why our intuitive psychology generally works smoothly when we interact with typical adults who would have been the cooperation partners that mattered most to our fitness, but is defeated by atypical minds, like those of infants or animals from another species. (Interaction with those two kinds of agents is handled by systems specialized in kin-selection and parenting (Hrdy, 2009) or predator-prey relations (H. C. Barrett, 2005), respectively).

This origin in cooperation has the important consequence that intuitive psychology is not just a descriptive mechanism that tells us what happened in other minds. It is also normative—it implies a description of the way a mind ought to work (Stich, 1983). But that also explains why our intuitive psychology alone does not produce any description or explanation of mental disorder. It just produces a 'mind not working' signal when it is defeated, a natural equivalent of the 'syntax error' of computer systems.

In this article I describe two consequences of these features of intuitive psychology. First, they allow us to predict which kinds of behaviors will be identified as evidence of underlying mental disorder, and which will remain 'invisible' to our intuitions. Second, the fact that intuitive psychology detects dysfunction but produces no representation of how it occurs creates an explanatory gap that is filled by all manner of culturally transmitted explanations, in many cases imagined agents like witches or spirits. Interestingly, people imagine those mystical agents as endowed with the kinds of minds that our intuitive psychology expects—minds that perceive what happens around them, form beliefs on the basis of perceptions, combine desires and beliefs to form goals, and so forth (J. L. Barrett, 2000; Boyer, 2003). So it seems that in most human societies, people cannot escape intuitive psychology when they want to explain behavior—first, it triggers the intuition of disorder, and second, it is used to explain disorder.

Isn't modern psychiatry often engaged in the same operation? Medical detection of mental disorder is of course framed by expectations of intuitive psychology. Patients are confirmed as patients because their behavior deviates from the expectations of intuitive psychology. Indeed, the catalogue of symptoms used by the American psychiatric profession, the Diagnostic and Statistical Manual (American Psychiatric Association, 1995), is mostly a list of deviations from the expectations of normative intuitive psychology. But beyond detection, the ideal of a scientific psychiatry would be to provide explanations, to describe the connections between observed behaviors and reported states of mind, on the one hand, and particular neuro-cognitive mechanisms, on the other (Murphy, 2006). Unfortunately, we are very far from having sufficiently precise computational descriptions of the neuro-cognitive processes that underpin mental dysfunction. Perhaps that is because the initial description, in terms of deviations from our theory of mind expectations, just does not capture the underlying similarities and differences in disorders. That discrepancy between our intuitions and possible underlying mechanisms is particularly clear in extreme cases of delusion, in which the patient seems to hold an irrational belief, e.g., that a part of their body is not actually theirs, that a relative has been replaced with a clone, and so forth. Interpreting delusions constitutes a formidable challenge, precisely because we cannot use any of the inferential tools supplied by our intuitive psychology (McKay, 2012). The most precise models for such delusions necessarily rely on neuroscience models that are completely alien to intuitive psychology (Gerrans, 2014). So intuitive psychology, which is indispensable to human interaction— its impairment in autism, for instance, has catastrophic consequences for the social life of patients (Lai et al., 2014)—may also constitute the most formidable obstacle to our understanding of mental disorder.

References

American Psychiatric Association. (1995). *Diagnostic and Statistical Manual of Mental Disorders, Vol. IV-R* (4th ed.). Washington, DC: American Psychiatric Publishing, Inc.

Barrett, H. C. (2005). Adaptations to Predators and Prey. In D. M. Buss (Ed.), *The Handbook of Evolutionary Psychology*. Hoboken, NJ: John Wiley & Sons.

Barrett, J. L. (2000). Exploring the natural foundations of religion. *Trends in Cognitive Sciences*, 4, 29–34. https://doi.org/10.1016/s1364-6613(99)01419-9

Boyer, P. (2003). Religious thought and behaviour as by-products of brain function. *Trends in Cognitive Sciences*, 7, 119–124. https://doi.org/ 10.1016/ s1364-6613(03)00031-7

Gerrans, P. (2014). *The Measure of Madness: Philosophy of Mind, Cognitive Neuroscience, and Delusional Thought*. Cambridge, MA: MIT Press.

Hrdy, S. B. (2009). *Mothers and Others: The Evolutionary Origins of Mutual Understanding*. Cambridge, MA: Belknap Press of Harvard University Press.

Lai, M.-C., Lombardo, M. V., & Baron-Cohen, S. (2014). Autism. *The Lancet*, 383, 896–910. https://doi.org/10.1016/S0140-6736(13)61539-1

Leslie, A. M., Friedman, O., & German, T. P. (2004). Core mechanisms in 'theory of mind'. *Trends in Cognitive Sciences*, 8, 529–533. https://doi.org/ 10.1016/j. tics.2004.10.001

McKay, R. T. (2012). Delusional inference. *Mind & Language*, 27(3), 330–355. https://doi.org/10.1111/j.1468-0017.2012.01447.x

Murphy, D. (2006). *Psychiatry in the Scientific Image*. Cambridge, MA: MIT Press.

Porter, R. (2004). *Madmen: A Social History of Madhouses, Mad Doctors & Lunatics*. Stroud: Tempus.

Stich, S. (1983). *From Folk-psychology to Cognitive Science: The Case against Belief*. Cambridge, MA: MIT Press.

Tomasello, M. (2009). *Why We Cooperate*. Cambridge, MA: MIT Press.

Intuitive Expectations and the Detection of Mental Disorder

A Cognitive Background to Folk-Psychiatries[1]

Abstract. How is mental dysfunction detected? How do cultural models of mental disorder affect this process of detection? Attempts to answer these questions have not often been made in the research, as they fall between two domains: that of cross-cultural psychiatry (which looks at the dysfunction itself) and anthropological ethno-psychiatry (which looks at cultural models of sanity and insanity). In this paper, I set out a model to illustrate this 'missing link' between behavior and cultural models, founded on experiential evidence for intuitive psychology. Typical adult minds contain certain intuitive expectations about mental function and behavior, and these are used to perceive certain sorts of dysfunctional behavior. It appears that there is a 'catalogue' of potential behaviors that activate this intuition, and therefore the symptoms that are present in culturally specific folk-understandings of mental dysfunction are also restricted. It is also suggested that certain mental dysfunctions are 'invisible' to folk-understandings due to their lack of obvious breaches of principles of intuitive psychology. This standpoint helps us to

---

1   Some of the contents of this chapter have been expressed earlier in Boyer, P. (2010) Intuitive Detection of Mental Disorder: Cognitive Background to Folk-Psychiatries, *Philosophical Psychology* 23(6): 821–844. https://doi.org/10.1080/09515089.2010.529 049

comprehend the cultural stability and spread of certain views of mental disorder.

1. Introduction

The concept of mental disorder is one which exists across the world—people in each and every country have a certain way of classifying and modelling this notion. This leads us to pose several questions: do those in different groups and communities view the concept of mental disorder as consisting of similar aspects? Are there limitless ways to envisage the concept or are our categorizations based on some common underlying principles? If these principles exist, where did they emanate from, and do they have influence over the purportedly scientific models and classifications in psychiatry?

These questions were traditionally approached by two disparate disciplines: cross-cultural psychiatry—a branch of mainstream psychiatry — and ethno-psychiatry, stemming from cultural anthropology. This disparity has led to various theoretical problems and uncertainties, which may yet be overcome by the advances in intuitive psychology (or 'theory of mind') and in the psychology of culture. We are now able to set forth a synthetic model which suggests that all normal adult minds across the world contain certain intuitive expectations about normative mental function and behavior, based on common underlying principles. These expectations are constrained by intuitive psychology, which influences both the detection of disorder (through affecting people's recognition of certain kinds of behavior as symptomatic of mental dysfunction) and the explanation of disorder. Thus, it seems that, despite the very different cultural conceptions of sanity and mental dysfunction, the underlying principles are simple and the same.

2. A Prototypical Scenario and a Question

The social interactions that we will consider throughout this paper usually take the following form:

1. An individual experiences some type of mental dysfunction.

2. Other people begin to notice that individual's behavior:

    a. At a certain point, the individual's behavior subverts the expectations of the other people involved in an interaction;

    b. The behavior cannot be easily or logically explained or repaired, and/or:

    c. The behavior is repeated, or similar behavior occurs, with similar results (lack of clear or logical explanation).

3. People perceive the individual to be experiencing an example of D, a local category or set of possible categories that fit(s) this type of discernible behavior.

4. A causal model of D is considered, which aligns with a locally, personally or culturally wide-ranging explanatory model M for these people.

5. People contemplate how the perceived issue could be effectively diminished.

Cross- (or trans-) cultural psychiatry predominantly focuses on step [1], attempting to discover the limits of variation within mental dysfunction, subject to cultural background (Stein, 1993). Inversely, ethno-psychiatry predominantly focuses on steps [3–5], delineating the models or suppositions lying beneath certain kinds of nosography and etiology, as well as contemplating treatment, the potential for specialist care, and the effectiveness of different techniques (Jovanovski, 1995).

It is notable that neither of these disciplines mentions the cognitive processes through which mental disorders are recognized (step [2] of the above scenario). Georges Devereux, a founder of modern ethno-psychiatry, comments:

The patient appears on scene—on the printed page [in ethno-psychiatric monographs]—as an already recognized and more or less completely diagnosed neurotic or psychotic, with no mention of the manner in which this status—for a status it is!—has been assigned to him. (Devereux, 1980) p. 247

While evidence from history and cultural anthropology has made us aware that steps [3–5] in the above scenario vary around the world, no principled model exists to illustrate the potential for variation in the area of detection ([step 2]), and there is additionally no formal research on the topic.

In order for us to understand how mental disorders are detected, we should examine whether common principles that underlie regular cognitive function play a part. In doing so, we extend the existing research program that explores cultural phenomena as bounded variations within limits set by human cognitive capacities (Sperber & Hirschfeld, 2004). Research performed by cognitive scientists and evolutionary anthropologists has found that the underlying principles we develop at a young age lead to suppositions that help us to acquire our specific cultural norms and ideas — for example, in the areas of folk-biology (Atran, 1990, 1998), kinship and ethnic categories (Hirschfeld, 1994a, 1996), racial categories (Kurzban, Tooby, & Cosmides, 2001), religious beliefs (Atran, 2002), social interaction (Cosmides & Tooby, 1992); (Fiske, 1992); (Tooby & Cosmides, 1996). As a result, we would expect that these underlying principles would also have an influence over how we determine what is acceptable versus atypical behavior.

3. The Background: Intuitive Psychology Expectations

The term 'intuitive psychology' straightforwardly describes the collection of cognitive capacities that help us to understand our own and others' behavior as the result of unobservable mental states and processes (Baron-Cohen, 1995), (Leslie, 1987), (Perner, Leekam, & Wimmer, 1987). The majority of these capacities are subconscious in function — we are unaware of the inferential processes that lead us to establish overt explanations of other people's behaviors. The capacities are likely to be situation-specific and distinct from each other, each with their own lower-level neural sub-capacities (C. D. Frith, 1996). We have only gradually begun to be able to (tentatively) describe the capacities involved in normal, adult intuitive psychology—our initial, more detailed descriptions came from instances where the system does not function, such as in autistic children or in animals from other species.

In this paper, we can limit our concentration to only the most basic intuitive principles involved in the process. Whilst there are key theoretical disparities between models of intuitive psychology, it is fortunate that its core standards are remarkably uncontroversial, and include:

[1] *Intentional states; representations of our existing apparent realities.* One notion of intuitive psychology is that people's minds have memories, beliefs, and perceptions 'inside' them, which represent or duplicate the conditions in a person's physical reality. Children realize from the age of three that mental representations are not physical objects (Wellmann & Estes, 1986). Beyond that age, we progressively cultivate the idea that our thoughts contain a representation of the circumstances surrounding us—there is a causal link between manifest states of affairs and mental representations (Leslie, Friedman, & German, 2004). Additionally, we use indirect cues — such as the extent to which people's gaze follows objects and other people's gaze—to subconsciously confirm the link between external objects and people's mental states (Friesen & Kingstone, 1998). Broadly speaking, by seeing that an object aligns with and seems to 'attend' to another object, we get a strong indication that it is an intentional agent (Johnson, Slaughter, & Carey, 1998).

[2] *Agency as internal causation.* One of the first assumptions that infants make is that agents, unlike other objects, decide their own behavior from within (Baldwin, Baird, Saylor, & Clark, 2001); (Rochat, Morgan, & Carpenter, 1997). This assumption is founded on the particular psycho-physics of animate motion (Michotte, 1963); (Schlottman & Anderson, 1993); (Tremoulet & Feldman, 2000) and on additional cues that reveal internal causation and production of behavior (Gelman, Durgin, & Kaufman, 1995); (Williams, 2000). Intentional agents' actions relate to objects and states in a principled way (Blythe, Todd, & Miller, 1999), and even infants can decode their orientations — for example, by reaching a specific object of interest and avoiding obstacles (Csibra, Gergely, Biro, Koos, & Brockbank, 1999); (Gergely, Nadasdy, Csibra, & Biro, 1995). Attributing more intangible intentions to objects is something that children learn to do at a young age, such as by emulating effective rather than ineffective actions in the handling of tools (Want & Harris, 2002) and using actors' visible emotions to deduce the effectiveness of the action (Phillips, Wellman, & Spelke, 2002).

[3] *Memory as a store.* Throughout the world, the inherent idea of memory as a store is pervasive and meaningful—to the extent that even certain scientific models of memory processes are based upon it (Roediger & Geraci, 2004). While research has not focused on this theme, intuitive psychology also appears to accept the copying of experiences

onto memory stores and their later retrieval in the configuration in which they were experienced, which is in conflict with a large amount of psychological research into human memory (Ross & Wilson, 2000); (Rubin, Schrauf, & Geenberg, 2003).

[4] *Inferential and communicate coherence.* In order to communicate, we must make inferences and follow strict, implicit pragmatic principles (Grice, 1975) which we develop at a very young age. These principles influence infants' communicative development (Trevarthen & Aitken, 2001) and acquisition of new vocabulary (Bloom, 2000). We generally cannot interpret others' utterances or communications without comprehending the speaker's intentions—the way in which they are trying to influence the listener's representations (Noveck & Sperber, 2004); (Sperber & Wilson, 1995). During conversations, implicit adaptations and small 'repairs' allow people to sustain comparable representations of the circumstances they are discussing.

[5] *Emotion, norms and empathy.* We build much of our information about other people's mental processes on the inadvertent reading of minute emotional cues — such as facial expressions, voice and gestures—and of the potential reasons behind them. Again, this ability evolves from a young age—at five months old, infants behave differently when faced with demonstrations of different emotions on a familiar face (D'Entremont & Muir, 1997). Different cultural groups develop comparable cues at similar times (Ekman, 1999). To detect and recognize certain kinds of emotions, specific neural circuitry is required (Kesler-West et al., 2001), separate from broader facial identity processing.

If cues are lacking, we use our inherent psychological principles to deduce what the emotional repercussions of certain circumstances would be. A substantial database of certainties about social relations is necessary in order to do this—we need to recognize the emotions that influence the different types of relationships, from family to partners, friends to acquaintances, and so on.

People tend to assume that those who are part of their cultural group adhere to the cultural norms to an equivalent extent—these norms explicitly prescribe behavior, which is connected to emotion or attitude (Nichols, 2002a). Assumptions about emotions originate from a broad ability to be empathic using simulation—such as internally simulating our own emotions resulting from a situation in order to perceive others (Decety & Sommerville, 2003). Our inherent expectations about emotionally relevant hypotheticals (such as deducing how somebody feels when their family is threatened, or when they are abandoned by their friends) could also be founded on this sort of simulation (Gordon & Olson, 1998).

[6] *Principled motivation.* Intuitive psychology comprises a particular model of how intentions are connected to available information and background preferences (Malle, 2004). It also differentiates desire and intention—desire is seen as a simple preference state, and intention is seen as the fusion of that state with available information to produce a plan of action (Malle & Knobe, 2001). Intentions are presupposed to make the attainment of desires and goals more probable. Children appear to develop their understanding of desire and intention before the age of three (Wellman, Phillips, & Rodriguez, 2000). They view desires as foundational when clarifying behavior, to a greater extent than physiological states (Moses, Coon, & Wusinich, 2000), but even young children appreciate that desires may clash (Bennett & Galpert, 1993).

And numerous other principles. This list of inherent principles is merely a summary of research in this area—it does not assert that there is concurrence on the functioning of intuitive psychological capacities in this field. With the completion of more research, we may be able to expand the list, but the key points at present are the generally undisputed findings above. Later in this paper, the restrictions of intuitive psychology will be further discussed, but it is now pertinent to discuss the way it is used to comprehend the perception of mental disorders.

4. Intuitive Catalogue of Detectable Mental Dysfunction

We can now attempt to detail the potential types of evident mental disorder using the broad inherent principles of intuitive psychology. Table 1 below details a list of assumptions and behaviors that defy these assumptions.

This list is not exhaustive—it is merely an initial attempt to illustrate that intuitive psychology does tacitly anticipate particular manifestations of mental disorder. Below, the items in the list are discussed in more depth, correlating with the categories introduced in the previous section:

[1] *Intentional states; representations of our existing apparent realities.* Our inherent presuppositions about intentionality are violated when an individual does not react to occurrences (for example, if they are in a vegetative state, hebetude, or coma) or to noteworthy stimuli (for example, if their reflexes are lacking or have declined, they neglect to gaze at moving objects, or display general indifference). Similarly, individuals who do not follow culturally appropriate types of gaze following and direct gaze cause a similar violation.

[2] *Agency as cause of behavior.* In this area, potential indications of atypical functioning comprise involuntary motor behavior (such as Vitus, tics, or alien hand), and circumstances where an individual's intention and action appear not to correspond (for example, if they are surprised by their own actions). Involuntary speech that flouts social norms (such as in Tourette Syndrome) are recognized in the same manner.

[3] *Memory as a store.* This model hypothesizes that memory impediments would be interpreted as leakage. Unlike in scientific models, failing to recall a recent, common occurrence would be viewed as a procedure of deletion, rather than a breakdown in organization or encoding.

Table 1. Inherent expectations and corresponding potential violations .
Table by P Boyer.

Intuitive assumption	Potential disruption
1a. Intentional states, representation of external states of affairs	Vegetative, unconscious states
1b. Direct perception of what is manifest	Failure to register or react to what's around, illusory perception of non-existent states of affairs
1c. Perception causes belief	Beliefs or other mental states causing perception
2a. Agency: Motor behavior as result of inner intentional states	Apparently unintended gestures or complex behaviors
2b. Agency: Speech controlled by intentions	Talking in strange voices, unexpected changes in intonation

Intuitive assumption	Potential disruption
2c. Agency: Self is the origin of intentions	Involuntary action
2d. Unitary self	Dislocation, appearance of different personalities
3a. Memory as a store	Loss of material
3b. Memories caused by experiences	False memories, memories influenced by beliefs
4a. Coherence in inferences from states of affairs	Inferential non-sequiturs, e.g. goals divorced from present situation
4b. Coherence in communication	Conversational non-sequiturs, unexpected changes of topic
5a. Emotions in tune with outcomes	No emotional reaction, emotions not suited to outcomes
5b. Emotional empathy	Failure to empathize
5c. Feelings towards kin	Hostility to kin, neglect
5c. Moral feelings towards non-kin	Behavior not driven by moral imperatives; opportunism; exploitativeness
5d. Feelings about cultural norms, within-group solidarity	Indifference to cultural norms & etiquette, deliberate violation
6a. Motivation towards external goals	Lack of motivation
6b. Motivation in tune with valence of potential outcomes	Desire to bring about negative outcomes / not cause positive ones
6b. Motivation proportional to value of outcomes	Excessive investment in low-value outcomes or converse misjudgment
Others...	Others...

[4] *Inferential and communicative coherence.* An inability to sustain coherence within a conversation would activate the perception of disordered mental processes, as we can see from the clinical accounts of many types of mental disorder—senile dementia and Alzheimer's are often both detected through the manifestation of violations of the principles of pragmatic relevance (Hays, Niven, Godfrey, & Linscott, 2004). As a result, caregivers must slowly modify their expectations of conversations with patients, adapting to their lack of responses, 'repairs', or strategies to diminish ambiguity or misunderstandings (Orange & Zanon, 2006). Likewise, the speech of schizophrenic patients often contains instances of wrong speech-acts, flouting of turn-taking, referential ambiguity (i.e. using pronouns without their referents), lack

of repair, referential incoherence—where multiple subjects are covered in the same statement (Corcoran & Frith, 1996); (Meilijson, Kasher, & Elizur, 2004)—and diminished comprehension of figurative speech and proverbs (Brüne & Bodenstein, 2005).

[5] *Emotion cues.* Individuals recognize when another person seems impassive in response to others' emotional cues, or exhibit unintelligible emotional cues themselves — for example, patients with dementia experience diminished control over emotional expression (Smith, 1995). Schizophrenic patients are often impeded in the perception and analysis of emotional cues, and in the same way, so are autistic children, even high-functioning or Asperger patients (Teunisse & Gelder, 2001). Those with autism find it extremely difficult to recognize emotional cues (Adolphs, Sears, & Piven, 2001), which is exacerbated by their struggle to comprehend the potential basis for others' emotions.

Any breaches of cultural norms or other emotional expectations should be conspicuous. While breaches of etiquette, for example, will not necessarily be perceived as indicative of atypical mental processes— they might instead indicate aggression or poor childhood experiences— persistent breaches with no explanation may be seen as confirmation of disorder (see Clement, 1981, #1956 for an account of this in Samoan culture). Breaches of familial expectations (for example, neglect or abuse towards family members) may also be seen as indicators of basal dysfunction.

[6] *Motivation.* Behaviours that seem to conflict with or oppose a person's own preferences would likely be detected as a disturbance in cognitive functioning. Additionally, individuals with low motivation ('indifference') or, in contrast, those who are highly motivated—to the point of mania—would be contenders for detection. For example, those with schizophrenia are often found to have low levels of motivation, just as high-risk children do (Watt, Grubb, & Erlenmeyer-Kimling, 1982). Similarly, Alzheimer's is frequently detected at an early stage via the degeneration of motivation, past what would be expected for those who are ageing (Ready, Ott, Grace, & Cahn-Weiner, 2003).

The above table does not constitute a list of potential types of mental disorder—it merely looks at the circumstances or behavioral events that could lead to the perception of atypical mental processes. At this point, we have no presuppositions about whether natural or sound instances of mental disorder can be detected consistently via intuition.

5. An Illustration: Mohave Cases

In order to connect a range of observed behaviours with the intuition of disorder, the dysfunction-detection model is suggested. Cases outlined by George Devereux in 'Mohave ethnopsychiatry and suicide' (1961) are useful demonstrations of the model—Devereux details a number of varying case-histories, in detail, separate from his and others' analyses of the behavior, which is an approach scarcely found in ethno-psychiatric ethnography. This permits us to notice the initial perception of the behavior as extraordinary and the later categorisation of it as an example of culturally specific dysfunction. In Table 2 below, all symptoms outlined within case-studies are set out—only behaviors described by participants, excluding the ethnographer and other investigators, are included.

We can presuppose that the disclosure of these utterances indicates that individuals thought the accounts of behavior were pertinent and indicative of an intrinsic disorder or condition. It is significant, therefore, that the majority of the utterances describe obvious breaches of inherent psychological expectations (compare Table 2 with Table 1). As mentioned previously, psychological contraventions often appear alongside other norm-contraventions, but the list additionally indicates that the psychological contraventions are recognized and acknowledged without fail. For example, a woman is reported to be a nymphomaniac (case-study 14), but for a Mohave onlooker, a salient aspect of the situation is that she was sometimes unaware of what she was doing. Similarly, losing consciousness during epileptic fits (case-study 6) is made significant by the individual not experiencing pain. An anti-social person (case-study 20) is additionally reported to be misled ('he seemed to believe he was going to war').

Naturally, this is not intended as overwhelming proof for the violation-detection model. That would necessitate a detailed examination of case-studies pertaining to a range of cultural environments, beyond what can be achieved in this paper. The intention here is to exemplify that breaches of psychological expectations are core to the perception of putative dysfunction. In fact, out of all the cases detailed by Devereux, only one (case-study 23) describes atypical or improper behavior (beating one's in-laws) that could be interpreted in any way other than psychologically.

Table 2. Collation of symptoms outlined in Devereux's case-studies. First column, case-study number; second column, page in Devereux (1961). Third column, quotation from the case-study. Fourth column, principles from Table 1 that may be breached in that case.

Case	p.	Description	#
C2	40	A certain man would get sudden fits of rage, take a stick and beat up people. He lived apart from others.	5a
C6	73	During one of his atcoo: r hanyienk seizures he fell into the fire, burning his hand quite badly. He did not seem to have any feeling (sensitivity) when he burned himself.	1b
C7	74	Suddenly he got up and made a choked, panting noise, which sounded like "ak'".	2a
C12	75	Suddenly he saw him fall down on the sidewalk and "act crazy."	2a
C13	78	When one spoke to her, she could not keep her head still, but kept looking around.	2a
C14	79	I was told that even in her old age Nyortc still "copulated around," and that she was ya tcahaetk, i.e., a nymphomaniac. She just did these things without knowing it; although sometimes she did know it.	5d
C19	87	One night, for no known reason, Uto : h cohabited with [had sex with] his younger daughter.	5d
C20	96	He became angry and began to say that he was constantly thinking of killing. [...] He painted his face black, like a warrior going on a warpath, and actually seemed to believe that he was going to war.	4a
			1c
C21	96	He cut off his long braids of hair, the way mourners do, and painted his face black. He declared that he would kill anyone who tried to come in.	4a
C23	97	She picked up a stick and went to her former husband's new residence and "just beat up everybody in that damn place."	4a 5c
C25	114	She just had a tired feeling all the time. She had no appetite.	6a
C31	142	Periods of excitement, during which it was necessary to chain or tie her to her bed.	2a
C32	144	While she was insane her father and her mother came to her. First they called her, and then they ran away. My mother ran away, people immediately ran after her. They must have been the ones she mistook for big balls that seemed to be chasing her.	1c

Case	p.	Description	#
C33	144	One day this old woman ran away from her daughter's house, went down to the riverbank, fell into the mud, and remained there for 2 days.	6b
C34	145	He was sane right up to his death and did no insane talking. He could not move at all.	2a
C35	146	He was unable to get around. He said just anything; sometimes he would even call out the names of all his dead relatives. He would try to get up and pick up anything with in reach and would then throw these objects around.	2a
C36	147	He dreamed that he was visiting his father and his mother, who had died, and toward the end of the dream he even ate food prepared by his dead relatives. Every time he ate anything, he would vomit it out again.	6b
C37	148	People who saw him asked him why he cried, but he replied that he did not know.	5a
C38	149	She began to talk- about anything at all-and kept on raving for about half an hour. At times she rose from her bed as though she were well, and then suddenly tore off her clothes.	4a
C52	203	The charm brought him luck for a while, but, in the end, it "turned against him," and paralyzed his tongue.	4b
C53	205	One of them became so indignant that he got drunk, came back to where his oldest brother kept his vigil and stabbed him.	5c
C58	207	He could no longer speak. He was in a kind of daze. He never acted as though he knew or understood what was going on. He just sat there.	1a
C61	218	She just kept on laughing and seemed unable to stop. We just watched her and let her laugh, until she sat down and fell asleep.	5a
C62	218	A Pueblo Indian girl of 17 began to laugh hysterically and could not stop laughing, even when people slapped her and told her to stop it. She didn't even seem to hear what was said to her.	5a 4b
C68	247	He had a tic since childhood. It consisted of occasional spastic movements of the face.	2a

6. Scope and Limits of Intuitive Psychology Principles

Intuitive psychology comprises a collection of critical inferential systems that function straightforwardly in general, giving us an analysis of perceived behavior with regard to beliefs, purposes, and emotional states—this is known and accepted. It is suggested here that, in the same way, intuitive psychology helps us to discern that a certain individual's mind is dysfunctional; this is the only clear explanation for the individual's behavior breaching the inherent psychology expectations. This model gives inherent psychological expectations the main causal role — it would thus be useful to define their key characteristics.

Are the principles universal? The core question is whether these principles are replicated across the world—do individuals in different cultures possess the same intuitive psychology? It is clear that much of our cognizance of behavior originates from local norms and beliefs about the right way to behave. As a result, individuals' overt interpretations of mind vary significantly (Lillard, 1997; Vinden, 1998), at least in the case of those individuals who attempt to produce an interpretation. However, there is no corroboration of comparable variation within the principles of intuitive psychology themselves—literature from around the world has not found that individuals in different communities decline to orient to the principles above (Table 1) or follow completely different principles (Leslie, 1994; Sperber & Hirschfeld, 2004). The majority of applied studies have looked at developmental features of intuitive psychology, discovering a large amount of overlap in early intuitive psychology principles (Astuti, 2001; Avis & Harris, 1991; Tardif & Wellman, 2000; Yazdi, German, Defeyter, & Siegal, 2006), the timescale of their development (Callaghan et al., 2005; Wellman & Fang, 2006), and their relationships to other mental processes (Chasiotis, Kiessling, Hofer, & Campos, 2006). If we observe the profuse amount of verification for early development of brain structures in line with intuitive psychology, this is to be expected (C. D. Frith, 1996; Luo & Baillargeon, 2007).

Are intuitive principles a conjecture of rationality? Psychological expectations should not be understood as an assumption of rationality, nor muddled with the broad presupposition that 'people generally behave rationally.' In fact, it seems clear that intuitive psychology is made up of exact, situational expectations and deductions—not an inferential hypothesis of the way individuals behave. Research has shown, for example, that even at an early age, we envision that people's beliefs are shaped according to their observations, rather than their observations being shaped by their beliefs (Leslie et al., 2004), and as a result, we have specific assumptions (e.g. 'X saw a dog here, so X believes there's a dog here'). However, this principle has not been shown to be related to a broader presupposition of people behaving logically the majority of the time—in contrast, we often expect others to behave illogically. Many cultures presuppose that in situations where an individual is angry (and other similar situations), they are likely to act in a way that they will find regrettable afterwards.

Intuitive principles are not fixed—they can be both reinforced or dismissed when additional context-specific considerations are taken into account. For example, while small children presuppose that the presence of an object A will be detected by everyone in the vicinity, this presupposition can be overcome if there is an obvious obstruction to other people's perception of object A (Luo & Baillargeon, 2007). Intuitive psychological analysis of behavior is, for the most part, a kind of relevance process, consisting of a detailed succession of presuppositions which lead to an optimal interpretation of the observable behavior (Sperber & Wilson, 1995). There is an unlimited set of circumstances where perceptions and beliefs do not match up—the principles of intuitive psychology are merely preset assumptions, with 'all else being equal' (Leslie, German, & Polizzi, 2005).

This should also be true for the discernment of dysfunction that occurs when presuppositions are breached, which would explain the variance of behaviors that precipitate such a discernment across culture and history. For example, in the past, speaking aloud in public when no other conversational partners were present was viewed as indicative of dysfunction in many parts of the world, but this behavior has come to be expected, and it is presupposed that the individual is likely to be on the phone. Mental dysfunction is perceived as a result of a network of illative operations, which may either support or weaken the original intuition.

Intuitive principles are not invariably correct. In the field of philosophy, it is still being debated as to whether the constructs that our psychological expectations predicate (such as beliefs, purposes, emotions, etc.) are 'really real'—whether our intuitive psychology has scientific value (Churchland, 1981). However, this discussion is immaterial for our purposes, as we are focusing on the way in which intuitive psychology functions, and not whether it does so correctly or not. This should be noted as we move to discussing our inklings of dysfunction. These inklings that are activated by an individual's behavior in a certain context may be erroneous. Broadly speaking, the set of behaviors that lead to such discernments may be divergent—in the fields of established neuro-psychology or psychiatry, they may be classified separately. Our perceptions of dysfunctional behavior might only have a minor overlap with true dysfunctionality. In fact, many types of dysfunction are likely to go undetected by intuitive psychology.

Are presumed dysfunction and broader norm-violation alike? It could be questioned whether breaches of psychological expectations are actually the basis for the perception of dysfunctional behavior—some might argue that they relate back to a more general defiance of social norms. For example, if someone declines to respond to a question, they are not only breaching a psychological expectation, but also flouting the rules of conversation; similarly, a sociopath who lacks remorse after causing pain is not only behaving atypically, but also flouting the social rules that surround violence.

However, this straightforward, domain-general analysis is not supported by research findings. Studies in the areas of behavioral and developmental neuropsychology and neuroscience show that intuitive psychology is domain-specific—its inputs and principles are separate from those contained within other mental systems (Blakemore et al., 2001; U. Frith, 2001; Leslie et al., 2004). There is an overwhelming lack of convincing affirmations for the existence of cognitive mechanisms that survey norms (and their violations). Instead, we find evidence for highly specific mechanisms that keep track of violations of moral imperatives as distinct from social conventions (Haidt, Kesebir, Plessner, Betsch, & Betsch, 2008; Turiel, Eisenberg, Damon, & Lerner, 2006); violations of exchange principles and economic fairness (Cosmides & Tooby, 1992; Kurzban, 2001); violations of incest revulsion (Lieberman, Tooby, & Cosmides, 2007); betrayal of the implicit requirements of friendship (Hess & Hagen, 2006), and violations of status and manners

(Nichols, 2002b). These kinds of violations all transpire in a certain type of situation, due to certain sorts of purposes. A broad operation that monitors their concurrent features does not seem to exist.

These conclusions lead us to suggest that manifest breaches of presuppositions lead to a certain sort of 'dysfunction intuition' that differs from the contravention of other norms. This intuition might be supported, altered, or weakened in reality due to the contravention of other non-psychological expectations. Additionally, we can assume that there are numerous instances where an individual is assessed as atypical due to psychological or non-psychological violations, but neither we nor the person who assesses this are aware of it.

7. Prediction of 'Invisible' Conditions

Our intuitive psychology comprises a group of presuppositions that allow us to comprehend and anticipate other people's behavior in the majority of everyday situations. However, it is not a fully comprehensive account of how and why intentional agents behave. Intuitive psychology wholly focuses on conspecifics. The majority of animals' motivation and conceptions are significantly disparate from our intuitive expectations (for example, see Grandin, 2005 #3976).

It happens that, even among conspecifics, our intuitive psychology frequently cannot help us to interpret behavior—for example, the behavior of young children, whose utterances and arrivals at certain conclusions can be perplexing. This can be explained by the assumption that, if intuitive psychology only accounts for a section of mental function, dysfunction within systems which it contains no presuppositions for will be 'invisible'. This assumption appears to be correct, especially when the dysfunction pertains to certain features of cognition, excepting reasoning, planning, and decision-making.

The condition of prosopagnosia—the failure to associate the visual stimulus of a person' face with information held in memory about the person (de Renzi, Faglioni, Grossi, & Nichelli, 1991)—serves as a good example. This handicap only applies to the global visual trace of the face, not to face-details or other aspects of an individual (Farah, Levinson, & Klein, 1995). Consequently, patients can overcome it by heeding facial features, voice, gait, and other characteristics in order to interact appropriately. It is improbable that this condition could be detected via intuitive psychology, because its only symptom is a prolonged interval before responding to an individual's presence. This is unlikely to be recognized—if it was, it may be misinterpreted as illustrating some sort of difficulty with vision, memory, or social interaction (i.e. an unwillingness to interact with others). In a similar way, the majority of kinds of visual agnosia—where an individual becomes confused when asked to name and describe common types of objects or animals (Dixon, 2000)—could be missed or misinterpreted.

Specific neuro-psychological conditions are generally expected to activate the sense that a dysfunction of some sort is present—however, it is hard for intuitive psychology to define what, exactly, this dysfunction is. For example, Tourette's syndrome causes breaches of etiquette that are detectable even in divergent cultures (Staley, Wand, & Shady, 1997), and these breaches are often not attributed to cognitive control, due to our intuitive psychology's unfamiliarity with the idea of distinct neural procedures and control loops connecting them. Another example is aphasia, which is frequently assumed to be a kind of insanity, due to the lack of meaning that can be derived from their utterances. Because intuitive psychology contains no detailed account of the intricate ways in which thoughts and speech are linked, disruption of speech is often assumed to represent disruption of thought.

8. From Intuitions of Disorder to Folk-Models

The operations that lead to the perception and analysis of mental disorder can be most accurately portrayed by describing causal links between disorder, the resulting behavior, the perception of behaviors controlled by intuitive psychology, and the patterns of acquisition and communication that cause models to be chosen. These links are illustrated in Figure 1 below.

8.1 What Makes Folk-Models "Folk"?

Up to this point, we have mainly concentrated on how intuitive psychology sorts the behaviors that are notable for their breaching of expectations from the others. This leads us to question whether this

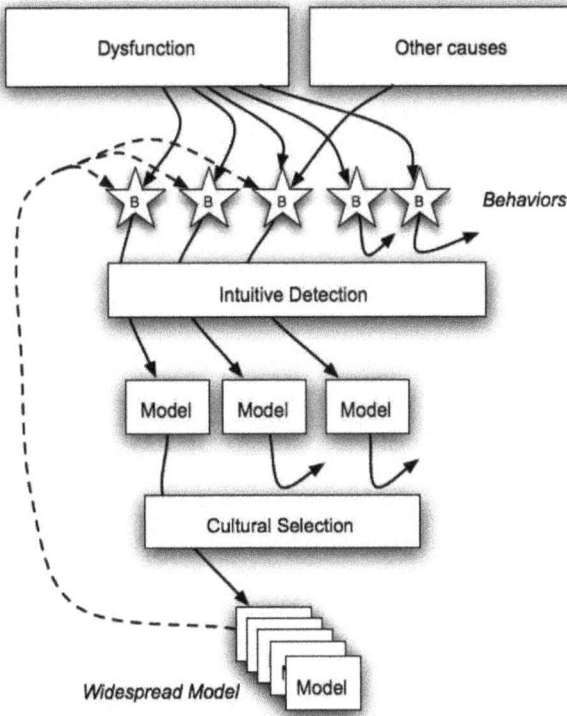

Fig. 1. A reduced model of the detection of mental disorder. Dysfunction sets off behaviors (stars), of which only a few can be perceived as breaches of intuitive psychology (many 'bounce off' intuitive perception). In certain cases, perception may be erroneous (where the origin of the behavior is something other than dysfunction). Perception of dysfunction notifies and limits people's models—only some of these complete the stages of acquisition and communication (ineffective models 'bounce off' transmission). Models which are often triggered may have feedback ('looping') effects both on themselves (transmission biases) and on certain people's behaviors. These are illustrated using dotted lines. (Figure by P Boyer)

system of perception induces general cross-cultural ideas of mental disorder.

In order to answer this question, we must first discuss contemporary anthropological models that illustrate the way cultural knowledge is transferred. How are certain models straightforwardly and customarily transmitted within a group? This sort of question is handled by present-day anthropological theory through cultural selection frameworks (Boyd

& Richerson, 1985; Durham, 1991; Sperber, 1985). A key presupposition is that, similarly to other kinds of human interaction, cultural transmission does not involve 'downloading' notions from one mind to another; instead, deductive processes are necessary, in which individuals notice signals in other's behavior, deduce their communicative purposes, and establish concepts founded on their deductions (Sperber, 1996; Tomasello, Kruger, & Ratner, 1993). Consequently, people are always generating modifications of others' representations. The unpredictability of communication and deductions leads us to seek an explanation for the presence of shared representations or 'cultural' information, where many varying models would be expected (Sperber, 1985). By terming certain representations 'cultural', we focus on the similar representations held by participants in a certain group. This similarity is indicative of certain notions and norms being chosen during the procedure of transmission, while others are altered, abandoned, and forgotten.

Cognitive predispositions go some way towards providing an explanation of the repetition of certain notions and norms (Sperber & Hirschfeld, 2004). Research and models originating from experimental and developmental psychology, linguistics, neuro-psychology, and the neurosciences are all unified in the contemporary cognitive anthropology approach, in an attempt to illustrate the power of cognitive predispositions in increasing the probability of specific types of notions and deductions appearing. Certain principles—the majority of which are implicit—accompany and arrange incoming data, which causes certain deductions to follow, regardless of their origin. As a result, we are left with statistical 'attractors' in the population dynamics of cultural transmission (Claidière & Sperber, 2007; Sperber & Hirschfeld, 2004).

8.2 A Basis for Dysfunction Intuition

The argument here is that a sizable amount of culturally transmitted folk-understandings of mental illness originates from cognitive dispositions, which impact cultural transmission significantly. This indicates that instincts about mental disorder are based on a cognitive network that is predominantly applicable across cultures, as opposed to the conventional presuppositions of ethno-psychiatry. Perceptions of atypical behavior are frequently called intrinsically 'cultural' (Gaines,

1992; Jovanovski, 1995) and, in all likelihood, differ to a large extent as a result. In the word of Anthony Marsella: 'mental disorders cannot be understood apart from the [culturally specific] concept of self, because it is the nature of the self which serves to identify 'reality' for a given cultural group and which dictates the definition of what constitutes a symptom [italics added]' (1981, p. 362; see also Good, 1994 #3892 and Sadowsky, 2003 for similar arguments).

It is useful to explore this statement in more detail. Here, the word 'symptom' could be interpreted in two ways—it could mean 'behaviors that people believe to be triggered by the mental dysfunction' or, alternatively, 'behaviors triggered by the mental dysfunction which are overtly built into a model of mental dysfunction'. Marsella appears to have intended the second meaning—in this sense, the statement seems totally justified. Our 'cultural models' of mental dysfunction unquestionably differ according to culture, within certain confines, as we will discuss below. However, we cannot assume that local models govern whether behaviors are or are not perceived as potential proof of mental dysfunction.

An assortment of the behaviors recounted above—including breakdowns in appropriate communication or motor control, incomprehensible emotions and self-destructive behaviors) could activate the instinct that an individual may have a mental disorder, no matter whether that can be related back to or clarified by a local cultural model or not. All European or Western individuals, even those who are not familiar with psychiatry, can interpret the motions of a Tourette's patient as indicative of dysfunction, though they often cannot diagnose what this dysfunction might specifically be. This is also true in other cultures—a range of other atypical behaviors are recognizable as symptomatic of mental disorder, even without the ability to carry out further analysis of it.

8.3 An Illustration: Haslam's Model of Folk-Psychiatry

Certain kinds of behavior are highlighted as representative of mental disorder in the majority of human groups—they correlate across cultures. The steps through which mental disorder is brought about are also hypothesized and locally agreed upon. Conventional ethno-psychiatry details these two stages in comprehending dysfunction (Kleinman, 1988), but may face the topic of culture in an overly 'culturalist' manner, believing culture to be an extrinsic network of representations that is considered from a theoretical point of view, separate from actual cognition (Jovanovski, 1995). Therefore, there is very little structured research into the cognitive procedures incorporated within it.

One anomaly is a sequence of conceptual and experiential papers by Haslam and colleagues that propose a psychological description of Western 'folk-psychiatry' (Giosan, Glovsky, & Haslam, 2001; Haslam, 2005; Haslam & Giosan, 2002). Their model details four different ways that perceptions of behaviors may fluctuate: [1] pathologizing, or in other words, the degree to which the behavior is interpreted as atypical due to it being difficult to clarify; [2] moralizing, where the behavior is thought to be governed by the person and having a certain moral valence; [3] medicalizing, where the behavior is thought to be a direct consequence of an implicit natural condition; [4] psychologizing, where the behavior is thought to be produced mentally but not intentionally — it is the consequence of a mental dysfunction, and the cornerstone is its origin, not its reasons, with decreased moral judgment (Haslam, 2005). Haslam and colleagues also recorded significant cultural variation in the comparative significance of these measurements. While US participants are more likely to prefer an 'internal' perspective of mental dysfunction (particularly 'psychologized' internal disputes), Romanian and Brazilian participants highlight external explanations for it (Giosan et al., 2001).

This model gives us a good foundation for exploring the cognitive procedures that are the basis of Western folk-understandings of mental disorder. Additionally, it gives us a guide for carrying out further experiential studies that build on conventional ethno-psychiatry—in other words, those that build on the accounts of the cognitive procedures involved in individuals considering mental disorder. In future research, it is important to appreciate that pan-specific aspects of human minds are probable authorities over cultural models.

8.4 "Looping Effects" from Models to Behaviors

Ian Hacking detailed the intricate network of links between pathology, its cultural context of appearance, its typical manifestations within that context, its popular categorization, and its scholarly description in a sequence of inquiries into past 'ways of being mad' (Hacking, 1995b, 1998). A 'looping effect' exists, where certain symptoms that have become core to scientific understanding of a condition guide people towards standard exemplifications of mental dysfunction. An instance of this phenomenon comes from Western psychiatry, when conditions such as female hysteria, long-lasting fugue states, and multiple-personality disorder were recognized in the research and thereafter spread throughout the culture (Hacking, 1995a). This examination of looping effects adds to the wealth of research focusing on historical and cultural procedures within the displays and models of dysfunction (see, for example, Porter, 1987 #7829 and Porter, 2004).

We can assist our comprehension of these feedback loops by looking at feed-forward links between the procedures discussed above. Hacking's statements about ideas of mental dysfunction actually constitute a broad evaluation of 'epidemiological' models of cultural transmission. The reality of a highly diffused representation within a certain group helps us to foresee the ways in which it might be transmitted in the future. For example, there is a 'frequency bias', in which it is probable that individuals will acquire and pass on representations that are already popular (Boyd & Richerson, 1985). Instances of disordered behavior overtly noted by others as being dysfunctional have a high probability— all else being equal—of being more salient and more memorable than other atypical behaviors. Just as in other areas of cultural transmission, behaviors that match up with an established pattern are much more likely to be understood and recalled (Bartlett, 1932), where alternative types of atypical or surprising behavior might be brushed off as behavioral 'noise'. Contemporary cognitive anthropology recounts the looping effect of popular ideas and norms in the area of 'race' concepts (Hirschfeld, 1994b), religious and supernatural beliefs (Boyer, 1994), and many more (see e.g. Hirschfeld, 1994 #4583).

9. Conclusion

Our models of behavioral dysfunction originate from culture, in the same way that narratives, scholarship, etiquette, politics, cuisine, musical traditions, and religious rituals do. Mental dispositions that make up a section of our common cognitive architecture govern these cultural formations (Sperber, 1996). This is the foundation of my argument that intuitive psychology should be considered to be the prime point of derivation of implicit presuppositions about other agents' behaviors and, as a result, a prime component in making us discern that an individual may have a mental disorder. While intuitive psychology does not describe why a behavior is atypical or the reasons behind its occurrence, it leaves a gap in which we can place a causal process that gives rise to this particular dysfunction. We may or may not fill the gap with a model of mental disorder that others in our cultural group subscribe to. Since some dysfunctions are invisible, and certain types of causal models are inherently more credible than others, intuitive psychology restricts the manner in which individuals form culturally pervasive ideas of mental disorder in two areas.

One objective of this model is to supply the 'missing link' between the incidence of certain behaviors (including those ascribable to mental disorder) and pervasive cultural models of mental disorder. The majority of cross-cultural psychiatry is centered around mental disorder without considering why certain forms of dysfunction are more noticeable than others, or why some recognizable atypicality is salient but some is not, or why certain recognizable atypicality is the focus of culturally transmitted models. In contrast, the majority of ethno-psychiatric research presupposes that the cultural models supply us with a notional grid, anything external to which will not be perceived as atypical or indicative of dysfunction. However, this is not correct—there are many instances where the detection of atypical behavior cannot be traced back to a shared model. The most plausible explanation for this is that inklings of mental disorder come from manifest, repetitive, and unaccountable breaches of implicit psychological expectations.

It is as yet unclear whether this proposal can clarify why such a high level of variation in individual and shared interpretations of mental disorder exists. However, it is suggested that a useful approach to further research is to involve intuitive psychology and its well-founded, intricate, early-acquired, implicit principles within our attempts to relate and comprehend the causal links between mental disorder and cultural representations.

References

Adolphs, R., Sears, L., & Piven, J. (2001). Abnormal processing of social information from faces in autism. *Journal of Cognitive Neuroscience*, 13, 232–240. https://doi.org/10.1162/089892901564289

Astuti, R. (2001). Are We all Natural Dualists? A Cognitive Developmental Approach. *Journal of the Royal Anthropological Institute*, 7, 429–447. https://doi.org/10.1111/1467-9655.00071

Atran, S. A. (1990). *Cognitive Foundations of Natural History. Towards an Anthropology of Science.* Cambridge: Cambridge University Press.

——. (1998). Folk biology and the anthropology of science: Cognitive universals and cultural particulars. *Behavioral and Brain Sciences*, 21, 547–569.

——. (2002). *In Gods We Trust: The Evolutionary Landscape of Religion.* Oxford; New York: Oxford University Press.

Avis, M., & Harris, P. L. (1991). Belief-desire reasoning among Baka children: Evidence for a universal conception of mind. *Child Development*, 62, 460–467.

Baldwin, D. A., Baird, J. A., Saylor, M. M., & Clark, M. A. (2001). Infants parse dynamic action. *Child Development*, 72, 708–717. https://doi.org/10.1111/1467-8624.00310

Baron-Cohen, S. (1995). *Mindblindness: An Essay on Autism and Theory of Mind.* Cambridge, MA: MIT Press.

Bartlett, F. C. (1932). *Remembering. A Study in Experimental and Social Psychology.* Cambridge: Cambridge University Press.

Bennett, M., & Galpert, L. (1993). Children's understanding of multiple desires. *International Journal of Behavioral Development*, 16, 15–33.

Blakemore, S.-J., Fonlupt, P., Pachot-Clouard, M., Darmon, C., Boyer, P., Meltzoff, A. N., Segebarth, C., & Decety, J. (2001). How the brain perceives causality: An event-related fMRI study. *NeuroReport: For Rapid Communication of Neuroscience Research*, 12, 3741–3746. https://doi.org/10.1097/00001756-200112040-00027

Bloom, P. (2000). *How Children Learn the Meanings of Words.* Cambridge, MA: MIT Press.

Blythe, P. W., Todd, P. M., & Miller, G. F. (1999). How motion reveals intention: Categorizing social interactions. In G. Gigerenzer & P. Todd (Eds.), *Simple Heuristics that Make us Smart.* (pp. 257–285). New York: Oxford University Press.

Boyd, R., & Richerson, P. J. (1985). *Culture and the Evolutionary Process.* Chicago, IL: University of Chicago Press.

Boyer, P. (1994). Cognitive constraints on cultural representations: Natural ontologies and religious ideas. In L. A. Hirschfeld & S. Gelman (Eds.),

Mapping the Mind: Domain-Specificity in Culture and Cognition (pp. 391–411). New York: Cambridge University Press.

Brüne, M., & Bodenstein, L. (2005). Proverb comprehension reconsidered--'theory of mind' and the pragmatic use of language in schizophrenia. *Schizophrenia Research*, 75, 233–239. https://doi.org/10.1016/j.schres.2004.11.006

Callaghan, T., Rochat, P., Lillard, A., Claux, M. L., Itakura, S., Tapanya, S., & Singh, S. (2005). Synchrony in the Onset of Mental-State Reasoning: Evidence From Five Cultures. *Psychological Science*, 16, 378–384. https://doi.org/10.1111/j.0956-7976.2005.01544.x

Chasiotis, A., Kiessling, F., Hofer, J., & Campos, D. (2006). Theory of mind and inhibitory control in three cultures: Conflict inhibition predicts false belief understanding in Germany, Costa Rica and Cameroon. *International Journal of Behavioral Development*, 30, 249–260. https://doi.org/10.1177/0165025406066759

Churchland, P. M. (1981). Eliminative Materialism and the Propositional Attitudes. *Journal of Philosophy*, 78, 67–90.

Claidière, N., & Sperber, D. (2007). The role of attraction in cultural evolution. *Journal of Cognition and Culture*, 7, 89–111. https://doi.org/10.1163/156853707X171829

Corcoran, R., & Frith, C. D. (1996). Conversational conduct and the symptoms of schizophrenia. *Cognitive Neuropsychiatry*, 1, 305–318.

Cosmides, L., & Tooby, J. (1992). Cognitive adaptations for social exchange. In J. H. Barkow, L. Cosmides, & J. Tooby (Eds.), *The Adapted Mind: Evolutionary Psychology and the Generation of Culture.* (pp. 163–228). New York: Oxford University Press.

Csibra, G., Gergely, G., Biro, S., Koos, O., & Brockbank, M. (1999). Goal attribution without agency cues: The perception of 'pure reason' in infancy. *Cognition*, 72, 237–267. https://doi.org/10.1016/S0010-0277(99)00039-6

D'Entremont, B., & Muir, D. W. (1997). Five-month-olds' attention and affective responses to still-faced emotional expressions. *Infant Behavior & Development*, 20, 563–568.

de Renzi, E., Faglioni, P., Grossi, D., & Nichelli, P. (1991). Apperceptive and associative forms of prosopagnosia. *Cortex*, 27, 213–221.

Decety, J., & Sommerville, J. A. (2003). Shared representations between self and other: A social cognitive neuroscience view. *Trends in Cognitive Sciences*, 7, 527–533. https://doi.org/10.1016/j.tics.2003.10.004

Devereux, G. (1961). *Mohave ethnopsychiatry and suicide: The psychiatric knowledge and the psychic disturbances of an Indian tribe* [microform]. Washington, DC: Smithsonian Institution. Bureau of American Ethnology.

———. (1980). Primitive Psychiatric Diagnosis: A General Thory of the Diagnostic Process. In G. Devereux (Ed.), *Basic Problems of Ethnopsychiatry* (pp. 247–273). Chicago, IL: The University of Chicago Press.

Dixon, M. J. (2000). A new paradigm for investigating category-specific agnosia in the new millennium. *Brain & Cognition*, 42, 142–145. https://doi.org/10.1006/brcg.1999.1185

Durham, W. H. (1991). *Coevolution. Genes, Cultures and Human Diversity.* Stanford, CA: Stanford University Press.

Ekman, P. (1999). Facial expressions. In T. Dalgleish & M. J. Power (Eds.), *Handbook of cognition and emotion* (pp. 301–320). New York: John Wiley & Sons Ltd.

Farah, M., Levinson, K. L., & Klein, K. L. (1995). Face perception and within-category discrimination in prosopagnosia. *Neuropsychologia*, 33, 661–674.

Fiske, A. P. (1992). The four elementary forms of sociality: Framework for a unified theory of social relations. *Psychological Review*, 99, 689–723.

Friesen, C. K., & Kingstone, A. (1998). The eyes have it! Reflexive orienting is triggered by nonpredictive gaze. *Psychonomic Bulletin & Review*, 5, 490–495.

Frith, C. D. (1996). Brain mechanisms for 'having a theory of mind'. *Journal of Psychopharmacology*, 10, 9–15. https://doi.org/10.1177/026988119601000103

Frith, U. (2001). Mind blindness and the brain in autism. *Neuron*, 32, 969–979. https://doi.org/10.1016/S0896-6273(01)00552-9

Gaines, A. D. (1992). Ethnopsychiatry: The cultural construction of psychiatries. In A. D. Gaines (Ed.), *Ethnopsychiatry: The Cultural Construction of Professional and Folk Psychiatries* (pp. 3–50). Albany, NY: State Unversity of New York Press.

Gelman, R., Durgin, F., & Kaufman, L. (1995). Distinguishing between animates and inanimates: Not by motion alone. In D. Sperber, D. Premack, et al. (Eds.), *Causal Cognition: A Multidisciplinary Debate.* (pp. 150–184). New York: Clarendon Press/Oxford University Press.

Gergely, G., Nadasdy, Z., Csibra, G., & Biro, S. (1995). Taking the intentional stance at 12 months of age. *Cognition*, 56, 165–193.

Gerrans, P. (2007). Mechanisms of madness: evolutionary psychiatry without evolutionary psychology. *Biology and Philosophy*, 22, 35–56. https://doi.org/10.1007/s10539-006-9025-y

Giosan, C., Glovsky, V., & Haslam, N. (2001). The lay concept of 'mental disorder': A cross-cultural study. *Transcultural Psychiatry*, 38, 317–332. https://doi.org/10.1177/136346150103800303

Gordon, A. C. L., & Olson, D. R. (1998). The relation between acquisition of a theory of mind and the capacity to hold in mind. *Journal of Experimental Child Psychology*, 68, 70–83.

Grice, H. P. (1975). *Logic and Conversation*. Cambridge, MA: Harvard University Press.

Hacking, I. (1995a). The looping effects of human kinds. In D. Sperber, D. Premack, et al. (Eds.), *Causal Cognition: A Multidisciplinary Debate* (pp. 351–394): New York: Oxford University Press.

———. (1995b). *Rewriting the Soul: Multiple Personality and the Sciences of Memory*. Princeton, NJ: Princeton University Press.

———. (1998). *Mad Travelers. Reflections on the Reality of Transient Mental Illnesses*. Charlottesville, VA: University Press of Virginia.

Haidt, J., Kesebir, S., Plessner, H., Betsch, C., & Betsch, T. (2008). In the forest of value: Why moral intuitions are different from other kinds. In Plessner, H., Betsch, C. & Betsch, T. (Eds) *Intuition in judgment and decision making*. (pp. 209–229). Mahwah, NJ: Lawrence Erlbaum Associates Publishers.

Haslam, N. (2005). Dimensions of Folk Psychiatry. *Review of General Psychology*, 9, 35–47. https://doi.org/10.1037/1089-2680.9.1.35

Haslam, N., & Giosan, C. (2002). The lay concept of 'mental disorder' among American undergraduates. *Journal of Clinical Psychology*, 58, 479–485. https://doi.org/10.1002/jclp.1158

Hays, S.-J., Niven, B. E., Godfrey, H. P. D., & Linscott, R. J. (2004). Clinical assessment of pragmatic language impairment: A generalisability study of older people with Alzheimer's disease. *Aphasiology*, 18, 693–714. https://doi.org/10.1080/02687030444000183

Hess, N. H., & Hagen, E. H. (2006). Psychological Adaptations for Assessing Gossip Veracity. *Human Nature*, 17, 337–354. https://doi.org/10.1007/s12110-006-1013-z

Hirschfeld, L. A. (1994a). The acquisition of social categories. In L. A. Hirschfeld & S. A. Gelman (Eds.), *Mapping The Mind: Domain-Specificity in Culture and Cognition*. New York: Cambridge University Press.

———. (1994b). Is the acquisition of social categories based on domain-specific competence or on knowledge transfer? In S. A. G. Lawrence A. Hirschfeld (Ed.), *Mapping the Mind: Domain Specificity in Cognition and Culture*. (pp. 201–233). New York: Cambridge University Press.

———. (1996). *Race in the Making: Cognition, Culture and the Child's Construction of Human Kinds*. Cambridge, MA: MIT Press.

Johnson, S., Slaughter, V., & Carey, S. (1998). Whose gaze will infants follow? The elicitation of gaze-following in 12-month-olds. *Developmental Science*, 1, 233–238.

Jovanovski, T. (1995). The cultural approach of ethnopsychiatry: A review and critique. *New Ideas in Psychology*, 13, 281–297.

Kesler-West, M. L., Andersen, A. H., Smith, C. D., Avison, M. J., Davis, C. E., Kryscio, R. J., & Blonder, L. X. (2001). Neural substrates of facial emotion processing using fMRI. *Cognitive Brain Research*, 11, 213–226. https://doi.org/10.1016/s0926-6410(00)00073-2

Kleinman, A. (1988). *Rethinking Psychiatry: From Cultural Category to Personal Experience*. New York; London: Free Press; Collier Macmillan.

Kurzban, R. (2001). The social psychophysics of cooperation: Nonverbal communication in a public goods game. *Journal of Nonverbal Behavior*, 25, 241–259. https://doi.org/10.1023/A:1012563421824

Kurzban, R., Tooby, J., & Cosmides, L. (2001). Can race be erased? Coalitional computation and social categorization. *Proceedings of the National Academy of Sciences of the United States of America*, 98, 15387–15392. https://doi.org/10.1073/pnas.251541498

Leslie, A. M. (1987). Pretense and representation: the origins of 'Theory of Mind'. *Psychological Review*, 94, 412–426. https://doi.org/10.1037/0033-295X.94.4.412

——. (1994). ToMM, ToBy, and Agency: Core architecture and domain specificity. In L. A. Hirschfeld & S. A. Gelman (Eds.), *Mapping the mind: Domain specificity in cognition and culture*. New York: Cambridge University Press.

Leslie, A. M., Friedman, O., & German, T. P. (2004). Core mechanisms in 'theory of mind'. *Trends in Cognitive Sciences*, 8, 529–533. https://doi.org/10.1016/j.tics.2004.10.001

Leslie, A. M., German, T. P., & Polizzi, P. (2005). Belief-desire reasoning as a process of selection. *Cognitive Psychology*, 50, 45–85. https://doi.org/10.1016/j.cogpsych.2004.06.002

Lieberman, D., Tooby, J., & Cosmides, L. (2007). The architecture of human kin detection. *Nature*, 445, 5. https://doi.org/10.1038/nature05510

Lillard, A. S. (1997). Other folks' theories of mind and behavior. *Psychological Science*, 8, 268–274. https://doi.org/10.1111/j.1467-9280.1997.tb00437.x

Luo, Y., & Baillargeon, R. e. (2007). Do 12.5-month-old infants consider what objects others can see when interpreting their actions? *Cognition*, 105, 489–512. https://doi.org/10.1016/j.cognition.2006.10.007

Malle, B. F. (2004). *How the Mind Explains Behavior: Folk Explanations, Meaning, and Social Interaction*. Cambridge, MA: MIT Press.

Malle, B. F., & Knobe, J. (2001). The distinction between desire and intention: A folk-conceptual analysis. In B. F. Malle & L. J. Moses (Eds.), *Intentions and intentionality: Foundations of social cognition* (pp. 45–67). Cambridge, MA: MIT Press.

Meilijson, S. R., Kasher, A., & Elizur, A. (2004). Language Performance in Chronic Schizophrenia: A Pragmatic Approach. *Journal of Speech, Language, and Hearing Research*, 47, 695–713. https://doi.org/10.1044/1092-4388(2004/053)

Michotte, A. (1963). *The Perception of Causality*. New York: Basic Books.

Moses, L. J., Coon, J. A., & Wusinich, N. (2000). Young children's understanding of desire formation. *Developmental Psychology*, 36, 77–90. https://doi.org/10.1037/0012-1649.36.1.77

Nichols, S. (2002a). Norms with Feeling: Towards a Psychological Account of Moral Judgment. *Cognition*, 84, 221–236. https://doi.org/10.1016/S0010-0277(02)00048-3

——. (2002b). On the Genealogy of Norms: A Case for the Role of Emotion in Cultural Evolution. *Philosophy of Science*, 69, 234. https://doi.org/10.1086/341051

Noveck, I. A., & Sperber, D. (2004). *Experimental Pragmatics*. Basingstoke; New York: Palgrave Macmillan.

Orange, J. B., & Zanon, M. V. (2006). Language and communication in adults with Down syndrome and dementia of the Alzheimer type: A review. *Journal on Developmental Disabilities*, 12, 53–62.

Perner, J., Leekam, S. R., & Wimmer, H. (1987). Three year olds' difficulty with false belief. *British Journal of Developmental Psychology*, 5, 125–137. https://doi.org/10.1111/j.2044-835X.1987.tb01048.x

Phillips, A. T., Wellman, H. M., & Spelke, E. S. (2002). Infants' ability to connect gaze and emotional expression to intentional action. *Cognition*, 85, 53–78. https://doi.org/10.1016/s0010-0277(02)00073-2

Porter, R. (2004). *Madmen: A Social History of Madhouses, Mad Doctors & Lunatics*. Stroud: Tempus.

Ready, R. E., Ott, B. R., Grace, J., & Cahn-Weiner, D. A. (2003). Apathy and executive dysfunction in mild cognitive impairment and Alzheimer disease. *American Journal of Geriatric Psychiatry*, 11, 222–228.

Rochat, P., Morgan, R., & Carpenter, M. (1997). Young infants' sensitivity to movement information specifying social causality. *Cognitive Development*, 12, 441–465. https://doi.org/10.1016/S0885-2014(97)90022-8

Roediger, H. L., III, & Geraci, L. (2003). How metaphors shape our understanding of memory [Review of the book *Metaphors of Memory: A History of Ideas about the Mind*, by D. Draaisma & P. Vincent]. *Contemporary Psychology*, 48, 829–831.

Ross, M., & Wilson, A. E. (2000). Constructing and apprasing past selves. In D. L. Schacter, E. Scarry, et al. (Eds.), *Memory, Brain, and Belief*. (pp. 231–258). Cambridge, MA: Harvard University Press.

Rubin, D. C., Schrauf, R. W., & Greenberg, D. L. (2003). Belief and recollection of autobiographical memories. *Memory & Cognition*, 31, 887–901. https://doi.org/10.3758/bf03196443

Sadowsky, J. (2003). The social world and the reality of mental illness: Lessons from colonial psychiatry. *Harvard Review of Psychiatry*, 11, 210–214. https://doi.org/10.1080/10673220303947

Schlottman, A., & Anderson, N. H. (1993). An information integration approach to phenomenal causality. *Memory & Cognition*, 21, 785–801.

Smith, M. C. (1995). Facial expression in mild dementia of the Alzheimer type. *Behavioural Neurology*, 8, 149–156.

Sperber, D. (1985). Anthropology and Psychology: Towards an Epidemiology of Representations. *Man*, 20, 73–89.

——. (1996). *Explaining Culture: A Naturalistic Approach*. Oxford: Blackwell.

Sperber, D., & Hirschfeld, L. A. (2004). The cognitive foundations of cultural stability and diversity. *Trends in Cognitive Sciences*, 8, 40–46. https://doi.org/10.1016/j.tics.2003.11.002

Sperber, D., & Wilson, D. (1995). *Relevance. Communication and Cognition*. Oxford: Blackwell.

Staley, D., Wand, R. R., & Shady, G. (1997). Tourette disorder: a cross-cultural review. *Compr Psychiatry*, 38, 6–16. https://doi.org/10.1016/s0010-440x(97)90047-x

Stein, D. J. (1993). Cross-cultural psychiatry and the DSM-IV. *Comprehensive Psychiatry*, 34, 322–329. https://doi.org/10.1016/0010-440X(93)90018-Y

Tardif, T., & Wellman, H. M. (2000). Acquisition of mental state language in Mandarin- and Cantonese-speaking children. *Developmental Psychology*, 36, 25–43. https://doi.org/10.1037/0012-1649.36.1.25

Teunisse, J.-P., & de Gelder, B. (2001). Impaired categorical perception of facial expressions in high-functioning adolescents with autism. *Child Neuropsychology*, 7, 1–14. https://doi.org/10.1076/chin.7.1.1.3150

Tomasello, M., Kruger, A. C., & Ratner, H. H. (1993). Cultural Learning. *Behavioral and Brain Sciences*, 16, 495–510. https://doi.org/10.1017/S0140525X00031277

Tooby, J., & Cosmides, L. (1996). Friendship and the banker's paradox: Other pathways to the evolution of adaptations for altruism. In W. G. Runciman, J. M. Smith, et al. (Eds.), *Evolution of Social Behaviour Patterns in Primates and Man*. (pp. 119–143). Oxford: Oxford University Press.

Tremoulet, P. D., & Feldman, J. (2000). Perception of animacy from the motion of a single object. *Perception*, 29, 943–951. https://doi.org/10.1068/p3101

Trevarthen, C., & Aitken, K. J. (2001). Infant intersubjectivity: Research, theory, and clinical applications. *Journal of Child Psychology & Psychiatry & Allied Disciplines*, 42, 3–48. https://doi.org/10.1111/1469-7610.00701

Turiel, E., Eisenberg, N., Damon, W., & Lerner, R. M. (2006). The Development of Morality. In *Handbook of Child Psychology: Vol. 3, Social, Emotional, and Personality Development.* (pp. 789–857). Hoboken, NJ: John Wiley & Sons Inc.

Vinden, P. G. (1998). Imagination and true belief: A cross-cultural perspective. In J. d. Rivera, T. R. Sarbin, et al. (Eds.), *Believed-In Imaginings: The Narrative Construction of Reality.* (pp. 73–85). Washington, DC: American Psychological Association.

Want, S. C., & Harris, P. L. (2002). How do children ape? Applying concepts from the study of non-human primates to the developmental study of 'imitation' in children. *Developmental Science*, 5, 1–13. https://doi.org/10.1111/1467-7687.00194

Watt, N. F., Grubb, T. W., & Erlenmeyer-Kimling, L. (1982). Social, emotional, and intellectual behavior at school among children at high risk for schizophrenia. *Journal of Consulting and Clinical Psychology*, 50, 171–181.

Wellman, H. M., & Fang, F. (2006). Scaling of Theory-of-Mind Understandings in Chinese Children. *Psychological Science*, 17, 1075–1081. https://doi.org/10.1111/j.1467-9280.2006.01830.x

Wellman, H. M., Phillips, A. T., & Rodriguez, T. (2000). Young children's understanding of perception, desire, and emotion. *Child Development*, 71, 895–912. https://doi.org/10.1111/1467-8624.00198

Wellmann, H., & Estes, D. (1986). Early understandings of mental entities: A re-examination of childhood realism. *Child Development*, 57, 910–923.

Williams, E. M. (2000). *Causal reasoning by children and adults about the trajectory, context, and animacy of a moving object.* Doctoral dissertation, University of California, Los Angeles, CA.

Yazdi, A. A., German, T. P., Defeyter, M. A., & Siegal, M. (2006). Competence and performance in belief-desire reasoning across two cultures: The truth, the whole truth and nothing but the truth about false belief? *Cognition*, 100, 343–368. https://doi.org/10.1016/j.cognition.2005.05.004

7. The Ideal of Integrated Social Science

Introductory Note

This essay starts with the question of why the discipline of cultural anthropology is marginal in public debates, when it should and might be central. (I provide data that may seem dated, but the trends described here have if anything become stronger.) The diagnosis is that this is a self-inflicted wound—and perhaps more interestingly, I try to describe how some kinds of social science do contribute to public discourse.

But this is not intended as a series of recommendations for anthropologists. To understand why, we must keep in mind a simple distinction between disciplines and intellectual projects. Disciplines are associated with university departments, teaching appointments, professional associations, etc. There is a discipline of anthropology, in that sense, in the same way as chemistry or biology. Intellectual projects are about a set of questions and methods. One example of such a project is the idea of explaining the diversity of human cultures in the context of the unity of human motivations and mental capacities. This was a central project for many (not all) professional anthropologists of the twentieth century. But the project of course existed long before that, in the works of Montesquieu or Ibn Khaldun, and many others before and after them. So the idea of explaining cultures in terms of human nature pre-existed the profession of anthropology, and persists, nowadays, largely outside professional anthropology, being pursued by people labeled biologists, linguists or economists, as well as historians in some cases.

This evolution is not uncommon. Projects can migrate into or out of disciplines. The idea of constructing mathematical models for genetic

 https://doi.org/10.11647/OBP.0257.12

evolution was first handled by professional mathematicians like Fisher, and only gradually became central to the discipline of biology. The arrival of some projects and departure of others is the reason why most academic disciplines, like the ship of Theseus, are incrementally modified to such an extent that in some cases nothing remains of the original set of ideas or methods.

In this essay, I try to describe the separation between professional anthropology (the discipline) and the goal of explaining the diversity of human cultures in terms of our common human nature (the project). This does not entail that actual anthropologists should abandon their current pursuits and join my favorite project—although I of course wish my tribe will increase and prosper. No, the only negative comment on the discipline of (cultural) anthropology is that it tends to create its own intellectual isolation.

What matters, then, are the projects. At the end of the chapter, I sketch a version of a research program that was advocated and implemented by many before me—a cognitive explanation of human cultures that is based on evolutionary principles (Boyd & Richerson, 1985; Sperber, 1985; Tooby & Cosmides, 1992). I described the main achievements of that research program in some detail elsewhere (Boyer, 2018).

Just as they crisscross or transcend disciplines, intellectual projects also ignore such common divisions as that between the sciences and the humanities, or Natur- and Geisteswissenschaften, which are descendants of those highly misleading and highly persistent distinctions between nature and culture, innate and acquired traits, etc. These segregation principles do not make much sense, as social sciences continue to become closely integrated, gradually realizing the ideal of consilience described by E.O. Wilson (1998).

References

Boyd, R., & Richerson, P. J. (1985). *Culture and the Evolutionary Process*. Chicago, IL: University of Chicago Press.

Boyer, P. (2018). *Minds Make Societies. How Cognition Explains the World Humans Create*. New Haven, CT: Yale University Press.

Sperber, D. (1985). Anthropology and Psychology: Towards an Epidemiology of Representations. *Man, 20*, 73–89.

Tooby, J., & Cosmides, L. (1992). The psychological foundations of culture. In J. H. Barkow, L. Cosmides, & et al. (Eds.), *The Adapted Mind: Evolutionary Psychology and the Generation of Culture*. (pp. 19–136). New York: Oxford University Press.

Wilson, E. O. (1998). *Consilience: The Unity of Knowledge*. London: Little Brown and Company.

Modes of Scholarship in the Study of Culture[1]

Why is it that the majority of cultural anthropology is no longer relevant? The debates within this specific field are generally absent from wider academic conversations, its scholars no longer rank amongst the most renowned and significant intellectuals of their day, and its contribution to non-academic discourse is basically nonexistent. This third aspect is even more alarming, given that the actual subject matter of cultural anthropology situates it at the core of pressing social issues.

Although I will qualify this stern appraisal, the aim of the present chapter is to investigate the causes and to propose a possible solution for (rather than to lament) the current status of cultural anthropology. My suggestion is that this condition is in large part self-inflected. Cultural anthropology lacks any function in wider discourse, since many cultural anthropologists have spoken and written themselves out of popular debates. This situation is on the verge of changing, although this change is occurring at the margins (rather than the mainstream) of the discipline.

I will begin by emphasizing that there is a considerable amount of reputable, and indeed, brilliant research in cultural anthropology— this is hardly in question. What is, however, of concern is a particular academic style (which entered the field of cultural anthropology relatively recently, but has dominated other fields for much longer) that has curtailed the creative vitality and social relevance of the discipline. It is also evident that by no means all anthropology scholarship is

---

1   Some of the contents of this chapter have been expressed earlier in Boyer, P. (2003). Science, Erudition and Relevant Connections, *Journal of Cognition and Culture*, 3(4): 344–358.

    https://doi.org/10.11647/OBP.0257.13

irrelevant: biological anthropology and archaeology are both alive and well. It is also worth noting that evolutionary biologists and economists are currently rejuvenating the established concerns of cultural anthropology in the public consciousness, which indicates the potential for a 'science of culture' field, or some emergent shift towards an integrated discipline of this sort.

1. Public Decline

Let us consider questions of public debate, such as the organization of marriage, gender and familial relations, the formation of social trust and cooperative norms, the outcomes of mass immigration, the impact of global cultural contact, the functions of religious persuasion, the links between civil society and religious institutions, or processes of ethical dispute. A whole range of disciplines—from history to evolutionary biology, and from neuroscience to economics—have much to contribute on all of these topics, but cultural anthropology is, for the most part, too readily introspective and concerned with obscure academic fads.

This is not merely an opinion. A brief scan of references to cultural anthropologists and anthropological themes within popular debates corroborates the field's declining relevance. For example, Richard Posner's painstaking study, *Public Intellectuals*, which lists prominent contributors to public debates (in books, magazines, newspapers, and journals) over the last twenty years in the United States, is instructive (Posner, 2001). Somewhat remarkably, in a list of 416 public intellectuals, only *five* are anthropologists, and *four* of these five (Margaret Mead, Ruth Benedict, Claude Lévi-Strauss, Ernest Gellner) are no longer alive. One could be forgiven for assuming that Posner prefers pundits to specialists, and politics to broader social debates, but this would be wrong. The study lists educational psychologists Jerome Bruner and Howard, psychologist and linguist Steven Pinker, literary critic and moral philosopher Tzvetan Todorov, philosopher Robert Nozick, and economist Thomas Sowell. It is worth observing that, save for Mead, the five renowned anthropologists listed are quite detached from the relativist, 'textual' trends of contemporary cultural anthropology.

Why this stark lack of influence? It is possible that cultural anthropology's recent propensity for academic fads is responsible for its declining relevance. Treatises on culture as text, postcolonialism, or more arcane and reflexive topics likely are not of much use to those concerned with matters of serious public debate, such as how non-traditional family units will raise children, how mass immigration might result in harmonious co-existence, or how we might overcome religious hatred.

'Mission creep' is the process by which a finite strategic goal snowballs into an excessively ambitious project, and is greatly feared by members of the military and certain politicians. Over the last fifty years, cultural anthropology has encountered the inverse issue, which we might term a dramatic 'mission shrink'. In contrast to its original scope and what is often referred to in textbooks as its 'mission', the focus of cultural anthropology has gradually waned to a few minor problems.

Anthropology's official mission over the last century, as emphasized in most textbooks on the subject, has been to understand human nature through the lens of the most challenging and typical features of the species, specifically, the production of vastly different norms, concepts, and social structures. Interestingly, however, nobody working in cultural anthropology pays much attention to these questions, and the majority of cultural anthropologists in fact consider such an approach to be either outdated or audacious. They have for the most part renounced the 'nature' aspect of human nature and cultural diversity. Instead of confronting so-called 'big' questions, the majority of cultural anthropologists gladly confine themselves to geographically specific, narrowly defined analyses.

What it worse is that this shift took place at exactly the moment when other fields began to produce many methods and results that could, when paired with cultural anthropological scholarship, revive our understanding of human cultures. Cultural anthropology has, far from embracing such advances, seemingly severed ties with other fields that could aid this progress (even the related fields of biological anthropology and archaeology). It has also doggedly ignored dramatic breakthroughs in the fields of psychology, economics, linguistics, and cognitive science.

2. Modes of Scholarship—Scientific and Erudite

What prompted this shift? I have a provisional diagnosis for this state of affairs that demands us to consider what I term *modes of scholarship*. These are the means by which we distinguish scholarly works from one another and acknowledge them as legitimate contributions to a given field, or recognize their authors as genuine members of the academy. In the present inquiry, the question is: how do scholars of cultural anthropology reach a decision on whether an individual may be awarded a position as a cultural anthropologist, or on whether their publications constitute valid contributions to the field?

The humanities-science binary is far too general and simplistic for a comprehension of the present situation. Instead, there are three different modes of scholarship: science, erudition, and salient connections.

2.1 The Science Mode

The science mode should not take too long to describe. This is not because scientific authority and authoritativeness are simple matters—far from it. Philosophy of science is difficult precisely because it is not easy to explain what this particular mode of scholarship consists of and what really makes it different from (and vastly more successful than) all other ways of gathering knowledge (Klee, 1999). This does not matter for present purposes, however, because the scientific mode, if difficult to explain, is very easy to recognize. You know it when you see it. Here is a short list of the common 'symptoms' by which we recognize a field that employs the science mode of scholarship:

a. There is an agreed corpus of knowledge. What has been achieved so far is taken as given by most practitioners. The common corpus also includes a set of recognized methods, and a list of outstanding questions and puzzles to solve. People also tend to agree on which of these questions are important and which only require some puzzle solving and some tidying up of the theoretical landscape.

b. The fundamentals of the discipline and its results are explained in textbooks and manuals that are all extraordinarily similar, as the essential points and the way to get there are agreed in the discipline.

c. It does not really matter who said what or when. Indeed, many practitioners have a rather hazy picture of the history of their disciplines.

Many young biologists would have a hard time explaining what the New Synthesis was, who was involved, and why a synthesis was needed in the first place. Revered figures from the past may be a source of inspiration, demonstrating how to make great discoveries, but they are not a source of truth. Darwin believed in continuous rather than particulate heredity and in some transmission of acquired traits—on both counts we think he was simply wrong, great man though he was (Mayr, 1991).

d. People typically publish short contributions. They do not need to establish why the specific problem addressed is a problem or why the methods are appropriate, since that is all part of the agreed background.

e. The typical biographical pattern is that the aspiring member of the guild is intensively trained from an early age in the specialized field and makes important contributions after only a few years of training.

f. There is a large degree of agreement (because of the various features already mentioned) on whether a given person meets the requirements for being a practitioner of the particular field, and there is also a large agreement on how important each individual's contribution is. Again, let me emphasize that this is by no means a description of *science*, but only of the scientific mode of scholarship, identified here on the basis of fairly superficial but sufficient criteria. By the same token, I am not claiming that all 'scientists' work in that way (more on that later) or that 'science' only occurs when these features apply. The point of all this is to draw a contrast with other modes of scholarship, where legitimacy and standards are established quite differently.

2.2 The Erudition Mode

Another mode of scholarship is erudition, understood as the requirement that specialists of the discipline should have detailed knowledge of a particular domain of facts. Consider, for instance, Byzantine numismatics or the history of Late Renaissance painting. We expect specialists of these fields to have knowledge of the corpus of coins or paintings. We turn to them to identify new findings. The erudition mode was essential to (and still plays a great part in) the development of many scientific fields. For instance biology started as natural history and still includes a large part of it.

The features of erudition are partly similar and partly different from those of science, as we can see by listing some of erudition's key features:

a. There is an agreed corpus of knowledge. There is also a large agreement on what remains to be done. For instance, only a small part of the extant corpus of Mesopotamian tablets has been deciphered. A great number of languages remain to describe. So the remaining tablets or languages are offered to the aspiring specialist as a possible domain of study.

b. A great deal of knowledge is not made explicit in manuals. One picks it up by working under the tutelage of more experienced practitioners and immersing oneself in the material for many years.

c. The history of the field matters and practitioners generally know it. There are some great masters, whose intuitions matter a lot, although they may have been wrong. For instance, to this day classical scholars know their Bachofen or Straus, religious scholars cite Otto or Eliade. But these are not considered infallible sources.

d. People often publish short descriptive contributions, e.g., the first description of a new insect genus or the phonology of a specific language. They also compile monographs that incorporate vast amounts of information about a particular domain (e.g., the comparative morphology of ant species, an encyclopedia of New-Guinean languages, a concordance of Ben Jonson's plays, a catalogue raisonne of Guido Reni).

e. Age is a necessary component of competence. Older experts are generally better, because expertise consists in the accumulation of vast amounts of specific facts, also because an expert needs the kind of intuition that is only shaped by long-lasting familiarity with the material. Only a seasoned Renaissance scholar can tell you that this particular painting is from the Venetian not the Milanese school. A younger scholar may be misled by superficial features.

f. Within a narrow field, people agree on whether a given individual is competent or not, generally based on that person's knowledge of a monograph-sized subfield.

Now, as I said earlier, there is nothing essential about these distinct modes—indeed, as we shall see, they are often found in combination, and this may be an index of 'healthy' disciplines. Also, whether a given field uses more or less of one of these modes can change with time. Technical change can have dramatic effects on the mix of modes. Classics used to be strongly based on erudition in the corpus. Knowing obscure (but relevant) textual sources was a *sine qua non*, and the outcome of many years of sustained training, the way it still is for, say scholars of Indian philosophy. Now that the entire Greek and Latin canon is available (and searchable) on CD-ROM, this particular form of knowledge cannot be used as a criterion for admission.

3. How Science and Erudition Combine

In healthy empirical disciplines, the science and erudition modes very often co-exist harmoniously. Two illustrative examples are biology and linguistics.

Today, molecular biologists principally employ the scientific mode. Conversely, evolutionary biologists often have a defined 'field' of research (for instance social organization amongst wasps, or lekking in antelopes), therefore necessitating a combination of both scientific and erudition modes. The two are not mutually exclusive, and certain fields, such as ecology, often demand scientific knowledge (such as how to apply optimal foraging models, how to run simulations, or awareness of epidemiological techniques) alongside erudite knowledge (such as the ways in which different species interact, the predators or prey of a certain genus, or the minimal density of resources required). Often, a productive information exchange between these two modes can take place. Natural history and evolutionary theory inform one another. E. O. Wilson is simultaneously one of the most significant evolutionary theorists of the last century and one of the world experts on ant behavior, to give just one example (Hölldobler & Wilson, 1990; Wilson, 1975).

Linguistics nowadays also combines these two modes in multiple ways, according to the particular sub-field. Whilst certain linguists exclusively work in the science mode (for instance, exploring which formal models might account for linguistic regularity), others employ a more field-oriented approach (for instance investigating Amazonian languages), and many others marry the two approaches. Erudite comparisons of creoles and pidgins have for example inspired certain scientific models of linguistic evolution (Bickerton, 1990).

Whilst we may observe these two modes within a single field, or even within the scholarly approach of a single person, their purposes and the manner in which they are applied nonetheless remain distinct. Biologists and linguists rely on empirical evidence for a proposed theory, as well as generating the relevant evidence, through experimentation or selection from a corpus, for example testing the notion that all languages have a noun-verb distinction by analyzing a large number of separate grammar systems. The erudition mode is driven by description, rather than by hypotheses or explanations. The aspirant scholar must catalogue the many forms of a particular genus of orchid, or the various coins found in a certain Byzantine palace because the given genus or collection has not previously been taxonomized. A 'pure' or 'a-theoretical' description does not exist, and particular hypotheses about what is or is not deemed to be relevant are usually established in a given discipline's existing descriptive methods.

It is crucial that the distinction between different modes of scholarship should not be conflated with the other (in my opinion) extremely confusing distinction between academic fields belonging to the humanities, the sciences or the social sciences. This institutional distinction operates on a different axis to the modal distinction. Examples of the erudition mode abound in the sciences, and there are also a fair few instances of the scientific mode found in the humanities.

In Humanities fields, scholars may for instance be working on a catalogue raisonné of a particular painter, a documentation of Greek coins (erudition), while others study how ecology constrains state formation or how visual perception influences aesthetics (science). In the social sciences, we find projects such as a study of comparative forms of nationalism (erudition) and formal models of cooperation and trade (science). In the so-called STEM fields, one could map the geological formations of England (erudition) while others study the physics of plate-tectonics (science). As I mentioned, erudition and science projects overlap. But the distinction between these styles of scholarship clearly cuts across the familiar humanities/sciences division.

4. A Third Mode of Scholarship: Salient Connections

The third mode of scholarship is the most elusive one, as it has not been systematically described, yet it is also most important to our understanding of many modern disciplines, including cultural anthropology. In this mode, people assess new contributions in terms of the connections they establish between facts or ideas which, by themselves, are not necessarily novel or even interesting. Although this way of judging new work has been around for a long time, it has become characteristic of many academic fields of a recent vintage and of the recent evolution of older disciplines. I call this the 'salient connections' mode. Again, I should provide examples before a model, because this is a phenomenon, we all know when we see it, even if we do not always reflect on the mechanism at work. For instance, a recent book reframes the discourse of love in Shakespeare's plays and sonnets as an expression of the colonial outlook. The lover's loving gaze transparently expresses the conqueror's prospect on a recently discovered, clearly gendered, and mythically virginal New World. A student is planning to work on Indian public executions during the Raj as a form of theater, a ritualized performance that constructs colonial power at the same time as it undermines it by exhibiting the gossamer of its dramatic texture. Another colleague has recently finished a study of gay fathers in the Caribbean in the framework of Benjamin's and Bourdieu's accounts of culture, technology, and late capitalism. Steel drums and strong rum prop up the local habitus of globalized self-empowerment.

What is the common thread in these disparate examples? They all seem to offer a new connection between elements that were previously known to everyone in the field and indeed, in many cases, to any educated reader. For instance, all literary scholars presumably know their Shakespeare and educated folk know a little about the conquest of America. But they (supposedly) had never considered Ophelia as American. In the same way, most historians know about the political organization of the Raj and its fondness for state pageantry. They are also cognizant of the 'comedian's paradox' from Diderot or some other source. The author's hope is in the fact that the connection between the two—between state ceremonial and precarious theatrical mimesis—is new. In the same way, most cultural anthropologists have some notion of the Caribbean as a place of contrasting influences and original cultural mixes. They also know a little about the various ways in which homosexuality is construed in different places, as well as cultural variation in fathers' duties or roles. The innovative point is to put all these together, creating salient associations, especially by throwing in Bourdieu and Benjamin—two rather dour, bookish, and strait-laced dead Europeans who would seem far removed from your typical Trinidadian gay dad.

One could multiply the examples, but it may be of more help to compare the features of this with the other two modes:

a. In salient-connections fields, there is no agreed corpus of knowledge. Indeed, there is no 'knowledge' in the sense of accumulated and organized information, but rather a juxtaposition of different views on different topics.

b. There are no manuals, no agreed techniques or methods. Indeed, each contribution constitutes (ideally) a new paradigm or method, each author is an island.

c. The history of the field, its self-definition, as well as the reframing of past theories, are crucial. A lot of scholarly activity in salient connections-based fields consists in citing various masters, commenting on their texts, finding some connection between what they said and the issue at hand. In cultural anthropological studies, authors like Walter Benjamin or Pierre Bourdieu or the entire Frankfurt school are part of this Pantheon (a very ephemeral one, with a high turnover rate). The masters are generally invoked as validating authority. That is, the particular fact that one is describing (the gay Caribbean father, etc.) is presented as illustrating the general principle laid down by Benjamin or some other luminary. (Incidentally, these authors are *never* shown to have been wrong. Indeed, their work is never discussed as having any connection to empirical fact that could make them right or wrong. Benjamin's or Bourdieu's conceptions of culture are not judged in terms of how much they explain). Also, there is a great deal of emphasis on the self-definition of the field, the ideas various practitioners have about what they do and what they ought to do, compared to what others do. Indeed, most important works are supposed to be not just contributions to the field, but also reflections on the field itself. For instance, a study of German post-Expressionist 1960s cinema will be praised, not just because it tells us a lot that we want to know about that specific genre, but also because it reframes our views of the connections between cinema or society. A study of recent rock songs is good because it establishes a new approach to popular culture.

d. Books are more important than articles. This, in part, reflects the fact that each contribution should ideally reframe a field as a whole, introduce a new way of looking at issues, and so on, something that cannot be done in a short article.

e. There is no specific developmental curve. Some authors produce interesting connections in their first piece of work, others are seasoned specialists of the erudition mode who, at some point, decide to let their hair down, as it were, and let salient connections govern their next project.

f. There is no agreement whatsoever on who a competent performer in this mode is, apart from the (generally dead) masters like Bakhtin or Benjamin or Raymond Williams for cultural studies, Derrida or de Man for literary criticism. A consequence is that there are tightly coalitional cliques and exceedingly bitter feuds about who should get what jobs, who is allowed to publish and where, and so on.

In the last three decades or so, some fields have dramatically evolved from almost pure erudition mode to the salient-connections mode. Literary criticism is a case in point. In the past, one could not really expatiate on Shakespeare's plays without thorough knowledge of the First Folio and Quartos and other such recondite source criticism. This kind of erudition is still practiced, but it is not the major criterion of a relevant contribution to Elizabethan studies (Garber, 2004). Saying something new about the plays is what matters. One could say that the specialists have (perhaps excessively) taken to heart Forster's dictum. They only connect.

There are various accounts of why this happened to literary studies, whether this is a Good Thing or not, and if not, whether it is all the fault of that awful Leavis or of the dreaded French structuralists (Kermode, 1983). I am not enough of an erudite to adjudicate between these normative interpretations of history. I can only comment that polemical narratives generally get in the way of a proper explanation. Neither jeremiad ('No-one knows the Canon anymore!') nor triumphalist epic ('We have overcome! The Canon is dead') is of great help here.

5. Effects of Salient Connections

The particular mode of scholarship I have described above could be explained by some as merely the outcome of a specific framework of ideas. For example, readers of earlier drafts of this essay highlighted similarities to postmodernist thought. This comparison is flawed, since the mode of scholarship I outline extends well beyond a certain intellectual trend (Gellner, 1992). Furthermore, and perhaps more significantly, assuming that an individual's actions (in this instance, the means by which academics validate scholarly contributions or acknowledge new academics) may be adequately accounted for by their own explanation of their rationale (in this instance, a certain intellectual trend). Such trends are no more intelligible than other social tendencies, and consequently we should also seek to explain them.

The results of the salient connections mode of scholarship are of greater concern than its sources, and are quite easily observed. For people with the correct grounding, the connections are salient, but they do not translate easily. Imagine explaining to a biochemist that the essays of Walter Benjamin provide an excellent context for a description of gay fathers in Trinidad. There is, understandably, a somewhat limited audience for salient connections, and these often pose a challenge even for scholars of a given field. Ernest Gellner mocked the pitiful Wittgensteinian philosophers propagating the idea that linguistic issues lay at the heart of any epistemological or metaphysical philosophy problems. They generally ended up teaching pupils who had never been particularly interested in philosophical problems *per se*, whether epistemological or not, and who consequently took on this idea with calm impassivity (Gellner, 1959). David Lodge has also drawn on the ample comic material in such a setup, through fictional professors forced to teach poorly-read students unfamiliar with the concept of the Canon that the margin is text, or the Canon is dead (Lodge, 1988).

An arguably more pressing concern is that writing like this does not solve any issues. It does not seek to generate a more accurate explanation of the world, nor even to highlight the boundaries of our knowledge. Salient connections ultimately are not sturdy or flexible knowledge. So what can we do about it?

6. Integrated Study of Cultures—An Incipient Program

Integrated scholarship is the basis of the most promising breakthroughs in comprehending human behavior. By 'integrated', I mean explanatory models that move beyond established oppositions between 'levels' or 'domains' of reality (Bechtel, 1993), so in this instance I have in mind 'culture' rather than human psychology, genetics, or economics. I also have in mind models that are steadfastly adaptable in using any available explanatory tools, irrespective of the specific disciplinary context from which those tools have originated.

There is now much greater potential for an integrated study of human culture, thanks to rapid progress on the three fundamental fronts of human cognition, economic models of behavior, and evolutionary biology. Contemporary findings in all three of these arenas are already changing perspectives on the study of culture:

One may regard the spread of cultural representations, concepts, and norms as forms whose limits are dictated by human cognitive abilities (Sperber & Hirschfeld, 2004). As evolutionary anthropologists and cognitive scientists have shown, cognitive principles that are developed early on form a framework of expectations that enable the acquisition of specific cultural concepts and norms (Boyer & Barrett, 2005) in a diverse array of domains, from folk-biology (Atran, 1990, 1998), to kinship and ethnic categories (Hirschfeld, 1994, 1996), to racial categories (Kurzban, Tooby, & Cosmides, 2001), to religious beliefs (Atran, 2002), and social interaction (Barkow, Cosmides, & Tooby, 1992; Fiske, 1992; Tooby & Cosmides, 1996).

Economic theory gives us the most accurate tools for describing opportunities and predicting options, and these tools are undoubtedly applicable beyond the bounds of exclusively economic issues (Gintis, 2000a). In particular, experimental and behavioral economics have demonstrated how we might move pas strict rationality assumptions (Smith, 2003), and how we might incorporate factors such as reputation (Sperber & Baumard, 2012) punitive feelings (Fehr, Schmidt, Kolm, & Ythier, 2006; Price, Cosmides, & Tooby, 2002) and intuitive standards of fairness (McCabe & Smith, 2001) into economic models. These models are responsible for the dissemination modes of cooperation specific to a given culture (Gintis, 2000b).

If we do not situate human culture within an evolutionary context, we cannot provide a thorough account of it. Evolution in humans (and other species) generates decision-making processes that are extremely context-dependent, meaning that environmental and social aspects may dictate the limits of an individual's personal preferences. An evolutionary framework can give a useful explanation of a wide range of cultural phenomena, e.g., reproductive strategies including teenage pregnancies (Ellis et al., 2003; Quinlan, 2003), different responses or uniform objections to cheating in social exchange—in both forager and industrial societies (Sugiyama, Tooby, & Cosmides, 2002); local particularities of 'race' categories (Kurzban et al., 2001; Sidanius & Veniegas, 2000); and many others (Barkow et al., 1992; Buss & Kenrick, 1998).

7. Back to What Matters

A vast domain is open to cultural anthropological investigation, provided that the practitioners accept substantive re-tooling and discard old fetishes. If slogans are needed, an integrated study of culture should proclaim the great values of *reductionism*, the ambition to understand the causal processes underpinning behaviors; *opportunism*, the use of whatever tools and findings get us closer to that goal; and *revisionism*, a deliberate indifference to disciplinary creeds and traditions. The integrated view of human culture—what some may call a 'vertical integration' in the field—will allow cultural anthropology to return to the highly ambitious set of questions it should have addressed all along.

For the sake of illustration, here is a far from exhaustive list of such questions:

- What are the natural limits to family arrangements? Will they shift with new reproductive techniques and economic change?

- Can we have an intuitive understanding of large societies? Or are our intuitive understandings of the social and political world limited to the small groups in which we evolved?

- Why are despised social categories essentialized? Why is it so easy to construct social stigma?

- What logic drives ethnic violence? Ethnic conflicts are more violent and seem less rational than traditional warfare. They sometimes involve whole populations as victims and perpetrators. What psychological processes fuel this violence?

- Why are there gender differences in politics? What explains womens exclusion from group decision making in most societies, and their reduced participation in other societies?

- How are moral concepts acquired? How do locally significant parameters affect general concepts of right and wrong?

- What drives peoples economic intuitions? Does participation in market economies create an understanding of market processes?

- Are there cultural differences in low-level cognition? Or do we find very similar ways of categorizing and assigning causation, with variable explicit cultural theories?

- What explains individual religious attitudes? Why are some individuals more than others committed to the existence of supernatural agents?

- Why is there religious fundamentalism and extremism? Why should people want to oppress or kill others in the name of a supernatural agency?

The list is not exhaustive but it is indicative, at least, of the potential scope and diversity of a vertically integrated approach to cultural anthropology. The list should also suggest why an integrated program is a Good Thing: because it finally allows cultural anthropology to talk about things that matter. Cultural anthropology is simply not heard in the public forum, and the simplest explanation is that it is not talking— or rather, not talking about anything of great importance. This should change soon.

References

Atran, S. A. (1990). *Cognitive Foundations of Natural History. Towards an Anthropology of Science.* Cambridge: Cambridge University Press.

——. (1998). Folk biology and the anthropology of science: Cognitive universals and cultural particulars. *Behavioral and Brain Sciences,* 21, 547–569. https://doi.org/10.1017/S0140525X98001277

——. (2002). *In Gods We Trust: The Evolutionary Landscape of Religion.* Oxford; New York: Oxford University Press.

Barkow, J., Cosmides, L., & Tooby, J. (1992). *The Adapted Mind: Evolutionary Psychology and the Generation of Culture*. New York: Oxford University Press.

Bechtel, W. (1993). Integrating Sciences by Creating New Disciplines: The Case of Cell Biology. *Biology & Philosophy*, 8, 277–300.

Bickerton, D. (1990). *Language & Species*. Chicago, IL: University of Chicago Press.

Boyer, P., & Barrett, H. C. (2005). Domain Specificity and Intuitive Ontology. In D. M. Buss & D. M. Buss (Eds.), *The Handbook of Evolutionary Psychology*. (pp. 96–118). Hoboken, NJ: John Wiley & Sons Inc.

Buss, D. M., & Kenrick, D. T. (1998). Evolutionary social psychology. In D. T. Gilbert, S. T. Fiske, et al. (Eds.), *The Handbook of Social Psychology, Vol. 2*. (pp. 982–1026). Boston, MA: Mcgraw-Hill.

Ellis, B. J., Bates, J. E., Dodge, K. A., Fergusson, D. M., Horwood, L. J., Pettit, G. S., & Woodward, L. (2003). Does father absence place daughters at special risk for early sexual activity and teenage pregnancy? *Child Development*, 74, 801–821. https://doi.org/10.1111/1467-8624.00569

Fehr, E., Schmidt, K. M., Kolm, S.-C., & Ythier, J. M. (2006). The Economics of Fairness, Reciprocity and Altruism—Experimental Evidence and New Theories. In S.-C. Kolm & J. M. Ythier (Eds.), *Handbook of the Economics of Giving, Altruism and Reciprocity (Vol 1.) Foundations*. (pp. 615–691). New York: Elsevier Science.

Fiske, A. P. (1992). The four elementary forms of sociality: Framework for a unified theory of social relations. *Psychological Review*, 99, 689–723.

Garber, M. B. (2004). *Shakespeare After All*. New York: Pantheon Books.

Gellner, E. (1959). *Words and Things: A Critical Account of Linguistic Philosophy and a Study in Ideology*. London: Gollancz.

——. (1992). *Postmodernism, Reason and Religion*. London; New York: Routledge.

Gintis, H. (2000a). *Game Theory Evolving: A Problem-Centered Introduction to Modeling Strategic Behavior*. Princeton, NJ: Princeton University Press.

——. (2000b). Strong reciprocity and human sociality. *Journal of Theoretical Biology*, 206, 169–179. https://doi.org/10.1006/jtbi.2000.2111

Hirschfeld, L. A. (1994). The acquisition of social categories. In L. A. Hirschfeld & S. A. Gelman (Eds.), *Mapping The Mind: Domain-Specificity in Culture and Cognition*. New York: Cambridge University Press.

——. (1996). *Race in the Making: Cognition, Culture and the Child's Construction of Human Kinds*. Cambridge, MA: MIT Press.

Hölldobler, B., & Wilson, E. O. (1990). *The Ants*. Cambridge, MA: Belknap Press of Harvard University Press.

Kermode, F. (1983). *The Art of Telling: Essays on Fiction.* Cambridge, MA: Harvard University Press.

Klee, R. (1999). *Scientific Inquiry: Readings in the Philosophy of Science.* New York: Oxford University Press.

Kurzban, R., Tooby, J., & Cosmides, L. (2001). Can race be erased? Coalitional computation and social categorization. *Proceedings of the National Academy of Sciences of the United States of America,* 98, 15387–15392. https://doi.org/10.1073/pnas.251541498

Lodge, D. (1988). *Nice Work: A Novel.* London: Secker & Warburg.

Mayr, E. (1991). *One Long Argument: Charles Darwin and the Genesis of Modern Evolutionary Thought.* Cambridge, MA: Harvard University Press.

McCabe, K. A., & Smith, V. L. (2001). Goodwill Accounting and the process of exchange. In G. Gigerenzer & R. Selten (Eds.), *Bounded Rationality: The Adaptive Toolbox.* (pp. 319–340). Cambridge, MA: MIT Press.

Posner, R. A. (2001). *Public Intellectuals: A Study of Decline.* Cambridge, MA: Harvard University Press.

Price, M. E., Cosmides, L., & Tooby, J. (2002). Punitive sentiment as an anti-free rider psychological device. *Evolution & Human Behavior,* 23, 203–231. https://doi.org/10.1016/S1090-5138(01)00093-9

Quinlan, R. J. (2003). Father absence, parental care, and female reproductive development. *Evolution & Human Behavior,* 24, 376–390. https://doi.org/10.1016/S1090-5138(03)00039-4

Sidanius, J., & Veniegas, R. C. (2000). Gender and race discrimination: The interactive nature of disadvantage. In S. Oskamp et al. (Eds.), *Reducing Prejudice and Discrimination.* (pp. 47–69). Mahwah, NJ: Lawrence Erlbaum Associates, Inc.

Smith, V. L. (2003). Constructivist and Ecological Rationality in Economics. *American Economic Review,* 93, 465–508. https://doi.org/10.1257/000282803322156954

Sperber, D., & Baumard, N. (2012). Moral reputation: An evolutionary and cognitive perspective. *Mind & Language,* 27, 495–518. https://doi.org/10.1111/mila.12000

Sperber, D., & Hirschfeld, L. A. (2004). The cognitive foundations of cultural stability and diversity. *Trends in Cognitive Sciences,* 8, 40–46. https://doi.org/10.1016/j.tics.2003.11.002

Sugiyama, L. S., Tooby, J., & Cosmides, L. (2002). Cross-cultural evidence of cognitive adaptations for social exchange among the Shiwiar of Ecuadorian Amazonia. *Proceedings of the National Academy of Sciences of the United States of America,* 99, 11537–11542. https://doi.org/10.1073/pnas.122352999

Tooby, J., & Cosmides, L. (1996). Friendship and the banker's paradox: Other pathways to the evolution of adaptations for altruism. In W. G. Runciman, J. M. Smith, et al. (Eds.), *Evolution of Social Behaviour Patterns in Primates and Man.* (pp. 119–143). Oxford: Oxford University Press.

Wilson, E. (1975). *Sociobiology: The New Synthesis.* Cambridge, MA: Harvard University Press.

List of Tables and Illustrations

Chapter 3

Chapter 4

Chapter 5

Chapter 6

Index

About the Team

Alessandra Tosi was the managing editor for this book.

Melissa Purkiss performed the copy-editing and proofreading.

Anna Gatti designed the cover. The cover was produced in InDesign using the Fontin font.

Luca Baffa typeset the book in InDesign and produced the paperback and hardback editions. The text font is Tex Gyre Pagella; the heading font is Californian FB. Luca produced the EPUB, MOBI, PDF, HTML, and XML editions — the conversion is performed with open source software freely available on our GitHub page (https://github.com/OpenBookPublishers).

This book need not end here...

Share

All our books — including the one you have just read — are free to access online so that students, researchers and members of the public who can't afford a printed edition will have access to the same ideas. This title will be accessed online by hundreds of readers each month across the globe: why not share the link so that someone you know is one of them?

This book and additional content is available at:

https://doi.org/10.11647/OBP.0257

Customise

Personalise your copy of this book or design new books using OBP and third-party material. Take chapters or whole books from our published list and make a special edition, a new anthology or an illuminating coursepack. Each customised edition will be produced as a paperback and a downloadable PDF.

Find out more at:

https://www.openbookpublishers.com/section/59/1

You may also be interested in:

Hanging on to the Edges
Essays on Science, Society and the Academic Life
Daniel Nettle

https://doi.org/10.11647/OBP.0155

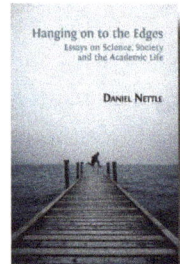

Foundations for Moral Relativism
Second Expanded Edition
J. David Velleman

https://doi.org/10.11647/OBP.0086

Knowledge and the Norm of Assertion
An Essay in Philosophical Science
John Turri

https://doi.org/10.11647/OBP.0083

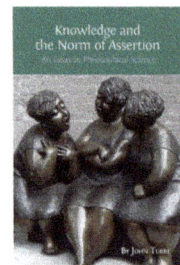

www.ingramcontent.com/pod-product-compliance
Lightning Source LLC
Chambersburg PA
CBHW040147270326
41929CB00025B/3410